12·9·79

THE DREAM STRUCTURE OF PINTER'S PLAYS
A Psychoanalytic Approach

THE DREAM STRUCTURE OF PINTER'S PLAYS
A Psychoanalytic Approach

Lucina Paquet Gabbard

RUTHERFORD • MADISON • TEANECK
FAIRLEIGH DICKINSON UNIVERSITY PRESS
LONDON: ASSOCIATED UNIVERSITY PRESSES

Associated University Presses, Inc.
Cranbury, New Jersey 08512

Associated University Presses
Magdalen House
136-148 Tooley Street
London SE1 2TT, England

The author wishes to thank: Doubleday & Company, Inc., for permission to quote from *The Peopled Wound,* copyright © 1970 by Martin Esslin. Reprinted by permission of Doubleday & Company, Inc.

International Universities Press, Inc., for permission to quote from *The Ego and the Mechanisms of Defense* by Anna Freud. Reprinted by permission of International Universities Press, Inc.

Library of Congress Cataloging in Publication Data
Gabbard, Lucina Paquet.
    The dream structure of Pinter's plays.

    Bibliograph: p.
    Includes index.
    1. Pinter, Harold, 1930-   --Criticism and
interpretation.   2. Psychoanalysis in literature.
I.   Title
PR6066.I53Z646   822'.9'14 [B]   75-26209
ISBN 0-8386-1848-0

PRINTED IN THE UNITED STATES OF AMERICA

To Gabby, Krin, and Glen

1952567

Contents

Acknowledgments

I would like to express my deepest thanks to Dr. James Hurt; his generous gifts of advice, time and patience made this book possible. I also want to thank my husband, Dr. E.G. Gabbard, for his time and energy spent typing my rough drafts and correcting my errors. For permission to use the quotations in this book, I would like to make the following grateful acknowledgments:

To Grove Press, Inc., for permission to quote from Plays:

THE BIRTHDAY PARTY: copyright ©1959 by Harold Pinter
THE ROOM: copyright ©1960 by Harold Pinter
A SLIGHT ACHE: copyright ©1961 by Harold Pinter
THE DWARFS: copyright ©1961 by Harold Pinter
THE COLLECTION: copyright ©1962 by Harold Pinter
LANDSCAPE: copyright ©1968 by H. Pinter, Ltd.
SILENCE: copyright ©1969 by H. Pinter, Ltd.
NIGHT: copyright ©1969 by H. Pinter, Ltd.
MAC (A MEMOIR): copyright ©1968 by Harold Pinter
OLD TIMES: copyright ©1971 by Harold Pinter
THE CARETAKER: copyright ©1960 by Theatre Productions Limited
THE DUMB WAITER: copyright ©1960 by Harold Pinter

To Eyre Methuen Ltd., Methuen & Co., Ltd., and Associated Book Publishers Ltd., for permission to quote from the following plays of Pinter: *The Birthday Party, The Room, The Dumb Waiter, The Caretaker, A Slight Ache, A Night Out, The Dwarfs, The Collection, The Lover, The Homecoming, Tea Party, Basement, Night School, Landscape, Silence,* and *Old Times.*

To Harold Pinter and Methuen & Co., Ltd., publishers, for permission to quote from *The Birthday Party, The Room, The Dumb Waiter, The Caretaker, A Slight Ache, A Night Out, The Dwarfs, The Collection, The Lover, The Homecoming, Tea Party, The Basement, Night School, Landscape, Silence, Old Times.*

To Sigmund Freud Copyrights Ltd., The Institute of Psychoanalysis and the Hogarth Press for permission to quote from the *Standard Edition of the Complete Psychological Works of Sigmund Freud,* revised and edited by James Strachey.

To George Allen & Unwin Ltd., publishers, for permission to quote from *The Interpretation of Dreams,* Volumes 4 and 5, and *Introductory Lectures on Psychoanalysis,* Volume 5, of the *Standard Edition of the Complete Psychological Works of Sigmund Freud,* revised and edited by James Strachey.

To. W.W. Norton and Co., Inc., American publishers of *Introductory Lectures* and *New Introductory Lectures* by

Acknowledgments/11

Sigmund Freud, translated and edited by James Strachey.

From *The Interpretation of Dreams,* by Sigmund Freud, translated from the German and edited by James Strachey, published in the United States by Basic Books, Inc. by arrangement with George Allen & Unwin Ltd. and The Hogarth Press, Ltd.

From *Three Essays on the Theory of Sexuality,* by Sigmund Freud, translated and newly edited by James Strachey, ©1962 Sigmund Freud Copyrights, Ltd.

Excerpts from *Collected Papers of Sigmund Freud,* Volume 4, authorized translation under the supervision of Joan Riviere, published by Basic Books, Inc., by arrangement with The Hogarth Press Ltd. and The Institute of Psychoanalysis, London.

To Martin Esslin and Methuen and Co., Ltd., publishers, for permission to quote from Martin Esslin's *The Peopled Wound: The Work of Harold Pinter.*

Selections from *The Peopled Wound: The Work of Harold Pinter* by Martin Esslin are reprinted by permission of John Cushman Associates, Inc., copyright ©1970 by Martin Esslin.

From *The Ego and the Mechanisms of Defense* by Anna Freud, published in Great Britain by The Hogarth Press. Reprinted by permission of Freud.

From *The Person: His Development throughout the Life Cycle,* by Theodore Lidz, ©1968 by Theodore Lidz, Basic Books, Inc., publishers, New York.

From *The Dynamics of Literary Response* by Norman Holland. Reprinted by permission of Oxford University Pres.

From *The Plays of Harold Pinter* by Simon Trussler. Reprinted by permission of Simon Trussler and Victor Gollancz Ltd., publisher.

THE DREAM STRUCTURE OF PINTER'S PLAYS
A Psychoanalytic Approach

1

The Key Dream: The Oedipal Wish

Seventeen plays—to date that is the sum of Harold Pinter's career as a playwright. Excluding the skits and the two short pieces, *Night* and *Monologue,* he has written five full-length and twelve one-act plays in the years from 1957 through 1971. This body of work has brought him critical acclaim, but it has also provoked controversy, for Pinter's plays present problems in understanding. Obscurity is the most immediate problem. The plays seem to move without regard to chronology. Characters are unidentified and seemingly unmotivated. Symbols are sometimes mysterious, and dialogue seems deliberately vague. The typical response is: What do these plays mean? Martin Esslin tells an amusing story that illustrates this reaction. Supposedly Pinter received a letter that read:

"Dear Sir, I would be obliged if you would kindly explain to me the meaning of your play *The Birthday Party.* These are the points which I do not understand: 1. Who are the two men? 2. Where did Stanley come from? 3. Were they all supposed to be normal? You will appreciate that without the answers to my questions I cannot fully understand your play." Pinter is said to have replied as follows: "Dear Madam, I would be obliged if you would kindly explain to me the meaning of your letter. These are the points which I do not understand: 1. Who are you? 2. Where do you come from? 3. Are you supposed to be normal? You will appreciate that without the answers to these questions I cannot fully understand your letter."[1]

Despite Pinter's clever reply, audiences and critics do find his plays baffling. Those who persist in attempting to understand them discover that one meaning blends into another; scholars continue to write new and differing interpetations of the plays. Alan Schneider, director of the New York production of *The Birthday Party*, remarked about the ambiguity of that play: "I think there are at least 249 meanings. You get the meaning you deserve, just as you get the wife you deserve."[2] Another problem of comprehension is that of the plays' interrelationships. The same characters and situations reappear from play to play but in various forms. The dramas seem to utilize the same themes and ideas but with altering emphases. Developmental patterns are like shifting sands.

The search for a comprehensive solution to these problems in understanding receives assistance from Northrop Frye's comment about archetypal criticism. He says that "the significant content is the conflict of desire and reality, which has for its basis the work of the dream."[3] Borrowing this idea and approaching Pinter's plays as dreams unlocks many of their secrets. Much of the obscurity in the plays can be illuminated by applying the mechanisms that Freud attributes to the dreamwork. The ambiguity can be understood as the result of the overdetermination so typical of dreams. The interrelationships can be viewed in terms of the grouping patterns of a dream series. It must be clearly understood, however, that in approaching these plays as dreams, there is no attempt to psychoanalyze Harold Pinter. Freud insists that the dreamer's cooperation is necessary to any accurate interpretation of the private symbolism of a dream. The aim of the analyses in this study is to identify the universal elements of these plays as dreams that, in turn, provide insight into everyman's inner self.

The various mechanisms of the dream-work can all be explained in terms of Pinter's first play, *The Room*, which contains the germ of all his other plays. *The Room* evolves out of the basic situation that Pinter varies for each of his dramas: two people are in a room and a visitor enters or threatens to enter. *The Room* introduces most of the characters to whom all the others are related in some degree. It introduces the oral, anal, and oedipal fantasies or anxieties that appear in one form or another in all of Pinter's works. It introduces most of the themes the reoccur in varying patterns of emphasis. It also introduces the dreamlike quality of incoherence that characterizes most of Pinter's plays. While *The Room* provides the basis for explaining the mechanisms of the dream, the mechanisms in turn illuminate the obscurities and ambiguities of *The Room* and its pivotal relationship to the succeeding plays. *The Room* is the key dream.

The dream mechanisms are the modus operandi for what Freud calls the *dream-work*. In *The Interpretation of Dreams*, Freud explains that the dream-work distorts and disguises the dreamer's threatening wishes so that they are not readily recognizable. As a result of these strange distortions by the dream-work, Freud concludes that there are two essentially different psychic processes operating during sleep: "One of these produces perfectly rational dream-thoughts, of no less validity than normal thinking; while the other treats these thoughts in a manner which is in the highest degree bewildering and irrational."[4] To the correct, normal method of thinking Freud gives the name *secondary process;* to the strange, improper one, he gives the name *primary process*. The mechanisms of this primary process, then, lend dreams their bizarre, incoherent quality; an understanding of these mechanisms can unlock some of Pinter's obscurities. Freud names *condensation* and *displacement* as the principal mechanisms of this primary process.

Condensation compresses several unconscious wishes, impulses, or attitudes into a single image in the manifest dream. It makes hidden analogies out of seemingly contradictory thoughts and ideas. It creates a montage out of current events, childhood memories, wishes, and fears. Freud explains condensation further:

> The material in the dream-thoughts, which is packed together for the purpose of constructing a dream-situation, must of course in itself be adaptable for that purpose. There must be one or more *common elements* in all the components. The dream-work then proceeds just as Francis Galton did in constructing his family photographs. It superimposes, as it were, the different components upon one another. The common element in them then stands out clearly in the composite picture, while contradictory details more or less wipe one another out.[5]

The most obvious example of condensation in *The Room* occurs under the image of the title itself. The montage consists of five layers. Just as dreams most often feature some real experience of the preceding day, so this montage begins with a realistic image. The room, first of all, represents the stage setting itself: "A room in a large house."[6] Second, the room represents the character Rose. Freud says: "Rooms in dreams are usually women; if the various ways in and out of them are represented, this interpretation is scarcely open to doubt."[7] As Bert's wife, Rose can then be envisioned as Bert's room. In this same context the room can be construed as a womb. It can be the womb in which Bert hides from the world. Here the image of mother replaces the image of wife in the previous layer of the montage. As a womb, the room can also be Rose's nurturing mother from whom she fears separation. Ultimately, the room becomes more literally a tomb for Riley who is beaten to death by Bert. The final image condensed under the title of *The Room* requires that Rose's house be perceived as her psyche. The room, then, becomes Rose's conscious mind as opposed to the basement, the subconscious strata.

Displacement is the second principal mechanism of the primary process. As Freud sees it within the dream-work, it is the transference of psychic energy from one element to another. It amounts, in other words, to a shift of attention that takes place in the service of the dream censor who must see that repressed wishes are disguised and distorted. For example, within the play Bert suffers from oedipal guilts. He defends himself against them by eliminating all sexual feeling from his relationship with his wife. Therefore, he displaces these feelings from Rose onto his van, which has the same symbolic association to women that a room has. Bert speaks of his van as though it were his woman: "She was good. She went with me. She don't mix it with me. I use my hand. Like that. I get hold of her. . ." (p. 120). Displacement on a broader scale refers to the degree to which the whole dream is disguised (or displaced) into a realistic situation. Northrop Frye uses the term in this sense when he speaks of the tendency "to displace myth in a human direction."[8] *The Room* is only slightly displaced; it remains close to pure dream. It has a very thin overlay of logic and chronology as compared to *A Night Out,* for example, which is highly displaced into realism. Norman Holland adds still another concept to the mechanism of displacement. He views all the defense mechanisms (repression, denial, regression, reaction formation, undoing, projection, introjection, turning against the self, identification with the aggressor, reversal, rationalization, and so forth) as kinds of displacement. For example, projection displaces some inner fear onto a person or object in the outer world. Rose's fear of the outside is a projection of her Oedipal fears. The little girl's wish to be rid of her mother still lives in Rose and frightens her so much that she projects it outside of herself. Therefore, every knock on the door becomes a potential threat that the danger outside has arrived at her threshold. Displacement then is a protective transformation that can take place outside the dream, affecting its overall character, or inside the dream, affecting the vision of a character within the play.

Four other primary process mechanisms that operate in the dream-work are by-products of condensation and displacement and overlap with them. The first, *symbolization,* suggests the creation of the single image under which many dissimilar but associated images are condensed. The room itself is such a symbol. *Concretization* is closely akin to symbolization. It represents the transformation of an abstract idea or verbalization into a concrete picture. Freud also refers to this "transformation of thoughts into situations" as *dramatization.*[9] Perceiving Rose's house as her psyche, her room as her conscious mind, and the basement as her subconscious mind concretizes the abstract concept of the two levels of consciousness within the psyche. Then, if Riley is perceived as a repressed wish rising from Rose's subconscious to her conscious mind, the concretization is dramatized. The third mechanism that springs out of condensation and displacement is *splitting.* Splitting refers to the division of one person into two or more, each representing differing character facets. Freud describes splitting: "In dreams the personality may be split—when, for instance, the dreamer's own knowledge is divided between two persons and when, in the dream, the extraneous ego corrects the actual one."[10] An example of splitting in *The Room* occurs when Mr. Kidd is viewed as a manifestation of Rose's father. He is, symbolically speaking, the landlord of her house. The other half, from which Mr. Kidd is split, is Riley. Riley is that fellow in the basement who disturbs and harasses Mr. Kidd by simply lying there wishing to see Rose. He also rises up to beg her to return to her father. Riley, then, is the fearsome side of Rose's father; Mr. Kidd is the harmless side. The final minor mechanism of the primary process is *klang associations* resulting from sound affinities. Freud's comment on these phonetic similarities is that they are "a pretty instance of the 'verbal bridges' crossed by the paths leading to the unconscious."[11] Puns fall under this heading, double entendres, and all kinds of connections springing from assonance and rhyme. The associations of room, womb, and tomb that link some of the condensations of the title symbol are an example of the last type. An example of double entendre occurs after Mr. Kidd has been reminiscing about his sister's beautiful boudoir. He tries to change the subject: "I've made ends meet" (p. 103). The primary process mechanism trips him up and subverts his intention. It creates the double entendre that reveals the incestuous fantasies associated with these memories of his sister. John Russell Brown has written at length about these Freudian slips in Pinter's dialogue and declares: "His [Pinter's] dramas cannot be received without a continuous intimation of the unconscious lives of his characters."[12]

These examples of the primary process mechanisms confirm their presence in Pinter's work and demonstrate their methods of functioning within the plays. The next link is between these mechanisms and overdetermination. These mechanisms create the ambiguity that constitutes overdetermination. As Freud describes it, overdetermination is essentially a synonym for ambiguity:

> Dreams frequently seem to have more than one meaning. Not only. . .may they include several wish fulfillments one alongside the other, but a succession of meanings or wish fulfillments may be superimposed on one another, the bottom one being the fulfillment of a wish dating from earliest childhood.[13]

Here Freud speaks of the overall interpretations of the dream, but overdetermination can also operate on individual elements within the dream:

> Not only are the elements of a dream determined by the dream-thoughts many times over, but the individual dream-thoughts are represented in the dream by several elements. Associative paths lead from one element of the dream to several dream-thoughts, and from one dream-thought to several elements of the dream.[14]

Clearly, overdetermination is the partner of condensation and displacement, and the "elements" Freud speaks of can be related to any one of the minor mechanisms. The overdetermined element can be an object, an action or idea, a person, or a word; the whole dream, of course, will also be overdetermined. It is the various determinations of a dream or dream element that are compressed by condensation into a single image. That image becomes the symbol (or concretization, split person, or klang association) whose associations unlock the various determinations (or ambiguities) it comprises. Once more *The Room* is illustrative. The room is a symbol with many meanings. In other words, it is overdetermined or ambiguous. However, all of these meanings have been grouped together, or condensed, because of a similar physical quality. Each meaning, like a room, is an enclosure—an area that can house something else. A room, a vagina, a womb, a tomb, a conscious mind—all are open spaces that can house what enters, even if it is only thoughts, as it is in the case of the mind. The contradictions and differences—such as between birth and death, body and mind—are glossed over and ignored. Each becomes a determination condensed under the one symbol. No one meaning is any more accurate than the other. The ambiguity of the symbol provides its depth and its wonder. So it is with the ambiguity of Pinter's play. A myriad of interpretations spring from the variety of associations that occur to differing individuals. It is this broad spectrum of appeal at many levels, an appeal simultaneously vertical and horizontal, that distinguishes Pinter's dramas. In general, no one of these interpretations or determinations is any more valid than another. However, one determination may be more meaningful or more recognizable to one individual than another, depending on his associations. To discover increasing numbers of interpretations, whether they be realistic, symbolic, or psychological, is to demonstrate the universality and power of the play.

The principal focus of this study is on the various overall interpretations of the plays that overdetermination allows and comprises. These multiple readings can also be demonstrated in *The Room*. The top layer of superimposed determinations is, of course, the realistic reading of the play that corresponds to the manifest dream. The manifest dream is the surface text of the dream. Behind it lie the latent dream-thoughts. The manifest dream usually features a residue of recent events to which the latent dream-thoughts attach themselves. Freud says: "almost every dream includes the remains of a memory or an allusion to some event (or often to several events) of the day before the dream, and, if we follow these connections, we often arrive with one blow at the transition from the apparently far remote dream-world to the real life of the patient."[15] So it is with *The Room*. The realistic reading can be compared to the manifest dream; it is concerned with current events. This current realism, however, conceals associated memories that are condensed beneath it. These hidden determinations are the unconscious or sometimes preconscious life of the play. They create its ambiguity, its depth, and its power.

Approaching *The Room* realistically, the spectator meets Bert and Rose Hudd. Bert is about fifty and Rose is about sixty. This difference in age is reflected in their personal relationship. Rose is a motherly wife. She fusses over Bert's food, wanting to be sure he has a hot breakfast before he goes out into the cold. She is a talker. Bert is a silent listener. Rose's talk discloses her anxiety; she is a fearful woman. She fears the world outside her room, and she shows an obsessive concern with the basement and whoever may inhabit it. She seems to recall having lived there once herself, and she constantly reiterates her preference for the room she currently occupies. Thus, she sets up an anxiety over being dispossessed that creates a moment of fear and suspense each time a knock comes on the door. She receives a succession of visitors. Mr. Kidd, the landlord, stops in to see about the pipes. He is a vague old man who neither hears well nor remembers well. He has forgotten how many rooms and floors the old house has. When he exits, Rose bundles Bert into warm clothes and sends him out for a speedy run in his van. Next, Mr. and Mrs. Sands come in, at Rose's invitation. They are looking for the landlord because they wish to rent a room like this one. They too are vague about the house—its stairways, halls, and basement. They place great attention on whether Mr. Sands is standing up or sitting down. When they leave, Mr. Kidd returns to tell Rose about a man in the basement who wishes to see her while Bert is gone. The man is a blind Negro, Riley, and he is Rose's next visitor. He brings a message from Rose's father that he later delivers in the first person: "I want you to come home." She insults and rejects him initially, but finally she relents and touches his eyes and head tenderly. At this moment Bert enters. At first, he ignores Riley; then without warning or explanation, he knocks him down and kicks his head against the stove until the Negro is still, ostensibly dead. Rose clutches her eyes and cries: "I can't see. I can't see" (p. 120).

The spectator who expects a traditional play is mystified and puzzled by this realistic determination. Who is Riley? Was he Rose's father? Why did Bert kill him? What was the meaning of the strange conversation of Mr. Kidd and the Sands? Approaching the play as a dream supplies most, if not all, of these answers, for they lie concealed in the other determinations of the play. The surface reality of the play, or the manifest content of the dream, is like a scrim—a gossamer curtain opaque only until it is lighted from behind. Then the scrim becomes transparent, and the stage setting, once so flimsily concealed, is illuminated and revealed as an eerie, dreamlike enclosure. Similarly, *The Room* is opaque and abstruse until attention is brought to bear on the unconscious content, or latent dream-thoughts, which lie beneath the surface. Then the play lights up with a multitude of penetrating meanings that explain the fearsome grip it has maintained on the emotions. These lower-level determinations are based on anxieties and fantasies that were experienced during the childhood developmental stages—oral, anal, and oedipal.

To take Freud's advice is to follow the connections established by the manifest content that are the transitions into the latent thoughts. Thus, the anxiety over leaving the room that can be seen in both Bert and Rose suggests oral fantasies associated with these individual characters. From one point of view, Rose herself can be recognized as the "all-powerful, maternal woman" who Norman Holland says is always present in literature based in the oral phase of development.[16] As Bert silently submits to her maternal care, he displays his own wish to return to the womb, to be one with the nurturing mother. He takes his nourishment from Rose, who provides him with bacon, eggs, bread, and tea. She tells him to "Eat it up," and he does (p. 95). As she talks to him, she sits in the rocking chair —traditionally associated with motherhood. She is concerned about his going out and dresses him warmly before he goes. He also shows anxiety over his separation from the womb-room. When he returns, his first words are: "I got back all right" (p. 119). And he repeats it twice for emphasis, explaining that he drove hard to get back. Frieda Fromm-Reichman confirms this unconscious connection between separations in adult life and those in infancy. She says "separation anxiety which people first experience at birth and subsequently throughout their lives [is] present at all phases of personality development. . . from weaning, that is, separation from mother's breast, to separation from one's fellow men, by death."[17] This separation anxiety and the wish to return to the womb can then be interpreted as Bert's reason for killing Riley. Possibly in his anxiety he views Riley as a usurper who would dispossess him from his room and Riley must, therefore, be destroyed.

Oral fantasy also attaches to Rose. The room also represents the womb that nurtured her. She, after all, never leaves it. Therefore, she shows her wish to be one with it. Rose, however, shows the ambivalence that comes in the second half of the oral phase—the sadistic half—when the child learns to bite as well as suck. Although Rose stays in the room, by means of her incessant talking she fights against being engulfed and overwhelmed. To quote Holland again: "A common defense against oral fusion and merger is putting something out of the mouth instead of taking something in; the something is usually speech."[18] Rose's memories of mother must then be tinged with hostility. Nevertheless, she clings to the security of the room. She makes this clear by repeatedly expressing her fear of the outside. Indeed, she states this fear most explicitly in the opening speech of the play: "It's very cold out, I can tell you. It's murder" (p. 95). Rose clings inside the womb because, in her view, murder lurks outside it.

In the overview of the oral content of the play, Rose and Bert together hide in the womb. Together they fend off all intruders. Rose, in this regard, is the weaker of the two; she seems almost to acquiesce in the face of pressure from outside visitors. Bert, however, resists these intruders with strength and violence. The repeated use of the antitheses—inside-outside, warm-cold, light-dark—are a constant reminder of the omnipresence of separation anxiety and oral fantasy that pervades this play.

There are determinations in *The Room* stemming from the anal and urethral stages of development also. The urethral element is perhaps relatively minor. It is centered in the sit down-stand up imagery that is tossed back and forth between the Sands. This imagery harks back to the young boy's learning to stand up to urinate and the young girl's concomitant sense of penis envy. Theodore Lidz, whose book is a standard text in many medical colleges, describes this development:

> The boy is likely to enjoy urinating and now stands up and imagines that he is shooting a machine gun — 'ack — ack — ack' — or hosing out a fire, gaining a feeling of masculine power. The girl who has watched boys may now also wish to stand up to urinate and expresses feelings of deprivation.[19]

This rivalry carries over into the struggle for dominance that is evidenced by the Sands and becomes an attempt on Mrs. Sands's part to castrate Mr. Sands symbolically. He in return fears sitting down, in the same way he fears castration itself. When she triumphantly catches him sitting on the table, he jumps up and insists he has only perched (p. 110). Mr. Sands shows a great need to assert his masculinity in this female place that he finds darker than outside. Mrs. Sands, on the contrary, finds Rose's room lighter than the rest of the house and would stay.

The struggle for dominance, however, is primarily associated with the anal period. At this time the oral polarity, activity-passivity, gives way to a new polarity, defiance-submission, which springs out of the child's battles with his parents over toilet training. Possessiveness is also born in the anal phase as a reaction against the child's feeling of being forced to give up his feces.[20] A third characteristic of anality is sadism. According to Mack and Semrad's summary of Freudian theory, the child perceives the pinching off of his feces as a sadistic act. Subsequently, he treats people as feces. Then his will to dominate, to possess, and to pinch off takes the form of a wish to "exert power over things and people and force them into a rigid and pedantic system." These feelings are also characterized by ambivalence—a "tendency to control and retain the object together with a desire to expel and destroy it."[21] Rose and Bert both display these qualities. Rose maintains the upper hand on Bert by mothering him; thus, she reduces him to a child. Her reluctance to send him out into the world, to let him out of her room, is also a form of possessiveness. On the other hand, Bert perhaps exerts the final control. Rose fears to allow Riley to enter the room until Bert is gone. Mr. Kidd also recognizes Bert's authority when he also expresses fear that Rily might come up to see Rose while Bert is present. Bert shows his sadistic impulse when he brutally kicks Riley until he is ostensibly dead. He seems to be motivated by the same will to have his way that he demonstrated on the road: "One [car] there was. He wouldn't move. I bumped him. I got my road. I had all my way" (p. 120). His ambivalence toward Rose now becomes clear in retrospect. He retains her in this room, forbidding any usurpers, but he lavishes on his van the affection he withholds from her.

An overview of the play as an anal fantasy, then, features a struggle for dominance in this room. Rose tries to dominate by mothering. As Lois Gordon points out, Rose "infantilizes" and "emasculates" the men who enter her room.[22] Bert dominates by his silent threat of violence. Each attempts to possess and retain the other by keeping him/her in the room. Bert maintains his possession by a sadistic murder. Rose's response to Riley, therefore, emerges as a protective device. She rejects him to protect him from the violence she knows will come. As she almost acquiesces to Riley's gentleness, she shows the longing for tenderness caused by Bert's cruel, silent withdrawal from her.

Oedipal fantasies provide still another determination of *The Room*. The sense of menace that pervades this play can be interpreted as the characters' fears of punishment for oedipal wishes. Rose has apparently repressed her erotic feelings for her father. Whether Riley is her father or her father's messenger, she reveals affection when her insults melt into tender touching of his head and face. Her inability to remember who lives in the basement, when she was down there last, and who Riley is—all these failures of memory indicate her repression. According to Freud, "the essence of repression lies simply in turning something away, and keeping it at a distance, from the conscious."[23] Her relationship with Bert also springs out of her oedipal fears. She has been unable to establish a wifely relationship. Her fear of her own erotic feelings still lives and presses her into the role of mother to her husband. This fear, in turn, determines her wish to castrate Bert and all male figures. She gives evidence of this castration complex as she spits out to Riley: "You're all deaf and dumb and blind, the lot of you. A bunch of cripples" (p. 117). All kinds of mutilation are associated psychologically with castration. Holland says: "amputations, mutilations, blindings, and the like symbolize this earliest feared punishment [castration]."[24] The mutilation is simply displaced to a less threatening part of the body. Further insight into Rose's castration complex comes from Max Schur. He explains that "castration is genetically linked with hunger" because both physical hunger and sexual hunger are satisfied by the female figure. He adds that "the predominance of 'orality' behind the phallic structure of so-called anxiety neuroses [is a] well-established clinical fact."[25] Rose is a true mixture of the nourishing mother and the castrating wife; Bert is an accurate picture of the silent, anxious victim. Rose's fears of the outside and of the basement can also be linked to her early oedipal fantasies. The little girl's wish to be rid of her mother is so fearful to her still that she projects it outside herself. Consequently, she fears mother will wish to harm her. By this displacement, outside becomes murder to Rose. A knock on the door arouses anxiety. The same anxiety persists when she looks out of the window and hears the wind (p. 95). Northrop Frye has commented on the wind as a symbol of "unpredictability or sudden crisis."[26] Immediately after her remark about the wind, Rose sits in her rocking chair. She tries to merge with her mother as a protection against her. In Freudian psychology this is known as *identification with the aggressor;* it is a mechanism of defense. Once this defensive measure is taken, Rose's mind skips immediately to that associated fear, the man in the basement—her repressed sexual drive—that could at any moment rise up and overwhelm her. Her speech and Pinter's stage directions reveal clearly these associated fears. "Just now I looked out of the window. It was enough for me. There wasn't a soul about. Can you hear the wind? *She sits in the rocking chair.* I've never seen who it is. Who is it? Who lives down there? I'll have to ask. I mean, you might as well know, Bert. But whoever it is, it can't be too cosy" (pp. 95-96).

Bert has oedipal fears, too. His condition is the necessary companion of Rose's. Having never outgrown the wish to marry his mother, he has allowed Rose to emasculate him and treat him as a helpless child. Eliminating sexual feeling from their relationship reduces his guilt over the fulfillment of this oedipal wish. Therefore, he displaces his sexual feelings onto his van, an inanimate object unable to compromise his impotent positon. He is capable of some control in the van: "I use my hand. Like that. I get hold of her. I go where I go" (p. 120). Nevertheless, his final remark returns him to the childhood state: "She brought me back" (p. 120). Bert's fear is seen first in his report of his actions on the road. When a car got in his way, he bumped him: "I got my road. I had all my way" (p. 120). Then when Riley gets in his way, he bumps him, too. Bert's violence can be viewed as the partner to his fear. Like Rose he has projected outside himself his wish to kill the father.

Thus, he fears physical attack by a father figure. So great is this fear that he strikes first in self-defense. Anna Freud calls this "'the reversal of the roles of attacker and attacked." She illustrates it in the case of a little boy who scolds the housemaid whom he expects will scold him. "The vehemence with which he scolded her—a prophylactic measure—indicated the intensity of his anxiety."[27]

Related to oedipal fantasies are the suggestions of promiscuity associated with Rose. Norman Holland comments that in the oedipal phase the child thinks his mother is "either absolutely untouchable, unattainable, pure, taboo, a virgin-mother, or she is a slut, common, fickle, available to anyone (notably the father)."[28] These hints are first suggested by Rose's knowledge of other rooms in the house. She reveals knowledge of Mr. Kidd's bedroom by denying she ever knew. She speaks off and on about her visits to the basement. She knows there's not room for two down there. She knows one man moved out and maybe two live there now. Mr. Kidd says Rose's room was once his, and he is a man who can take his pick of rooms in the house. All this talk of going in and out of rooms corresponds to Freud's contention that walking through rooms "is a brothel or harem dream."[29] Rose promotes the idea of her own promiscuity when she says to Riley: "Oh, these customers. They come in here and stink the place out. After a handout. I know all about it" (p. 117). Later she says to him: "You think I'm an easy touch, don't you?" (p. 118). Earlier to an innocent remark of Mr. Kidd's, she has replied indignantly: "Mr. Kidd, do you think I go around knowing men in one district after another? What do you think I am?" (p. 115).

Also related to oedipal anxiety are primal-scene fantasies. Norman Holland explains that in these fantasies "the child imagines that he watches or hears his parents in the act of love."[30] The fear also arises from having witnessed what the parents consider taboo and from imagining himself in the role of the parent of the same sex. Among the images that Holland says give the cue to such fantasies are "darkness, a sense of vagueness and the unknown, mysterious noises in the night. . ., vague movements, shapes shifting and changing, . . .things appearing and disappearing. . . ."[31] Some of the primal-scene imagery is provided by the Sands. They roam about in the dark halls. They move up and down the stairs. According to Freud, "Steps, ladders, or staircases, or, as the case may be, walking up or down them, are representations of the sexual act."[32] In a footnote Freud elaborates:

> staircases (and analogous things) were unquestionably symbols of copulation. It is not hard to discover the basis of the comparison: we come to the top in a series of rhythmical movements and with increasing breathlessness and then, with a few rapid leaps, we can get to the bottom again. Thus the rhythmical pattern of copulation is reproduced in going upstairs. Nor must we omit to bring in the evidence of linguistic usage. It shows us that "mounting" is used as a direct equivalent for the sexual act.[33]

If the Sands are accepted as transformations of the mother and father figures, then the confusion about when they were coming up and when they were going down suggests the vagueness of the memories of the primal scene. Also, Mrs. Sands's wish to have Rose's room and Rose's concern over that possibility take on new significance. Mrs. Sands's wish can be interpreted as evidence of reversal and projection on Rose's part. She wishes to be in her mother's place, but she displaces this fearful wish and imagines instead that her mother wants to be in her place. As a result of this projection, the mother figure becomes so threatening that she must be transformed into a harmless visiting stranger—a reversal. Moreover, thoughts about visitors sometimes project a wish that the father were not here to stay, Holland explains.[34] If Rose is to defend herself against her incestuous fantasies, she must wish that the father was not here. All of these oedipal and primal-scene fantasies generate the guilt and anxiety from which springs the feeling of menace that pervades *The Room*.

Backing away from the details to survey the oedipal content of this play reveals another overall determination. Bert, the Oedipus figure, lives in the room with a mother figure, Rose, whom he has taken as wife. Riley, the embodiment of Rose's repressed sexual feelings, returns to claim her again. As such he becomes the rival father to Bert. Consequently, Bert acts out the rest of the classic oedipal wish: he kills the father. The blindness, traditionally associated with Oedipus, is displaced onto the other two principal characters. By reversal, they are blind and Oedipus is not.

A consideration of the house as a concretization of Rose's psyche provides still another determination of *The Room*. If the house is viewed as Rose's psyche, her inner self, then the room becomes her conscious mind. Here she lives. Here then is light, warmth, security. Here she exercises some measure of control. The basement, the subconscious strata, is the place of discomfort, uncertainty, danger. There are darkness, dampness, and the unknown. There reside forgotten and forbidden thoughts—particularly repressed erotic feelings for the father. The old house is full of other shadowy areas that she only half remembers. These memories sometimes come to the threshold of her consciousness—her door. In this vein, Bert becomes another manifestation of Rose's self—split from her. He represents her violent tendencies that she tries to control in her conscious mind. To live with these tendencies she has had to transform them into their opposites. By the defense of reversal, she has displaced them into something helpless, to be fed and cared for. Periodically, however, they must be let out. When they are let out, they *drive* hard and fast, out in the dangerous world, at night. Her female spirit goes with them, however, and brings them back, ultimately, into conscious control. Mr. Kidd then becomes the third element of Rose's self—her harmless instincts, free to roam through various levels of the mind at will. He is harmless because he can not hear temptation and he is forgetful of sin. Mr. and Mrs. Sands are transformed memories of mother and father who come to the threshold of consciousness. Rose can only let them in when her violent spirit is outside herself. She can only entertain them by keeping their real identities out of her conscious mind. Finally, there is Riley. He has already been characterized as the repressed erotic feelings for her father. He has lain silent in the basement of her psyche. But he rises to the surface. John Pesta views Riley in similar fashion: "Riley's emergence from the basement may represent the rising of an unconscious impulse in Rose to return home to a haven of true security."[35] In this determination, however, what rises from the unconscious is not an impulse for security but a return of erotic feelings. When Riley arrives at her door, he is black and blind. Norman Holland says that "the forbidden love objects can be symbolized by any dark, unknown, obscure, banished, or debased persons."[36] Riley's blindness can be interpreted as a sign of castration. As the concretization of her repressed sexual drives, dark and forbidden, she has had to castrate him in order to release him from repression. When he has almost returned her to tenderness, her violent spirit returns and protects her from incest by murdering the father image. Then she defends herself by denial. Anna Freud explains that denial is a companion defense to repression. Repression operates against internal dangers (fearsome instinctual drives), and denial operates against external dangers. Denial is sustained against overthrow from without by "fantasies in which the real situation is reversed."[37] This explanation is very appropriate to Rose's case. The repressed erotic feelings have risen to consciousness. They have been concretized at this point into external form in the person of Riley. The violent spirit that lives within her, Bert, kills Riley. Rose has always denied this violence. She has by reversal transformed it into a child to be cared for. When it has committed murder, she must deny even the sight of it. She clutches her eyes and calls out, "I can't see" (p. 120). Her blindness is the concrete realization of her denial.

Concretizing the house as psyche and viewing Bert and Rose as products of splitting leads to one final determination. Bert is the ego; Rose is the superego, distressed and fearful over the sinful thoughts existing in the basement. Mr. Kidd and Riley are the split father toward whom Bert/Rose is ambivalent. The harmless, unremembering father is acceptable; the other one, who demands to be seen through the superego, is the hated, feared half. Bert tries to keep him repressed. When the superego is about to forgive him and reaccept him, the violent side takes control and carries out the wish of the id; Bert kills the father.

This analysis of these levels of fantasy in *The Room* suggests the themes of the play. The first, the realistic, reading of the play makes some general sense despite the unanswered questions that remain. Rose has been observed to fear the outside world and an unknown person or persons from the basement. At the same time she treats Bert as a helpless child. Ultimately, however, the outside world—the Sands and Mr. Kidd—proves harmless and friendly. Even the man from the basement, Riley, is gentle and welcoming. It is Bert who is dangerous and violent. It is Bert—living inside the room with her—who needs to be feared, but Rose is unwilling to see it. The play seems to support the old axiom that the danger to oneself is from within. If the spectator is willing to ignore the loose ends, false leads, and omissions that seem to remain, he can be satisfied that he has found meaning in the play. However, once he has turned on the lights behind the scrim, he discovers there is more to discern. First of all, it is clear that these dream images of the play reinforce the intellectual meaning already determined. In each of these interpretations,

Rose, or the central consciousness, fears the outside while she nurtures the violence within her own room. Even though she refuses to see it, it is there, as silent as Bert, waiting to erupt at some subrational signal. At this point, however, we also have some feasible explanations for the mysteries of Riley's identity and the reasons for Bert's killing him. Riley is a repressed father image come to reclaim Rose or dispossess and punish Bert. Bert kills him to protect his room or to fulfill the oedipal wish. Moreover, the play seems to have taken on additional meaning. Some of the workings of inner man have been revealed. The irrationality of his fears and the automatic response of his defenses have been partially bared. The play has shown that man is consciously confused and unconsciously controlled, that his actions have less to do with the interpersonal relationships of the moment than with the forgotten events of infancy. Man still seeks refuge from a fearful world. He still longs for the security of the womb; yet, he still strives to dominate. He still fears to love. He still expects punishment that reflects his own guilts rather than the enmity of others. He still acts on his old yearnings to marry the parent of the opposite sex and to kill the parent of the same sex. Thus, Pinter's characters are not unmotivated at all. They are indeed motivated, as people in real life are motivated, by the psychological phenomena of the unconscious. Approaching Pinter's play as a dream has provided a glimpse of the psychological realities of life.

In the following chapters it will be shown that the rich dream structures of *The Room* are equally evident in Pinter's subsequent plays. Furthermore, the plays follow a progression that corresponds roughly to that of a series of dreams. Freud explains that dreams tend to occur in groups or series through the night. Perhaps the lapses between are lapses in the dreamer's memory, but what he recalls presents a series. The order in which these dreams occur in the series frequently reveals the logical relationships between them. Freud describes several possible relationships that are implicit in these clusters. First, a group of dreams can represent different views or focal points of the same material. Freud says:

> It often seems as though the same material were presented in the two dreams from different points of view. . . .Or the two dreams may have sprung from two separate centers in the dream material, and their content may overlap, so that what is the center in one dream is present as a mere hint in the other, and vice versa.[38]

Second, a grouping can imply condition or consequence. In Freud's words:

> A short introductory dream and a longer main dream following it often stand in the relation of protasis and apodosis [conditional and consequential clauses]. . . .[39]

For example, a dream grouping can imply the causal relationship of wish fulfillment and punishment:

> Another and similar relation between the two members of a pair of dreams is found where one represents a punishment and the other the sinful wish fulfillment. It amounts to this: "If one accepts the punishment for it, one can go on to allow oneself the forbidden thing."[40]

Third, a group can produce a wish fulfillment in separate stages:

> Franz Alexander (1925) has shown in a study on pairs of dreams that it not infrequently happens that the two dreams in one night share the carrying-out of the dream's task by producing a wish fulfillment in two stages if they are taken together, though each dream separately would not affect that result. Suppose, for instance, the dream wish had as its content some illicit action in regard to a particular person. Then in the first dream the person will appear undisguised, but the action will be only timidly hinted

at. The second dream will behave differently. The action will be named without disguise, but the person will either be made unrecognizable or replaced by someone indifferent.[41]

Although Pinter's plays are separate and individual works of art, the chronology of their public appearances does follow an arrangement comparable to these grouping patterns Freud describes in dreams. *The Room* provides the stepping-off point. As the first play it begins the pattern and thereby is the key to the focal relationship to the others. The most striking thing that happens in *The Room* is the murder of Riley. The determinations based on the play's oedipal fantasties reveal that this murder is the fulfillment of the oedipal wish to kill the father. An attempt by the dream censor to disguise the murder victim as Rose's father rather than Bert's adds additional force to the choice of this oedipal act as the key fantasy of the play. In the following three plays — *The Dumb Waiter, The Birthday Party*, and *A Slight Ache* — the figure who constitutes the key male consciousness — Gus, Stanley, Edward — is invariably punished or rendered helpless. These plays then correspond to the punishment dreams that result from the sinful wish fulfillment of *The Room*. These plays also share a translation of the basic Pinter situation into fear of dispossession. In each play this fear seems to spring from the repressed oedipal guilt embodied in the intruder — Riley in *The Room*, Goldberg and McCann in *The Birthday Party*, the one who will give the call in *The Dumb Waiter*, and the Matchseller in *A Slight Ache*. Each play also shows the struggle for dominance as typical of the anal conflict. Thematically, these plays center on fear and violence and their interlocking guilts. These four plays, then, comprise the first group.

In general, the remaining plays fall into three additional groups. The second group consists of *A Night Out, The Caretaker, Night School*, and *The Dwarfs*. These plays soften the wish to kill into the wish to be rid of someone. Or, by purging and rejecting parental figures, they soften the wish to be rid of father into the wish to be someone else. The plays adopt differing focal points on this material. They also exploit the oral, anal, and oedipal anxieties inherent in *The Room,* but they extend and refocus these anxieties to include character conflicts and the resultant splittings and identity crises. Thematically, the plays center on ambivalence and impotence. The third group consists of four short plays — *The Collection, The Lover, Tea Party,* and *The Basement* — and one long play, *The Homecoming.* These plays are based on the oedipal wish to have the mother. In the four short plays, the wish is modified or softened into the wish for a change of lover. In *The Homecoming* the wish to have mother is fulfilled; wish fulfillment seems to develop in stages. This group also complicates the basic Pinter situation set forth in *The Room* with its oral, anal, and oedipal conflicts and anxieties. In the short plays splitting, however, is reduced to role playing and conscious fantasizing as introduced in *Night School.* A thematic focus of these plays is the ever-changing quality of individual character in response to shifting interpersonal relationships and perceptions. Women move among the roles of mother, wife, and whore. Men shift among father, husband, and lover. In this group, violence and rejection are avoided by adaptation, adjustment, or acceptance. The fourth group consists of *Landscape, Silence, Old Times,* and *No Man's Land.* These three plays are punishment dreams in consequence of the fulfillment of the sinful wish to have mother in *The Homecoming.* The punishment can be readily seen in the rejection of the male figure — Duff, Bates, Deeley, and Hirst — which occurs in all four plays. These people, however, do not anticipate violence and love, nor do they act out fantasies as do the characters in the preceding groups of plays. These people look back on their anxieties and struggles. They linger in the effects of their losses — effects that amount to incompatibility, isolation, alienation, and finally self-destruction. These are the thematic emphases of this final group of plays.

2

Punishment Dreams: For the Wish To Kill

The murder that occurs at the end of *The Room* is the most violent in any of Pinter's plays, and it provides the motive force that sets off the following three plays: *The Birthday Party*, *The Dumb Waiter*, and *A Slight Ache*. These four plays are linked, at least metaphorically, by the causal relationship of wish fulfillment and punishment. In *The Room* both aspects of the oedipal wish are fulfilled: Bert lives with a mother figure, Rose, and he kills a father figure, Riley. In the subsequent three plays the central figure is punished or rendered helpless. Each time the catastrophe seems to come from an intruder who has paternal associations. Each time, however, the punishment seems also to be self-inflicted. As the fulfillment of the wish to have mother is understated in *The Room*, so is the failure to win or keep mother present but not focal in the other three plays. These plays can, then, be called *punishment dreams*.

Freud states that dreams can be either wish fulfillment, anxiety fulfillment, or punishment fulfillment. He explains that all dreams are an attempt by "the dream-work to get rid of a mental stimulus, which is disturbing sleep, by means of the fulfillment of a wish."[1] The fulfillment of a wish can occasionally result in a need for punishment. Thus, punishment becomes in itself a wish fulfillment. A dream that fulfills the wish for punishment will be accompanied by anxiety; all three elements — wishing, anxiety, and punishment — will be present. Freud adds that "the anxiety is the direct opposite of the wish, that opposites are especially close to one another in associations and that in the unconscious they coalesce; and further, that the punishment is also the fulfillment of a wish — of the wish of the other, censoring person."[2]

The Birthday Party, The Dumb Waiter, and *A Slight Ache* seem related to *The Room* in the same fashion. Since the repressed wish won out in *The Room,* punishment wishes are expected in the plays that follow. This wish is fulfilled in each case, and it is accompanied by anxiety, just as anxiety precedes the realization of the wish to kill in *The Room.* This anxiety is expressed as the "menace" that inspired the name *comedies of menace* so often given to Pinter's early plays. Arnold Hinchliffe calls the first three plays by this name and explains that "in Pinter's plays, the potency of menace derives from an inability to define its source or reason even though it is all pervasive."[3] Another similarity of the plays in this group is their minimal displacement into realism. Like *The Room,* the succeeding three plays are characterized by the quality of surrealistic dream distortion. As the source of their menace is undefinable, so are the origins of their characters. As their anxiety springs from danger that is not immediate, so their actions spring from causes that are not clearly discernible.

THE BIRTHDAY PARTY

The Birthday Party, Pinter's second play, can be viewed as an alteration of the basic Pinter situation of *The Room.* The play begins with two people in a room, Meg and Petey. Like Bert and Rose, they are at breakfast, and like Bert and Rose, they have visitors. Stanley Webber, the principal character, has already arrived. There are also threatening visitors, Goldberg and McCann, whose arrival is vaguely anticipated as Riley's is. They threaten Stanley, however, not Meg. At the end of the play, Goldberg and McCann have done violence to Stanley, and may have greater violence in store for him. Thus, the play contrasts with *The Room,* in which the violence is done *to* the threatening visitor not *by* him. In short, in *The Room* the son figure kills violently; in *The Birthday Party* the son figure suffers violent punishment.

The Birthday Party, however, is much more than just the punishment of Stanley. Like *The Room,* it has many levels of meaning; it is overdetermined. The surface or realistic determination presents Stanley, a seedy young man of doubtful talent but apparent sin, hiding in fear and shame from the retribution of the organization he has wronged and deserted. He takes resentful advantage of the foolish but disgusting infatuation of his landlady, Meg. Thus, he could, if he chose, willfully displace Petey, her kindly old husband. The certainty with which he expects his pursuers reveals his own wish for the punishment by which he will expiate his guilt. The punishment comes in the form of Goldberg and McCann, who appear to be hired killers sent by the secret organization Stanley has fled. They all but kill him, depriving him of mind, speech, and sight, forcing him into their chosen mold, and then whisking him away to Monty. They tell Petey that Monty is a doctor. But the audience do not believe it; the audience recognize that Stanley's morning suit is his funeral costume and that he is dead. Observers are reminded of Nazi storm troopers carting off Jews in the night while neighbors stood by fearful and helpless, or of deserters from the I.R.A. being captured and subdued for their return to final retribution. An escapee—

from prison, from an asylum, from a stultifying society, from some hell—is being forced back into the confining world he has fled. His brief freedom has been marred by guilt and dread, and his future promises to be more suffocating and restraining than his past. His shelterers offer neither help nor notice, except Petey; but he is too ineffectual to provide any real protection at all. Stanley Webber is the victim of the external forces that have captured him.

As it is with *The Room,* this realistic determination leaves many unanswered questions. Most obvious, who are Goldberg and McCann? What group do they represent? Why do they want Stanley? What has he done? Most puzzling of all are the strange litanies of Goldberg and McCann. Most startling are the bizarre events of the party. All of these gaps in the play's logical overlay create the aura of a dream and cry out for exploration of the latent content below.

The first overall determination of the play at this hidden level reveals the anxieties of the latency stage of maturation. Near the end of the play Goldberg tells Petey that the birthday party was too much for Stanley, that he has had a nervous breakdown. And well Stanley might! His ego has been assaulted by a configuration of fears from latency as well as from the oedipal, anal, and oral phases. Mack and Semrad confirm that anxieties from all these periods do accumulate inside the psyche: "Freud. . .noted that, although each of these determinants of anxiety was appropriate to a particular period, they could exist side by side."[4] The anxiety of Stanley's current crisis in reality has reactivated, through association, all his old anxieties. Dominant among these are the fears he experienced as he attempted to move from latency into puberty or adolescence. Theodore Lidz describes the regression that psychological growth precipitates:

There is often a pause before a child achieves the confidence and vitality to venture into the strange uncertainties of a new phase of life. . . . .There is an inner impetus to expansion and the mastery of new skills and situations, a desire for greater independence and new prerogatives, and a wish to become more grown up like the parental figures he seeks to emulate; but movement into new areas brings insecurity, inability to manage the new situation creates frustrations, and independence means giving up dependency. The ensuing anxieties tend to direct the child toward regaining the security of shelter and dependency and to renounce for a time further developmental movement.[5]

Just as on the conscious level Stanely has fled from danger and responsibility to the refuge of Meg's seaside home, so on the unconsious level he has fled from the dangers of oncoming adolescence back to the security of fusion with the mother.

The play contains abundant evidence of Stanley's psychological position between latency and adolescence. Mack and Semrad declare that: "In the latency period, the characteristic fear is that the parental representatives, in the form of superego, will be angry with, punish, or cease to love the child."[6] This fear is so extreme in Stanley that he has projected it outside himself and concretized it in the form of Goldberg and McCann. They are split representations of Stanley's father figures who are so angry with him that they have come to punish him. At Meg's house they occupy together the room with the armchair — the father symbol. They have many names because they are a composite construction created by the dream-work. Freud says that the "construction of collective and composite figures is one of the methods by which condensation operates in dreams."[7] Goldberg and McCann are incorporations of a multifaceted father — uncles, grandfathers, teachers, and perhaps the many lovers of a promiscuous mother. Frieda Fromm-Reichman confirms that "this fear of disapproval may be transferred from the original significant people who trained and educated the anxious person to their emotional successors."[8] Thus Goldberg calls himself both Simey and Nat; he speaks intimately of Uncle Barney; McCann is also called Dermot and Seamus. Goldberg says to him:

> And I knew the word I had to remember—Respect! Because McCann— *Gently*. Seamus—who came before your father? His father. And who came before him? Before him? . . . *Vacant—triumphant*. Who came before your father's father but your father's father's mother! Your great-gran-granny.[9]

In these words Goldberg indicates that he and McCann speak the attitudes and beliefs of generations of parent figures. Each child along the way has introjected his parents' admonishments into his own superego and passed them on by the same process to his son. These accumulated judgments have become more than Stanley can bear. He has projected them outside himself and has tried to escape their menace. It is interesting to note here that the withdrawn, weak aspect of the father has been separated from these demanding, punishing aspects. Petey is the third element in the three-way split of the father figure that Martin Esslin points out,[10] but Petey is not involved in the threat. Nevertheless, this threat is so severe that it could well result in emotional collapse. Stanley's condition corresponds to a prepsychotic state described by Arieti:

> It is no longer the whole world which is against the patient; "they" are against him. He no longer has a feeling of being under scrutiny, under the eyes of the world; no longer a mild sense of suspiciousness. The sense of suspiciousness becomes the conviction that "they" follow him.[11]

Stanley continually speaks of a fearsome "they." "They're coming in a van" (p. 24); "What do they want here?" (p. 37). On the other hand, some of what Goldberg and McCann actually say and do to Stanley is more typical of parental recrimination and concern than of murder by hired killers. "What were you doing yesterday?" . . . Why are you wasting everybody's time? . . . Why do you behave so badly? . . . What would your old mum say, Webber? . . . Did you take anything for it [the headache]? . . . When did you last have a bath?" (pp.

50-51). These verbal beatings are the main punishment Goldberg and McCann mete out to Stanley. But they do express Stanley's great sense of inadequacy. Other parts of the litany hit at Stanley's lack of industry. "Why don't you pay the rent? . . . What's your trade? . . . No society would touch you. Not even a building society" (p. 54). Goldberg's and McCann's final promises echo this same criticism of Stanley's lack of ambition; they'll make him a success, a magnate, a statesman.

Erik Erikson describes the conflict between industry and inferiority as central to the latency period, and concerns about identity or role confusion as integral to adolescence.[12] Stanley is beginning to show this concern with identity when he says to Meg in their opening scene together: "Tell me, Mrs. Boles, when you address yourself to me do you ever ask yourself who exactly you are talking to? Eh?" (p. 22). He tells McCann: "the way some people look at me you'd think I was a different person. I suppose I have changed . . ." (p. 43). Goldberg, as the externalization of Stanley's fears, is not sure of his son's name. He says it was Emanuel, but he called him Timmy. In the next breath, he calls him Manny. In the interrogation, Goldberg demands to know why Stanley has changed his name. A closer examination of the father images will reveal that Stanley's retreat from adolescence is abnormally severe because his identity problems are unusually complicated. Stanley does not wish to identify with his father images. This is one reason he has run away and changed his name. He does not wish to be like McCann—a bully and strong-arm man who, in the service of others, uses his muscle instead of his brain. He does not wish to be like Goldberg either—pompous, maudlin, unfaithful, and unfit. Goldberg's image represents Stanley's projection of him as a hollow man puffed up with pretended beliefs in homespun philosophy, a deceitful man spouting family sentiment and indulging in extramarital affairs, a lost man clinging to commercial slogans that have smothered the soul within him. Even the chest he strives to expand lacks the easy breath he himself claims to know the secret of.

Stanley's problem with identity extends also to his career goals. He has tried to be a concert pianist, but "they" have forbidden him this role; "they" have locked him out. "They" want him to be rich, successful, a magnate, a statesman. Finally, it must be remembered that all these values that Stanley finds so objectionable originate within him. He had to introject them in earlier years to be able to project them at this point. Stanley despises himself as well as his fathers. The resulting confusion about his role shows up in almost every major event of the play. At breakfast with Meg, he alternates between her son and her wooer, between accepting her mothering and rejecting it. When Meg gives him the drum, he hangs it around his neck like a little boy, then rejects childishness by beating the drum savagely. At the party he sits silently and watches like a child; then he attempts the adult sexual act with Lulu.

At the end of the play the father figures march Stanley off into the world again. They are forcing him to accept the identity they wish to give him. He is to become their "pride and joy." Whether he likes it or not, they are pushing him out of latency and into adolescence. But Stanley goes as a dead man. The self he would have chosen has given in to Goldberg's prophecy: "You're dead. You can't live, you can't think, you can't love. You're dead. You're a plague gone bad. There's no juice in you. You're nothing but an odour!" (p. 55). Ironically, he is forced into this acceptance by his own guilt over abandoning the values of Goldberg and McCann that he had once introjected. Stanley's fears and guilts, externalized as Goldberg and McCann, have made him what he feared to be. It was their gift at the birthday party to celebrate his passage into a new phase of growth. Stanley's current reality crisis as a fugitive from a sinister organization indicates that he never recovered from this birthday.

An overview of these anxieties from latency gives new meaning and dimension to Martin Esslin's comment that the play is a "metaphor for the process of growing up."[13] Although Esslin makes this comment in reference to expulsion from the womb—the oral content of the play—it seems doubly pertinent in regard to Stanley's retreat from adolescence. On this level, the play is about a young man hiding from the forces of maturation. A surrogate mother, Meg, protects him in his retreat and compounds his confusion by her own ignorant disregard of his needs. A surrogate father, Petey, also protects him by his permissive withdrawal from the difficult situation. Finally, when the alternate images of parental authority, the fearsome ones whom the child has introjected and projected, have almost completed the unpleasant task, the gentle father would stop them if he had the strength. The gentle father's final advice, "Stan, don't let them tell you what to do" (p. 90), resounds with irony. He cautions wisely against demands for conformity by an overzealous superego, but the wise advice comes from a man too ineffectual to accomplish his own will.

In Stanley's attempts to resist maturation, he resorts to regression, an extreme regression all the way back to the oral period of life. Martin Esslin says Stanley "has regressed to the status of a babe in arms."[14] Indeed, the play reveals a regression even greater than that; the play contains a birth fantasy. The setting is "a house in a seaside town" (p. 9). Freud says presence at the seashore usually indicates a birth fantasy and that "the delivery of a child from the uterine waters is commonly represented, by way of distortion, as the entry of the child into water."[15] Stanley tells Lulu he was "in the sea at half past six" (p. 26). It is a significant lie: symbolically, he was taken from the uterine waters at 6:30 *A.M.* Goldberg later makes a speech that blends into one the image of the emergent embryo at birth and the waking man in the morning. Ultimately, like Beckett's birth astride a grave, the two images fade into a corpse. The whole speech is introduced by the play's title image:

> What a thing to celebrate—birth! Some people don't like the idea of getting up in the morning. I've heard them. Getting up in the morning, they say, what is it? Your skin's crabby, you need a shave, your eyes are full of muck, your mouth is like a boghouse, the palms of your hands are full of sweat, your nose is clogged up, your feet stink, what are you but a corpse waiting to be washed? (p. 48)

The seashore also connotes a place of pleasure which, of course, is what Stanley wishes to gain by regression. Meg's house is a boarding house—a place where people are fed and nourished. At Stanley's first appearance, he comes to be fed his breakfast. His entrance is preceded by the conversation about his incessant sleeping. He is pictured then as spending his time as babies do—sleeping and eating. The strongest clue to orality is Meg's mothering presence. She calls Stanley by infantile names—"little monkey," "Stanny," "good boy." Pinter prepares the way for this mother-son relationship by Meg's expression of regret that Lady Mary Splatt has given birth to a girl. Meg would rather have a boy. This birth story all but begins the play.

In connection with the birth fantasy there are in the play elements of separation anxiety—fear of dispossession. The earliest danger situations the child experiences are loss of the mother's breast and later of the mother herself. Meg's teasing indicates the presence of the first mentioned anxiety. She taunts Stanley by refusing to feed him—"No breakfast" (p. 15). He protests that he has been dreaming about this breakfast all night long. The presence of the second anxiety is evidenced by

Stanley's never going out. Lulu encourages him to come out and get a bit of air. And leaving the house is immediately associated with food. He tells Lulu, "I'm a big eater, you know" (p. 27).

Stanley also shows the ambivalence of the oral-sadistic stage. He rejects Meg and her food. He spits out that the "milk's off," that "the cornflakes are terrible" (p. 15). He insults Meg by calling her a "succulent old washing bag" (p. 19). The klang associations here reveal a reference to her nourishing breast and her bag of waters in which the embryo is carried. Moments later he shows that the jocular tone of these rejections conceals inner conflicts that are exhausting him. He puts "his head in his hands" and says: "Oh God, I'm tired" (p. 19). She assumes the role of mother-seductress and asks coyly: "Am I really succulent?" He reacts "violently" and resumes his symbolic insults. He calls her house a pigsty and says he needs a new room. Thus, his residue of guilt begins while he defends himself against engulfment and indicates his attempt to move into the next stage of life.

These oral elements provide the play with its most popular interpretation, man's fear of expulsion from the womb. A variety of critics have recognized these associations in the play. Indeed, the title forces notice of them and lends emphasis to this determination. The play emerges as the story of a man who has attempted to escape the world's guilt and responsibility by returning to a place of womblike security. Here Meg offers him what James T. Boulton characterizes as "a childhood world that has gone to seed."[16] Goldberg and McCann are again the externalization of Stanley's own guilts and fears. Lois Gordon calls them "projections of Stanley's guilt, driving and uncompromising internal furies."[17] They pursue him to his refuge and force him out of it into the deadly world he fears; he fears it because there lies his final punishment for his sin. All too often, however, a simplistic view of this determination overlooks the tension provided by the oral-sadistic elements. At the same time that Stanley clings to Meg's protection, he is revolted by her. At the same time that he fears the punishment of his projected father figures, he welcomes it and acquiesces to it at the end of the party. Consequently, at the same time that the spectators pity Stanley for his final destruction, they participate in his sense of relief that his dangerous flight from inevitability is ended.

Norman Holland says that the "oral fantasies of being engulfed or devoured become, in anal writing, fears of being enveloped by what is foul, dirty, or sordid."[18] Thus, the oral and anal elements of this play overlap. Even more indicative of anal anxieties, however, is Stanley's constant alternation between defiance and submission that Holland says creates "lifelong habits about rage, giving up, or giving in. . . ."[19] He accepts Meg as confidante; he pours out to her the story of his first concert and his dreams of a world tour. Then he rejects her. She responds to the recital of his dreams by a concern for his elimination: "Aren't you feeling well this morning, Stan? Did you pay a visit this morning?" (p. 24). "He stiffens" and defies her attempt to turn him into a little boy by turning her into a frightened little girl. He tells her that "they" are coming for her in a van with a wheelbarrow. Further instances of Stanley's defiance and rage are in his reactions to Goldberg and McCann. In the conversation with McCann, he objects to a birthday party; he objects to being called "sir." He calls Goldberg a "dirty joke" and fights both their attempts to make him sit down. The elaborate conversations about sitting down and standing up also reflect the struggle for dominance. The residue of anxiety and guilt from this period builds on this defiance and centers on failures to keep clean. The litany of Stanley's guilts includes references to his not bathing, to his stinking and his sweating.

These anal factors emphasize the play as a struggle for

command of Stanley's soul. Several critics point out the battle between the artist and society that is inherent in *The Birthday Party*. As if in a dream, the artist fades into a son while society fades into a father. The combat is between father and son— the generation gap. In either case, the play does encompass a fatal battle for Stanley's future way of life. Stanley's defiance has caused his break from his former life. He had not invited his father to his concert: "I—I lost the address, that was it" (p. 23). It was after that that they locked him out. When he got there, "the hall was closed" (p. 23). Stanley fled, then, from their demands: they wanted him to "crawl down on [his] bended knees" (p. 24). His defiance ends, however, in submission. Ultimately, society or the father figures capture Stanley, and he submits to their rehabilitation.

There is also overlapping of the anal anxieties and the phallic anxieties. When the child is born into the phallic phase, the concerns with standing up and sitting down take on added significance. Holland explains it: "The phallus with its power to stand erect becomes identified with the boy's own recently acquired power to stand up and [with] his other skills, such as talking."[20] To be forced to sit down becomes connected at this point with loss of manhood. This is what happens to Stanley at the birthday party. For approximately forty-five consecutive speeches, Goldberg and McCann struggle to make Stanley sit down. He refuses; he tricks *them* into sitting down; he argues; but eventually he sits in silence. Thus, he becomes a child at his birthday party; he has lost his manhood. The other way to lose manhood is by castration; therein lies the root of the overlapping between anal and phallic concerns. These phallic concerns grow into oedipal and primal-scene fantasies that increase castration fears. Animism—the belief in "magical thinking, which affects all the developmental phases"— complicates castration fear still further. As a result of animism, the child fears he can be punished for his thoughts as well as his deeds. Among the literary representations of animism Holland lists verbal formulas and rituals, fears of the dark, and the "child's sense of helplessness in the face of some other nameless power (adult or supernatural)."[21] The litanies that Goldberg and McCann recite, recounting parental admonitions and Stanley's violations of them, certainly are verbal formulas or rituals. Moreover, during the birthday party in Act II, frightful things occur while the stage is plunged into darkness. Finally, Stanley is rendered helpless by the powers of Goldberg and McCann.

Oedipal fears are Stanley's principal problem. Lidz states that "oedipal strivings with the ensuing guilt. . .create anxiety over punishment by castration, abandonment, or death. . . ."[22] Stanley fears all of these, and his self-accusations about oedipal sins resound throughout the verbal punishments of Goldberg and McCann: "Why are you driving the old lady off her conk? . . .You contaminate womankind. . . .Mother defiler!. . .You verminate the sheet of your birth. . . .You betrayed our land" (pp. 50-55). Likewise, every major scene of the play contains oedipal imagery. The flirtation between Stanley and Meg needs no documentation. It is, however, worth noting that when one of Freud's female patients dreamed of preparing for a birthday party, Freud equated it with readiness for coitus.[23] And it is Meg who first declares that it is Stanley's birthday. Moreover, her birthday present to Stanley is a toy drum, a musical instrument shaped like a box and covered with membrane. Stanley beats on this drum with the phallic drum sticks, and later he puts his foot into the drum, breaking the membrane. The sexual imagery is obvious. Stanley's account of his concert career and its demise contains oedipal undertones, too. He says he had a "unique touch" and "they" were grateful. But in the next breath, he admits his father was not there. He had mentally banished him; he had lost his address. As a result, "they" had carved him up; mutilation symbolizes castration. When he arrived for his next concert, the hall was locked. "They'd locked it up" (p. 23). In discussing the representation of the woman as a room, Freud says: "The interest as to whether the room is 'open' or 'locked' will be readily understood in this connection."[24]

At the party the game of blindman's buff can be viewed as an extravagant primal scene. Stanley, at first, sits on the side and watches while the other figures move about, touching and fondling one another. McCann takes Stanley's glasses and breaks them, signifying that watching adult sex play is taboo for the child. Then when Stanley is blindfolded for the game, he steps into Meg's drum. Almost immediately thereafter, he expresses his revulsion by trying to strangle Meg. In these incidents Stanley has acted out two of the deepest sources of oedipal guilt: the wish to interact sexually with the mother and the wish to punish her for her infidelity with the father. At the end of the game Stanley is discovered hunched over Lulu's prone figure. Since Goldberg has been fondling Lulu while Stanley watched, Stanley appears once more to be trying to replace the father in the sexual act. As the light is shone on Stanley, the prepsychotic fear of being under scrutiny is concretized, adding to the picture of inner hysteria that Stanley is experiencing. When his attempted rape is disclosed, he resorts to the childish feint of giggling. Then the father figures threaten him again. They converge upon him, backing him up against the wall. Stanley makes no move to resist. However, before the party he had tried to escape from the house, and McCann had prevented him. Later he had kicked Goldberg in the stomach. At this point he submits. It appears that here he has relinquished his oedipal desires. He has given up his desire to replace his father and surrendered to the superior power of their images. He pauses in his defiance to receive the punishment that will relieve his guilt.

The next morning the fathers have carried Stanley upstairs, listened to him talk, and sat with him until he has fallen asleep. Then they have cleaned him up and dressed him up; and now they lead him off to home and a doctor. Such treatment can not fail to suggest that given to the errant child. Stanley has been punished in other ways as well. His glasses have been broken, and he has lost the power of speech. He can no longer see what he should not, and he can no longer spit back his defiance. He has lost his manhood; he has been symbolically castrated. He has also suffered psychological death, according to Freud's equation of dumbness with death.[25] Stanley has received the punishment his superego demanded as it shouted his self-hate and self-effacement through the litanies of Goldberg and McCann. Stanley's own fears and wishes have been realized.

An overview of this oedipal determination of the play reveals its strength. Stanley, like Sophocles' hero himself, has fled from the incestuous and murderous desires toward one set of parents to the security of another home. Here he engages in flirtation with a second mother figure. As he had banished the first father from his thoughts and his concert, he ignores the husband of his new mother/wife. Both men are dead to him. His guilt and sins, however, pursue him relentlessly. As Oedipus worked blindly toward his own defeat, so does Stanley. As each new messenger told another chapter of Oedipus' crime, so do Goldberg and McCann continually chant new verses of Stanley's shame. As projections of his punishing fathers and his own self-indictments, Goldberg and McCann, like Teiresius, bring the criminal face-to-face with the final truth. Oedipus plucked out his own eyes in punishment for his sins and went voluntarily into exile. Stanley accepts blindness and banishment from the father figures who are, in fact, his own externalized superego.

From an even longer view, *The Birthday Party* emerges as a concretization of the birth and death cycle within the psyche.

As such this play, called a *party*, is clearly a punishment dream with all its accompanying anxieties. The play focuses on the desire for punishment that accompanies the accumulated guilts of the developmental stages. The title derives from the idea that a child must be born into each new phase of his growth and suffer its corresponding fears and punishments before he can be reborn into the next phase. This life and death cycle, repeating itself within the psyche, occasions in the dramatic imagination a series of intrapsychic birthdays. They do not follow each other in linear order as they do in outer reality; they are condensed by the primary process into a crazy quilt of images: a birth fantasy brought to an end by separation anxiety, an anal wish for dominance brought to an end by submission to vanquishing fathers, an oedipal wish brought to an end by castration fears and final acquiescense to the demands of the superego. *The Birthday Party* is a paradoxical celebration of birth into destruction and death.

As a final determination, the play is also a concretization of regression itself. It depicts man's inability to be born out of infantilism. This party given by adults to chastise the wayward child into a more mature life features the repressions and self-indulgences that characterize the regression of these same adults. In Lois Gordon's words: "the party becomes a celebration of original sin and guilt in all men."[26] Meg begins the party by coming downstairs "holding sticks and drum." She is dressed in the dress her father gave her. She persists in forcing each of the men to compliment her. In her toast to Stanley she cries out her lack of maternal fulfillment. To McCann she babbles out her childhood erotism for her father. She remembers her little pink room with all its musical boxes. There she was cared for and had no complaints. Yet she also admits her father was going to take her to Ireland, but went away by himself. The cause of Meg's problem becomes clear. She was rejected by her father and never able to develop emotionally beyond her oedipal days. This rejection was so painful that she learned to transform pain and unpleasantness into their opposites—pink rooms and protection. At the end of the play, all she can remember of the macabre party is that she was the belle of the ball. But she has to convince herself it it true: "Oh, it's true. I was. *Pause.* I know I was" (p. 91). Meg has the wishes of child, woman, and mother all rolled into one. Her readiness to apply to herself Stanley's adjective, "succulent," reveals her subconscious awareness of these repressed wishes. The klang associations of the word cover all her would-be roles. Succulent means juicy and rich. Suckling means an unweaned infant. Suck refers to the function of her mothering breast. Succuba is a female demon reputed to have sexual intercourse with men in their sleep. Succor is the help or aid she gives to Stanley, the refugee. Ironically, Stanley first used the word to refer to the fried bread. Such is the way that life has passed Meg by.

Lulu also reveals repressed oedipal feelings when she offers to fill Goldberg up, and to sit in his lap and bounce to the ceiling. As the alcohol warms her, she admits she has always liked older men, and she finds Goldberg the "dead image of the first man" she "ever loved" (p. 64). It is she who suggests they play blindman's buff. Then while the blind men stumble, she allows Goldberg to fondle her. But when she sees Stanley moving toward her, she screams and faints. That night she sleeps with Goldberg. But the next morning, the party over, she resumes her inhibitions and retreats with indignation and threats.

Goldberg and McCann indulge themselves, too. Goldberg is no more maudlin than usual, but he does slather about infancy—what "our mums taught us in the nursery" (p. 59). However, at the party he acts out his sexual desires; he plays games with Lulu and reminisces about having played with her in the past—piggyback and pop goes the weasel. McCann is normally tight with an aura of contained violence. At the party, however, McCann relaxes and remembers "Mother Nolan's." Thus, he joins the regression to orality. He refrains, however, from sex play with the women, and instead recalls his parties with the boys—"singing and drinking all night" (p. 63). He recites about the night "poor Paddy was stretched" and the boys "all paid him a visit" (p. 64). And he sings a song—a love song about the Garden of Eden—where all of these children would like to return. It's calling him home.

There is one exclusion from the party—Petey. Petey reneged. He preferred to go out to a quiet game of chess. Petey has always reneged from life. As an element of Stanley's father image, he withdrew from the problems of child rearing except for a gentle concern on occasion. He withdraws from Meg each morning by hiding behind his paper. He reads about life rather than living it. He attends the deck chairs, another waiting and watching operation. At the end he is moved to protect "Stan," but the simple threat of being taken along causes him to retreat to a mild offer of advice. He has never outgrown the childish defense of restricting the ego. Anna Freud explains this defense with a story of a little boy who was eagerly drawing with a colored pencil. She began to draw, too, and the little boy was pleased until he glanced at her paper. Then he abruptly put down his pencil and said, "You go on doing it; I would much rather watch." When he had seen that her drawing was superior, he had decided not to compete. He abandoned the activity even though it had brought him pleasure. "He adopted the role of the spectator, who does nothing and so cannot have his performance compared with that of someone else. By imposing this restriction on himself the child avoided a repetition of the disagreeable impression."[27] So it was with Petey; he never came to the party—not to Meg's, not to Stanley's, not to life's.

These various determinations disclose the thematic messages of the play. The realistic reading reveals the play's general meaning. Goldberg and McCann are external forces that Stanley is anxious to evade. Three times they ask him: "Do you recognize an external force?" (p. 53). Each time he answers evasively. But the play shows man can not continue to evade these forces. They will seek him out and shape him to their measure. They will take away his clear vision so that he must stumble into his choices like a blindfolded child. They will brainwash his thoughts and silence his speech. They will dress him in clothes appropriate to the funeral of his real self and drive him away in a hearse. When the rebirth they celebrated occurs, he will be what they make him. The play also demonstrates that such human destruction can take place inside man's own secret refuge. The enemies can come right in. They need only knock at the door and give a party to celebrate the new life they will build on the death of the old.

The birthday fete, the title symbol of *The Birthday Party*, also shows life as a wild, erotic party where perpetual children dance and play, punish and suffer, while they yearn for home and Eden. It is a party of bitter irony because the child whom the party pushes toward maturity watches from the sidelines while the adults indulge in the infantile behavior they chastise him for. Life's birthday party is a giant orgy of regression.

From the intrapsychic point of view, *The Birthday Party* shows life as a cycle of births and anxieties, punishments and deaths. The child is born into each successive stage, learns its fears, suffers its guilts, seeks its punishments, and through the death of some part of his inner self, he is born into the next stage. In this fashion, the births and the fears, the punishments and the deaths build on one another, and who can say where the cycle begins. "Which came first? Chicken? Egg? Which came first?" (p. 55).

The play also picks up on some of the minor themes of *The Room*, holding them in abeyance until they will be the focus of future plays. Man's impotence is echoed. Petey's ineffectuality echoes Mr. Kidd's. Stanley's sexual impotence echoes Bert's, and over all of the men in both of the plays hangs the cloud of personal inadequacy. The women are ignorant and promiscuous. They emasculate by their overprotectiveness. Thus, they satisfy their own needs while they imagine themselves to be satisfying their mates. And around them all is the aura of promiscuity. As *The Room* hints at Rose's former promiscuity, so *The Birthday Party* reveals Meg's promiscuous desires and fantasies, and Lulu's actual indulgences with Goldberg.

Principally, this play enlarges on the theme of *The Room* — the danger to oneself lives within. The dream dynamics in *The Birthday Party* reveal that the external force man fears, the force that finds him out and shapes him, is not external at all. The nameless "they" who menaces man is his own sense of guilt and inadequacy. No flight is possible from this menace. It goes with man wherever he goes because it lives in the unconscious by which man is controlled. Thus, it makes man what he fears to be. What's more, man welcomes this punishment as a relief from its inevitability. If guilt and fear are strong enough, they can blind man to reality, castrate him, cause him to relinquish his own dreams by forcing him back into the pattern of his fathers. Goldberg said it to McCann: "And I knew the word I had to remember — Respect! Because McCann — Seamus — who came before your father? His father. And who came before him? . . . Who came before your father's father but your father's father's mother! Your great-gran-granny" (p. 81).

THE DUMB WAITER

If moving backward from Goldberg and McCann leads to "great-gran-granny," moving forward leads to Ben and Gus in

The Dumb Waiter, Pinter's third play. *The Dumb Waiter* was written later in the same year, 1957, as *The Room* and *The Birthday Party,* so its similarities are not surprising. It seems to focus on a segment of *The Birthday Party,* the hired killers. Ben and Gus appear, at first, to be Goldberg and McCann waiting for another assignment. Goldberg and McCann drove up to Meg's house in their car, rented a room in her house, took care of Stanley, and left the next morning; Ben and Gus operate in the same manner. Gus explains their routine: "I mean, you come into a place when it's still dark, you come into a room you've never seen before, you sleep all day, you do your job, and then you go away in the night again."[28] They have other similarities as well. One talks a great deal more than the other; one busies himself with a newspaper; one seems to be in charge. These relationships, however, are reversed in some ways. In *The Birthday Party,* Goldberg talks and commands, and McCann tears newspapers into strips and carries out orders. Ben is the boss of this new duo. He looks up from his newspaper long enough to give orders. Gus is the doer and the talker. Ben and Gus, however, are not the menacing intruders of *The Dumb Waiter.* They are the two people in a room who are menaced from outside. The play, then, repeats the basic Pinter situation. Instead of a man and wife as it is in *The Room,* there are two men, but again they are confined in a small room of a large house about which they know nothing. Again they concern themselves with eating, while they tensely await an expected visitor. They do not, however, expect to be the victims; they expect to be the killers. Or do they? The element of menace and uncertainty is the same as it is in *The Room* and *The Birthday Party. The Dumb Waiter's* visitors, however, never appear on stage. They remain mysteriously unseen, but they do make their presence known. They give the order that Gus is to die.

Gus, then, becomes the one punished and assumes the

role of the central figure in the dream. Therefore, his resemblance shifts to Stanley; he is the sinner who must pay for his crimes. In this play, however, the dream-censor allows a more positive identification of the crime. Stanley's crimes were left vague, unstated. Gus's crimes are known; he is a killer, and he is punished. Thus, *The Dumb Waiter* takes its place with the first group of plays.

Like the other two plays of this group, the surface reality of *The Dumb Waiter* is tense and broken in continuity. Ben and Gus await their assignment in a basement room of the unknown house. Ben lies on the bed alternately reading the paper and watching Gus. Gus is more restless: he paces, shows constant concern with food, gives continuing attention to the lavatory, and complains about his work and his treatment by his superiors. Ben counters these complaints and gives orders. It soon becomes obvious, however, that Ben's commands conceal his fears, while Gus, though tense, has the courage to take action and even to think about his work. His questions only irritate Ben. Soon the two men are frightened by a loud clatter; they discover a dumb waiter in the wall between their beds. The dumb waiter returns again and again with orders for food placed there by an unknown presence upstairs. Ben and Gus send up all they have—Gus's store of snacks. The people upstairs send back complaints: the Eccles cake was stale and the chocolate was melted. Gus is disgruntled. He is hungry and thirsty, too. He does not like "doing a job on an empty stomach" (p. 114). Ben insists that the time for the job is near, and he gives Gus instructions. These are "stated and repeated" like a ritual. Finally, while Gus is offstage, in the lavatory, Ben gets the message that the time has come to do the job. Ben calls to Gus and levels his revolver at the door. Gus stumbles in, stooped and stripped of his upper clothing and his revolver. Pinter says: "*He raises his head and looks at Ben. A long silence. They stare at each other. Curtain*" (p. 121).

This play reveals the terror of the terrorists. The fear and tension that barely showed behind the violence of Bert, the killer, is here emphasized in killers, Ben and Gus. They are indeed no less afraid than was Stanley, the victim. And, of course, if Stanley was, like all little boys, a killer in thought, then he, like Gus, was killer turned victim.

Again the realistic determination of the play leaves questions and confusion. With Gus the spectator asks: who slipped the envelope under the door? who sent the orders down the hatch? He also wonders about the significance of the demands for food. Most of all, he wants to know if Ben knew from the outset that Gus was the intended victim. Some of these questions are answered when the play is approached as a dream.

In this case, the various determinations of the dream are condensed under the title symbol. Lois Gordon recognizes the ingenuity of this title but finds it misleading. She notes that "Unless the author has carelessly misused two words instead of one, the *dumb waiter* cannot refer to the mechanical object, a single or hyphenated word." She speculates, therefore, that it refers to Ben and Gus, each of whom "is the waiter, the servant, to his internal drives."[29] Actually, however, *dumb waiter* can be a pun of multiple meanings, one of which can surely be the mechanical object despite the evolution of its spelling into one word. With this referent, the title alludes to the apparatus that is central to much of the action of the play. It links Ben and Gus to the mysterious powers outside the room. It conveys symbolically the idea of taking from them—Gus, particularly, because it is his food—the last that they have to offer and finding it unsatisfactory. Dealing with the realistic determination of the play, Ben and Gus are the dumb waiters—in a dual sense. They attempt to serve Gus's meager hoard of morsels to the unknown diners upstairs even though they are unfamiliar with the exotic dishes being ordered. They are dumb waiters also because they have always made themselves available, unquestioningly, for the moment when the powers will order them to eliminate the next victim.

Moving to the unconscious meanings beneath the surface of the montage, the dominant latent image of *The Dumb Waiter* is a little boy waiting silently in the night to be taken to the bathroom. This image is presented in a profusion of manifest images of an anal character. First, the identification of Ben and Gus as killers has anal overtones; Freud establishes a direct link between varieties of bogeymen and toilet-training anxieties.

Robbers, burglars, and ghosts, of whom some people feel frightened before going to bed, and who sometimes pursue their victims after they are asleep, all originate from one and the same class of infantile reminiscence. They are the nocturnal visitors who rouse children and take them up to prevent their wetting their beds, or who lift the bedclothes to make sure where they have put their hands in their sleep. Analyses of some of these anxiety-dreams have made it possible for me to identify these nocturnal visitors more precisely. In every case the robbers stood for the sleeper's father, whereas the ghosts correspond to female figures in white nightgowns.[30]

The play's emphasis upon obedience to orders is also an indication of the anal phase of development. According to Freudian theory, during the anal period the child is expected to relinquish one aspect of his freedom and "accede to his mother's demand that he use the toilet for the evacuation of feces and urine."[31] His feelings are complicated by a libidinal attachment to his feces as part of himself; he is loathe to give them up. Consequently, he expresses resentment; he attempts to frustrate his mother by holding back, that is, by being anal retentive. On the other hand, the child fears loss of parental love, and so alternately he submits; this is the defiance-submission antithesis, characterized by the struggle for mastery and control.[32] In *The Dumb Waiter* Ben and Gus are under constant demands to give up their food. Gus is loathe to part with it. He tries to hold back the tea bag; he asks to keep the Eccles cake; he tries to conceal the crisps (pp. 105-106). Only at Ben's insistence does he put them all out on the plate. Ben's role is thereby recognized as the superego, and the superego constantly asserts its control over Gus. Splitting of this kind is also typical of the anal period. Lidz explains that this is a "time of notable ambivalence." The child "cannot really contain opposite feelings at the same time," so he "vacillates from one to the other." He is apt to split his mother into a loving mother and a frustrating mother. "Similarly, he is apt to consider himself as two children: a good, pleasing child and a naughty, contrary one. The 'good child' may wish to renounce responsibility for the 'bad child.' He has difficulties with his unity and with accepting responsibility to the same parents for all of his behavior."[33] Then, Ben's frequent alarm at Gus's behavior takes on deeper meaning. For example, when Gus shouts up the tube: "The larder's bare!", Ben grabs it and says with "great deference": "Good evening, I'm sorry to — bother you, but we just thought we'd better let you know that we haven't got anything left. We sent up all we had. There's no more food down here" (p. 111). The fact that Ben and Gus send food up the hatch instead of feces down the intestinal track indicates displacement in the concretization. Toilet-training fantasies are accompanied by great anxiety and so distortion is a necessary defense. Feces are therefore transformed into uneaten food and the downward direction is displaced upward.

The Dumb Waiter abounds in other evidences of anality, including the recurring emphasis on neatness and cleanliness. Ben is disgusted with the news story of the little girl killing a cat; Gus begins to wonder who cleans up the messes their victims make. Gus is also disgruntled over not having clean sheets. The play begins and ends with auditory anal imagery.

Before a word is spoken, the sound of the lavatory chain being pulled is heard offstage (p. 85). Again at the end, just before Gus's final entrance, "the lavatory flushes off left" (p. 120). Afterwards, Gus stumbles into the room stripped of his upper clothing—jacket, waistcoat, tie—and his holster and revolver. This could be another case of displacement upward, averting attention from the missing lower garments. He has been ignominiously placed on the toilet. He has been stripped of his pants and his revolver—his defiance and his manhood. Before him stands Ben, the good boy. Ben still has his revolver and is holding it in his hand. The defiant side of the child has received the punishment that his guilt required.

The anal content of the play confirms, then, its character as a punishment dream. It also undoes some of the dream's displacement by identifying the antagonists more clearly—father and son, son split into good boy and bad boy. The source of the antagonism is still disguised, however. Here it appears to be toilet-training resentment. Although the crime is displaced, the feelings of guilt and fear and the attendant wish for punishment are the same.

The title symbol of *The Dumb Waiter* holds still another image—a little boy silently waiting while sounds and images of the primal scene mingle in his head. Freud says that "the portions of the dream in which people are busy *upstairs* and *downstairs*, 'above' and 'beneath,' point to fancies of a sexual content. . . ."[34] The powers that order Ben and Gus are busy upstairs with thoughts of exotic food. They are busy downstairs slipping envelopes under doors. The oedipal fantasies that always accompany the primal-scene fantasies are in evidence when Gus sticks his head into the hatch and looks up. Holland associates phallic fantasies with "poking or prying into things."[35] The accompanying oedipal wish to kill the father is embodied in the central identity of the boys in the dream: they are killers. This wish is also discernible in the instruction ritual;

the "bloke" is trapped between Ben and Gus, each of whom points his revolver at the hypothetical victim.

Castration fear is so strong in this play that there is an overlapping fantasy of impotence and inadequacy. This is the next image condensed in the phrase—*dumb waiter*. *Dumb* implies mental impotence, and removing mental potency is a castration symbol.[36] Alrene Sykes expresses this theme of the play in realistic terms. Sykes says Gus suffers because he is inefficient.[37] On the unconsciouis level, however, the picture is of a child waiting in impotence to be husband to his mother. Ben and Gus are ordered to put exotic foods into the box, but they have only ordinary things to give. Their ordinary things are unsatisfactory: their cakes are stale; their chocolate is melted; their milk is sour. Unmistakably, the box equals a vagina, and the exotic orders represent the imagined sexual demands of the mother; the rejected food is the child's inadequacy. Other symbols of impotence are the "deficient ballcock" (p. 89) and the teakettle that Gus can not light. Ben tells him he will have to *wait* — "for Wilson" (p. 100). Wilson, of course, is the possible owner of the house, the man who will give the call—the father figure.

The oedipal content of the dream reveals the greater source of the child's guilt—the forbidden fantasies about mother and the hostility toward father. The resultant feelings of mother's promiscuity and the child's own impotence take on added strength in this third play. The feeling of impotence is itself part of the punishment that this determination also stresses.

The punishment wish inherent in *The Dumb Waiter* is even clearer in another of its determinations. At the center of this whirlpool of images of the dumb waiter is a death wish. Remembering Freud's equation of dumbness with death[38] suggests that the little boy is a fearful figure anticipating his own death. Martin Esslin also sees a death wish in *The Dumb Waiter*. Speaking of "the final confrontation" between Ben and Gus—

"executioner and victim"—he says: "There is always a death wish at the bottom of these insoluble tensions. The supernatural forces driving us to murder our fellow human being are our subconscious desires and fantasies of aggression."[39] This idea appears in the first exchange of dialogue in the play. Ben tells Gus about the newspaper item in which an eighty-seven-year-old man crawls under a lorry to get across the road. "The lorry started and ran over him" (p. 86). The story makes Ben want to "puke"; Gus finds it incredible. They react to the essence of the story: an old man found what seemed to him a rational way to bring about his own death. The presence of the death wish gains additional support from Gus's feeling that his bedroom is like a tomb. It has no window; he can not see outside. It is a basement room—underground and damp.

This death wish suggests a major interpretation of the play as a whole. At the unconscious level, the child turns his fatal wish for the father onto himself. At the conscious level, Gus, who has come to wonder about his work, to feel dissatisfied with it, to feel emptied by it, yearns to be free of guilt and shame. He, therefore, asks for punishment, death, by a route he knows to be certain—asking questions.

The thematic revelations of *The Dumb Waiter* echo those of the other two plays. On the realistic level, Ben and Gus, like Bert in *The Room*, illustrate the partnership of violence and fear. They commit violence out of fearful, blind obedience to mysterious unknown powers. For these powers they have emptied themselves—emotionally and morally. Their intellects have been silenced long ago with their wills, and the reward for Gus's awakening curiosity is destruction. Like Rose and Stanley, Gus fears destruction from the outside; but, like them, he finds it lives with him: the mysterious powers have ordered Gus's destruction at the hands of his friend, Ben.

The dream life of the play reinforces these themes and adds new meaning as well. *The Dumb Waiter* picks up on the regression theme of *The Birthday Party*. Gus and Ben appear to be hardened killers, but inside they are only children, like the people at Stanley's party. They have carried into adulthood the guilts and fears of infancy. Their killer instincts stem from their toilet-training days; their hostility toward men and women stems from old oedipal feelings. What is more, even these terrifying killers yearn to return to the secure womb. This infantilism that Pinter shows persisting in men's inner lives puts him in agreement with Wordsworth's, "The child is father of the man," and with Freud's discovery that the child lives on, almost unchanged, in the waking man as well as in the dreamer.

A SLIGHT ACHE

The final play of this first group, *A Slight Ache*, was written for radio and first produced by the B.B.C. in July 1959. Despite the lapse of time between this play and the other three, it remains inextricably interwoven with them. Simon Trussler exclaims that in this play Pinter suddenly "moved out of town and. . .out of doors."[40] However, this seeming departure from the characteristic setting of a room is only an illusion. Radio sets very few physical limits; therefore, *A Slight Ache* spreads out over more space. The setting is a country house with an eating room, a scullery, a study, and a garden. At the end of the garden is a gate; beyond that gate is the outside world. Edward and Flora establish it as such just as clearly as Rose and Bert define the areas beyond their window and door as the outside world. Moreover, the Matchseller blocks Edward's gateway. He and Flora are confined within their space by this physical fact as well as by the dialogue and imagery of the play. Their enclosure is merely more elaborate, and Edward and Flora are more affluent. As Martin Esslin points out, this is "the first of Pinter's plays based on a middle-class idiom."[41]

Within this setting the basic Pinter situation is reenacted. When the curtain opens, "*Flora and Edward are discovered sitting at the breakfast table. Edward is reading the paper.*"[42] They are familiarly old. As Riley lay in the basement waiting to see Rose, the Matchseller lurks at the gate until he is summoned by Edward. The prospect of this visitor creates great anxiety in Edward, as it did in Rose, Stanley, and Gus. After the visit has become reality, Edward, like Stanley and Gus, is near death.

As usual, the characters are unique but bear some basic resemblance to those who came before. Flora is a motherly wife, always fussing over Edward's physical well-being. Edward is an insecure man. Like Stanley, he seems at the outset to be in a prepsychotic state. Flora is more sensual than Rose or even Meg; Edward is talkative and irritable. Thus, he pairs with Stanley and Gus instead of Bert or Petey. The Matchseller parallels Riley in many ways. Both are dark; one is blind and the other is mute. Both are relatively passive. John Russell Taylor notes that the Matchseller is a "passive menace," more a "disruptive force in the mind" than an active agent.[43] His description is accurate, and it fits Riley, too, to a lesser degree. Both characters are acted upon. The Matchseller, however, is not immediately the victim. He may well be Flora's next victim, but in the confines of the play, it is Edward who suffers collapse. It is Edward who is the central figure wishing for and receiving punishment. Basically, Edward, like Stanley and Gus, wants to be punished for his sins against the father.

Edward's anxiety is immediately apparent even in the manifest content of the play. At breakfast there is an undertone of tension between Edward and Flora. Edward's irritability comes to light when he traps a wasp in the marmalade jar and scalds it with boiling water poured down the spoon-hole. His fear of the Matchseller seems irrational from the outset. As Flora says, the man is old and harmless, but Edward finds him a great threat. He has been watching him daily from a window in the scullery. Then he insists on bringing him into the house to "get to the bottom of it" and "get rid of" the Matchseller. James R. Hollis analyzes it very well: "He [Edward] invites the Matchseller in so that he can deal with him as a master deals with a subordinate, as a man deals with a wasp."[44] However, once the Matchseller is inside the house, Edward subverts his own intention. In private conversation with the Matchseller, Edward reveals himself by his accusations against the Matchseller. Edward projects all of his own inadequacies onto the old tramp. While the Matchseller sits mute, Edward reviews his own past. When his monologue has exhausted him, Flora comes in for her private session with the old man. She finds him attractive. He reminds her of a poacher who once raped her in the mud. As she warms to his dirty, muddy presence, she becomes overjoyed at the prospect of keeping him to bathe and bed and pamper until he dies. Edward returns for a final monologue of sensual memories about his physical contacts with nature. As he talks he is stricken with fever. The slight ache he has had in his eyes turns into complete physical collapse. As he lies on the floor weakening, the Matchseller appears more youthful and vigorous to him. He asks: "Who are you?" Flora's voice answers, "Barnabas?"—the name she has given the Matchseller. She enters, takes the Matchseller out to see her garden, and leaves Edward holding the tray of matches.

Here again is the familiar story of a man who brings about his own displacement and destruction through his own fear. Also familiar is the Pinteresque absence of Aristotelian logic. Esslin characterizes the play as "the coexistence of extreme realism and the symbolism of the dream."[45] By this time even the tone of the questions is familiar: Who is the Matchseller? What causes Edward's slight ache? What is the significance of the wasp in the marmalade? Like the other plays, this one features unusual conversation, disconnected images, fragmentary memories. Knowledge of the dream dynamics in the other plays, however, clarifies some of the mystery of this one. Except for the difference in the ending—Bert inflicts death while Edward accepts it—*A Slight Ache* is in many ways a more elaborate and complex replay of *The Room*. The subtexture is denser, but the similarities are so great that some of the determinations of *A Slight Ache* can be dismissed briefly by reference to those in *The Room*.

Edward's confinement in these quarters with Flora, the "all-powerful mother," discloses oral fantasy. Flora's garden is clearly a female symbol. Freud confirms it: "*Gardens* are common symbols of the female genitals."[46] Thus, they are the entrance to the womb. Freud cites numerous cases of dreams in which landscapes represent the female body.[47] Edward yearns for the security of the womb, and he suffers from fears of dispossession. Flora fosters Edward's anxiety over separation by coddling him. Like Meg, she yearns to be a mother—to Edward and later to the Matchseller. This fragmentary evidence represents the wealth of oral imagery in the play that establishes it as another example of the dispossession theme. Edward, like Bert, fears dispossession; unlike Bert's, Edward's fears become reality. He is dispossessed.

Like *The Room*, *A Slight Ache* contains the struggle for dominance inherent in its anal content. Edward would like to be masterful. He shows it in his killing of the wasp, in his summoning of the Matchseller, in his irritability to Flora. He shows his anality also by his possessiveness; he collects curios and he strives to maintain possession of Flora. Flora shows her will to dominate in the same way that Rose does. She reduces Edward to a child. Thus, she fills her own desire for a child and simultaneously emasculates Edward. She shows this compulsion to motherly emasculation in her attentions to the Matchseller. She promises to bathe him, put him to bed, and buy him little toys to play with. Her words correspond closely to Freud's words about a patient's birth-fantasy: "Thinking of the boy going into the water induced a reverie in which she saw herself taking him out of the water, carrying him to a nursery, washing him and dressing him, and installing him in her household."[48] In Flora's unconscious, Edward and the Matchseller are little boys, babes, to play with. Thus, they become at the same time, children, sex objects, and representations of her feces. Her words to the Matchseller make this clear. She says seductively:

> Speak to me of love. *Pause.* God knows what you're saying at this very moment. It's quite disgusting. Do you know when I was a girl I loved. . .I loved. . .I simply. . .what *have* you got on, for goodness sake? A jersey? It's clogged. Have you been rolling in mud? (p. 32)

In these lines she associates his making love to her with his disgusting dirtiness and with her former pleasure at being raped in the mud. The unspoken pleasure from her childhood is, undoubtedly, having played with her feces. At the end of the speech she transforms him into a child and a thing as she exclaims: "I'm going to keep you. I'm going to keep you, you dreadful chap. . ." (p. 32). The constant references to cyclical recurrence in this play leave little doubt that Edward has received this same treatment from Flora. Consciously or unconsciously, she makes her men into things and dominates them. At the end of *The Room*, Bert emerges as the stronger. By his violence, he keeps Rose in greater subjection than she keeps him. At the end of *A Slight Ache*, however, it is Edward who is the loser. Flora abandons him and takes the Matchseller in his place. Thus, the anal determination confirms the play as a punishment dream.

The overlapping roles of mother and wife by which Flora relates to Edward lead into the oedipal content of the play. Edward's oedipal desires toward Flora as mother are implicit in his description of her garden: "The pool must be glistening. In the moonlight. And the lawn. I remember it well. The cliff. The sea. The three-masted schooner" (p. 39). The sexual symbolism of the garden and the uterine symbolism of the pool and the sea are already clear. The three-masted schooner can be associated with the male body. Freud asserts: "In any case the number three has been confirmed from many sides as a symbol of the male genitals."[49] Another instance of Edward's consideration of Flora as mother/wife occurs in his confusion between her honeysuckle and her convolvulus. The klang associations of honeysuckle with suckle (mother) and convolvulus with vulva (wife) clearly show the condensation of mother and wife into one. Moreover, Edward's father images are so threatening that in the confrontation with the Matchseller he displaces them as chairs. Chairs have been parent symbols in all of Pinter's plays so far, and in this one the composite father image is repeated from *The Birthday Party*. Edward's father images were all bought on sale, like the chairs he collects. Then, he associates himself with the many roles his borrowed fathers played—philosopher, theologian, traveler, student of flora and fauna. The Matchseller represents the guilts attached to all these father images. Ultimately, the Matchseller is the instrument of Edward's loss. Flora gives Edward the match tray and takes the old tramp in Edward's place. Edward collapses—weak and spent. He has been punished for his sin against the father. Unlike *The Dumb Waiter*, where Ben/Gus's crime is obliquely indicated by the characters' identity as killer, the real sin is not mentioned in *A Slight Ache*. As with Stanley Webber, the dream-censor has not allowed mention of a father's actual death. Edward's father figure, like Stanley's, is merely absent until his specter appears at the gate to haunt him.

There are many other determinations in this play as well. The density of the ambiguity is indicated by the two major symbols, the slight ache and the Matchseller, each containing its own montage of images and fantasies that link and tie off into interlocking cycles. The first major symbol is the title *A Slight Ache*. Its major reference is to the interlocking illnesses of Edward and Flora. He suffers from impotence and she from emptiness. In her emptiness, she aches for the fulfillment that he can not give because of his impotence. In his impotence he aches for youth and vigor, but she who would share it emasculates him by her smothering love. Thus, each one aches with mutual pains and longings. These aches are cyclical. They have grown before the play and do grow within it from slight aches to fully realized aches.

Edward's growing impotence is both psychological and physical. His headache and eyeache symbolize the beginning of a growing mental imbalance. It is slight at the outset; like Stanley Webber, he seems prepsychotic. His own sense of personal inadequacy seems to overwhelm him, and it creates what Arieti describes as a "gloomy web of feelings."[50] When the imbalance worsens, "The patient projects to the external world the evaluation of the self he now rejects."[51] This externalization is the "they" who menace. For Edward, "they" is the Matchseller, standing threateningly at his gate. Edward reveals the synonymity of his sense of inadequacy, the Matchseller, and "they" when he admits having watched and studied the old man through a span of time:

> In fact every time I have seen you you have looked quite different to the time before. *Pause*. Even now you look different. Very different. *Pause*. Admitted that sometimes I viewed you through dark glasses, yes, and sometimes through light glasses, and on other occasions bare eyed, and on other occasions through the bars of the scullery window, or from the roof, yes in driving snow, or from the bottom of the drive in thick fog, or from the roof again in blinding sun, so blinding, so hot, that I had to skip and jump and bounce in order to remain in one place. (p. 37)

The speech indicates both the persistence and the anxiety of Edward's examination of his inadequacies. Arieti says this kind of inadequacy usually springs out of the failures of basic trust in infancy.[52] Edward shows the results of an insecure infancy in his continuing need to be mothered. This anxious infancy has developed into an impotent adulthood, and, according to Arieti, "the path toward mental delapidation continues."[53] Edward's head and eye aches, therefore, symbolize mental deterioration and the distorted perception that causes him to see impotence and death standing before him. Moreover, both loss of mental competence and loss of sight are symbols of castration—another form of impotence. Edward's associations of the Matchseller with his own maleness, his castration, and his impotence are evident in his discussion of the Matchseller's balaclava. The Matchseller is, among other things, a projection by Edward of his own phallus, and the balaclava, as a head covering, suggests that his maleness is hidden, that he is impotent. The associations of beheading, castration, and the balaclava are represented in Edward's speech:

> For when I first saw you you wore no balaclava. No headcovering of any kind, in fact. You looked quite different without a head—I mean without a hat—I mean without a headcovering, of any kind. In fact every time I have seen you you have looked quite different to the time before. (p. 37)

Edward's aching for youth and vigor is the companion to this sense of impotence.

Flora shows her emptiness in her constant sexual demands. She continually calls to Edward to join her under the canopy, to work in her garden. She aches not only for a baby to coddle but also for a man to fulfill her desire. She reveals this desire by projecting it onto the Matchseller. She identifies him with her own forgotten sexual encounter with a poacher who once raped her in the mud. The word *poacher* reinforces the image of a "ghastly rape" or "a desperate battle," which are the descriptive phrases she uses. A poacher is a trespasser on someone else's land, which supports his identification with the Matchseller. A poacher is also one who takes game or fish illegally. The poacher took Flora illegally as the Matchseller soon will. The nature of Flora's projection upon the Matchseller is suggested by the name she gives him: "Barnabas." Hinchliffe cites the meaning of this name, "son of exhortation," as Flora's solution to the Matchseller's identity. He says Barnabas becomes her "Desirable and submissive combination of child, husband, and lover."[54] Kathleen Burkman, on the other hand, sees a different meaning in the name. She notes that:

> The day of Saint Barnabas, June eleventh in the old-style calendar, was the day of the summer solstice, and Barnaby-bright is the name for the longest day and the shortest night of the year. Flora merely recognizes her new god as the incarnation of summer itself. . . .[55]

This name has still another determination. Barnabas is the name of the man who sold his field and laid the money at the feet of the apostles to supply their physical needs (Acts 4: 32-37). Ananias, by contrast, kept back part of the proceeds from the sale of his property. Peter upbraided him for this deception saying: "You have not lied to me but to God." When Ananias heard these words, he fell down and died. When Edward's slights toward Flora increase, she rejects him and takes in his place Barnabas, who will sell all to supply her needs. As the play closes, Edward is lying on the floor, sick and gasping. Flora, who has always tended him, ignores him. She takes Barnabas by the hand and leads him out to see her garden: "You must see my japonica, my convolvulus,. . .my honeysuckle, my clematis" (p. 39). As they exit, she pauses to put the tray of matches in Edward's hands.

The second major symbol that is significantly overdetermined is the Matchseller. Already it is clear that this enigma shapes itself to the slight aches. Specifically, the Matchseller's identity changes and develops with Edward's and Flora's feelings. He is a screen for their projections, becoming, in R. F. Storch's words, "whatever is most desired or feared or regretted."[56] Edward and Flora have both noticed him, but only Edward has been disturbed by him. He has been there, at Edward's gate, since early morning. In other words, he has been at the threshhold of Edward's consciousness since childhood when Edward's insecurity began. At that stage the Matchseller was merely Edward's gloomy feelings, his matches unable to banish the dark and gloom. Edward has observed him through both time and space. As Edward grew, the Matchseller grew into his debased self-image that became so painful, ached so, that Edward had to project it outward where it was his match, his external self. Then it was that the Matchseller took up his post at Edward's actual gate where Edward could observe him from the scullery. There he also became a prison guard; his fearful image forbade Edward's former pleasures. Edward could no longer "stroll along through the long grass," and "pass into the lane" (pp. 15-16). The Matchseller denied him that pleasure. The Matchseller at this point has become the symbol of Edward's impotence. His passions can no longer be fired. Edward complains that once the Matchseller stood without moving while the summer storm raged about him. As Edward grows older his fear of the Matchseller begins to include death. He can no longer be called harmless. Edward wants to speak to him, to drive him away. Here Edward's unconscious wish to be punished for his guilts begins to overtake his rationalizations. He invites the Matchseller into his house. As the Matchseller stands before him, Edward engages in an orgy of projection. At first the Matchseller becomes Edward's own father image. Next, he sees the Matchseller as the personification of his early struggles from which Flora saved him. He was once destitute like the Matchseller. She took him in and stuck by him through thick and thin. When the Matchseller drops his tray, Edward finds the matches wet and funguslike. Edward's view of the Matchseller as his own debased manhood, his own phallus, emerges here before all the other images. Sweating with fear and shivering with cold dread, he projects these feelings onto the Matchseller. He sees his own image there again—jellylike, glass-eyed, nearly deaf—an impostor. He begins to feel nearly smothered and calls for Flora. When he returns, he has begun to accept his coming death and that becomes the dominant image in the Matchseller. Edward, therefore, reviews his life. As he falls, feverish, and growing weaker, the Matchseller becomes the fulfillment of his fears and wishes. Edward's impotence and death are almost complete, so the Matchseller becomes the personification of real youth and vigor, the virility Edward always longed for, and as such he usurps Edward's mother, wife, and home. Life has come around full circle. Edward is the dispossessed, punished for having dispossessed the old squire.

In Flora's eyes, the Matchseller has been only a harmless old man at first. She has seen him realistically, for what he is. When she views him through the scullery window, however, she sees him through Edward's eyes—a bullock, a large full-grown castrated ox. It was easy to see him thus, after Edward's slights and rejections. As these slights grew in her, her emptiness and aching grow. Finally, when she is alone with the Matchseller, she sees him through her own desires. He becomes first the embodiment of her sexual fantasies—the poacher. Then the Matchseller becomes the embodiment of her anal and phallic pleasures. He's a solid old boy, not at all like jelly. She names him Barnabas and takes him away to nurse to death under the canopy in her garden. As the play ends there is a sense that another cycle has begun. Flora will mother another man into impotence. She is caught in a repetition compulsion.

This cyclical sense is an echo from *The Birthday Party*. It is strengthened by Flora's reminders to Edward that this is the longest day of the year. She refers to June 21, the solstice, the middle of summer. This is the day when, owing to the annual revolution of the earth, the sun is at its greatest distance from the equator, and seems to begin to turn back. Edward's study of time and space also coincides with the cyclical feeling of *A Slight Ache*. Freud explains that the transposition into childhood is expressed in dreams "by the translation of time into space. The characters and scenes are seen as though they were at a great distance, at the end of a long road, or as though they were being looked at through the wrong end of a pair of opera-glasses."[57] Edward says of his observations of the Matchseller: "I've been engaged in the dimensionality and continuity of space. . .and time. . .for years" (p. 17). In other words, he has been watching his fears grow and transform from childhood repressions to adult externalizations. He has somehow sensed that these fears would someday bring about his castration and death.

Overall *A Slight Ache* concretizes a growing illness based on a growing fear. The illness grows from a slight head or eye ache to a total feverish collapse. The fear grows from a vague gloomy feeling of inadequacy to sexual impotence. These fears are concretized in the continuing transformations of the Matchseller in the aching eyes of Edward. Both the illness and the impotence end in the psychological death, which is the fulfillment of Edward's death wish. Freudian theory claims that the validity of the death wish is substantiated by "the tendency of individuals to repeat past behavior, a phenomenon he [Freud] described as the 'repetition compulsion,' even if such behavior has proved to be ill-advised."[58] Edward's compulsive movement toward the impotence and death that he fears is seen in his deliberate acts to diminish the distance between himself and the Matchseller. While the Matchseller is only a gloomy, threatening feeling, Edward has been observing him from the scullery window. As the menace and the illness grow, Edward invites the Matchseller into his house where he projects upon him father images. Then, Edward brings the Matchseller closer by identifying him with aspects of himself. Ultimately the Matchseller is transformed into Edward's dream of youth and power, and in this guise he walks away with Edward's wife-mother-home, Edward's life. This concretization is then an exact picture of Freud's words: "Let us be clear that the hallucinatory wishful psychosis—in dreams or elsewhere—achieves two by no means identical results. It not only brings hidden or repressed wishes into consciousness; it also represents them, with the subject's entire belief, as fulfilled."[59]

Much of this is capsuled in the smaller concretization that opens the play—the drowning of the wasp in the marmalade. This practice of prophesying the theme of the play in an initial image is by now a familiar Pinter technique. Just as Edward has voluntarily stepped into Flora's garden and become one of her hot-house plants, so the wasp goes voluntarily into the marmalade pot. Then Edward himself claps on the lid. The wasp is trapped in the sweet sticky marmalade. Flora is afraid to release it for fear it will "bite" her. Edward insists the wasp will sting not bite; therefore, he asserts the wasp's maleness and suggests the oedipal wish. He also dispels her fear by pointing out that this wasp can not escape. It is stuck in the marmalade and will drown there; just so is Edward suffocating in Flora's garden. When she replies: "What a horrible death," he answers: "On the contrary" (p. 12). Thus, he reveals the death wish. He immediately associates death with his aching eyes and begins clenching and blinking them. She notices and comments that he is tired, but he denies this sign of declining virility. Their attention shifts again to the wasp who is trying to escape through the spoon-hole. Again the death wish is his: "Well, let's kill it, for goodness sake" (p. 12). So he decides to scald it. But before he does, he contemplates the wasp's viciousness and notes that no such creature—by now established as male and vicious—has come to his attention all summer. Just so, he recognizes his docile, feminine state. She urges him to get on with the killing. So he pours scalding hot water down the hole, blinding the wasp. Then he lifts the lid and exclaims: "There he is! Dead. What a monster." Then, as if to prove he can still be vicious, that he is still male, he removes the dead wasp and squashes it on the plate. The wasp has been castrated, blinded, and killed. By contrast, Edward feels well; he exclaims that it is a beautiful day. His sense of impotence has been relieved; he feels powerful for having killed the wasp. More important, however, his guilt has been relieved. He has killed the wasp with whom he identifies. Punishment is complete.

This concretization has other ramifications. If the marmalade pot is analogous to Flora's house and garden, and if the drowning wasp is analogous to the declining Edward, then the spoon-hole is analogous to the garden gate. This analogy is valid not only on the level of female symbolism, but also as a link to the Matchseller and Edward's fears. As Edward stands powerfully over the spoon-hole, pouring in the scalding, castrating, murdering water, so the Matchseller stands threateningly at the garden gate.

Drawing back to look at the whole picture makes clear some of the play's major themes. First, there is the familiar one: fear lives within, but by tricks of the psyche it appears to live without. Man can fool himself this way and spend his time hiding from phantoms while unconsciously he courts his own punishment and realizes his own fears. The play also repeats *The Birthday Party's* stress on the ironic cycles of life. Man begins life in anxiety over returning to dust and ashes — mother earth. In between he suffers through many births and deaths, and it is the dead selves he leaves behind that rise up to control the life before him. The special theme of *A Slight Ache* lies in the demonstration by Edward and Flora of the residual peripety in human life. Each works blindly toward his own defeat as he interacts and responds to the other. She castrates her husband as she mothers him, leaving him unable to provide the sexual fulfillment she craves. He sacrifices the manhood he longs for by accepting the womb pleasures she offers. Thus, ambivalence is set up, and each longs to escape the other, while at the same time each yearns for the satisfactions of the other. The slight aches of life grow and multiply into and unto final death.

A Slight Ache has restated the major themes of the other three plays in its group, and it has developed the minor theme of impotence as well. It keeps alive the other minor theme, mother's promiscuity, by Flora's relationships with the poacher and the Matchseller. Stanley's problem with identity is also kept alive. Edward is a role player. He pretends to study and write while he spies from the scullery. He masquerades as a squire. He is an imposter. By emphasizing ambivalence and impotence and incorporating promiscuity and identity, *A Slight Ache* becomes a link to the plays of group two that stress these themes.

3

Anxiety Dreams: The Wish To Be Rid of Someone

A Night Out, The Caretaker, Night School, and *The Dwarfs* were all produced or published in 1960. Likewise, *The Room, The Birthday Party,* and *The Dumb Waiter* were all born in the same year, 1957. *A Slight Ache,* 1959, is therefore the transition piece in time as well as theme. Falling chronologically between these two groups, *A Slight Ache* ends the series of plays that focus on the wish to be punished and begins the series that focus on problems with impotence, ambivalence, and identity. These thematic concerns translate into the wish to be rid of someone. In other words, the fantasies behind the first group of plays are related to those underlying the second group by condition or sequence, at least metaphorically. In Freud's words: "It amounts to this: 'if one accepts the punishment for it, one can go on to allow oneself the forbidden things.' " [1] In the last three plays of group one, punishment for the wish to kill has been accepted; in group two a softened version of this forbidden wish is therefore allowable. The fantasy need no longer involve murder, only riddance. Pinter, himself, seems to say as much when discussing *The Caretaker* with Kenneth Tynan: "The original idea. . .was. . .to end the play with the violent death of the tramp. . . .It suddenly struck me that it was not necessary."[2] Instead of killing Davies, Mick and Aston merely turn their backs on him.

Within group two the wish to be rid of someone is spurred by ambivalence and directed against both parties. With this focal point the plays have a dual relationship to one another. They present differing views of the same material, and they also achieve wish fulfillment in separate stages. From *A Night Out* to *The Dwarfs* there is a progressive softening of the wish to kill; and as the wish softens, it moves closer to fulfillment. In *A Night Out* ambivalence appears in all of the characters, but principally it is presented between mother and son. Father is already dead, and Albert wishes to be rid of mother. The wish is naked and raw. He lifts the alarm clock over his head in a gesture of promised violence, but he does not kill her or even leave her. At the end of the play he has returned to mother and to his filial posture. *The Caretaker* examines ambivalence toward a father. In this play mother is dead, but a disguised father figure has presented himself and his demands. Mick and Aston show no wish to kill him. They wish only to be rid of him, so they reject him by turning their backs on him. Nevertheless, when the curtain falls, Davies is still there; he is not gone; Mick and Aston are not rid of him yet. In *Night School* ambivalence is again universal. The wish to kill retreats beyond physical rejection to a more oblique disavowment. Wally has no mother or father, but the wish is not complete because he does have surrogate parents. His two aunts behave very much like a mother; they nourish him and betray him by giving his room to Sally. Mr. Solto is a father substitute who plays a part in Wally's loss of Sally. In *The Dwarfs* ambivalence is transformed into self-hate and distintegrating friendships. Parental figures have no physical presence at all, but to borrow Ibsen's term, their *ghosts* remain in a lingering sense of inadequacy. The wish to kill has no physical realization either; it has evolved into an emotional purging. By the end of the play Len has purged himself of his past. His yard is empty—bare and clean. Only new growth remains—a shrub and a flower. Len is rid of Pete and Mark and the dwarfs; he is rid of his old identity—his parents and his heritage. He is a new man, reborn without benefit of parents. The wish to be rid of them is fulfilled.

The completion of wish fulfillment in these plays inspires the query: why are these plays called *anxiety dreams* if they bring about wish fulfillment? Freud was asked this question frequently. He explains that first of all, "it may be that the dream-work has not completely succeeded in creating a wish fulfillment; so that a portion of the distressing affect in the dream-thoughts has been left over in the manifest dream."[3] This first point seems highly applicable to the plays in group two because their group relationship is in part the progressive achievement of the wish. The wish, therefore, is not completely achieved until the fourth play. Freud adds that this lingering of distress is aided by the "fact that it is so much harder for the dream-work to alter the sense of a dream's *affects* than of its *content*."[4] Consequently, the distressing affects remain even after the content has been transformed into wish fulfillment. Then, Freud presents a second factor that he considers "more important and far reaching":

No doubt a wish fulfillment must bring pleasure; but the question then arises 'To whom?' To the person who has the wish, of course. But, as we know, as dreamer's relation to his wishes is a quite peculiar one. He repudiates them and censors them—he has no liking for them, in short. So that their fulfillment will give him no pleasure, but just the opposite; and experience shows that his opposite appears in the form of anxiety. . . .[5]

This phenomenon is particularly noticeable in *The Dwarfs*. In this play that contains the final fulfillment of the wish to be rid of parents and their heritage, more anxiety appears than in the other three plays. Moreover, Len seems singularly unsatisfied by the realization of the wish.

As anxiety dreams based on the same wish, the plays of group two are closely interrelated. The wish also relates them consequentially to the plays of group one. However, there is also a sharp difference among these plays. *The Room*, *The Birthday Party*, *The Dumb Waiter*, and *A Slight Ache* retain the dreamlike character. Overall they present a minimal displacement into realism. The first three plays of group two, however, are highly displaced and move sharply into psychological realism. In *A Night Out* the logical overlay is a whole cloth. There are no gaps to puzzle the audience. John Russell Taylor declares that "the question of verification and its problems does not arise; the motivation of all the characters is made quite clear. . . ."[6] This is only slightly less true of *The Caretaker*. Harold Clurman states that "one barely notices the degree of the play's abstractness."[7] Of *Night School* Simon Trussler says: "It so happens that here the loose-ends are all tied up. . . ."[8] But with *The Dwarfs* comes a sharp break in this pattern. This fourth play of the group reverses the trend and takes the most extreme position on the other end of the continuum. It is the nearest to pure dream of any of Pinter's plays. The explanation for this may be that *The Dwarfs* is a reworking of an earlier manuscript for a novel. Nevertheless, Pinter himself admits that this play is a "most intractable, impossible piece of work."[9]

The realism of these first three plays and the extreme surrealism of the fourth is apparently not unusual for anxiety dreams. Freud explains that "anxiety dreams often have a content entirely devoid of distortion."[10] Such dreams have somehow evaded the dream-censor, and anxiety takes the place of censorship. The anxiety is, of course, the result of the escape of the repressed wish. By the use of the word *often*, however, Freud indicates that this is not an invariable pattern. A later statement confirms this inference: "what is true of undistorted anxiety dreams applies also to those which are partly distorted as well as to other unpleasurable dreams. . . ."[11]

A NIGHT OUT

The first of these anxiety dreams, *A Night Out,* is probably the most realistic of them all. It is interesting to note however, that this retreat from obscurity still leaves critics divided. George Wellwarth calls *A Night Out* "a small masterpiece";[12] R. F. Storch calls it "a dull play because the theme is out in the open."[13] Both of these comments seem exaggerated. The play is certainly not a masterpiece, but neither is it dull. The play is actually quite interesting, although it can probably be called *minor* Pinter.

Nevertheless, despite noticeable alterations, the basic Pinter pattern is there. Like its immediate predecessor, *A Slight Ache,* this play was written for radio. Consequently, it moves freely from place to place. Albert Stokes is not even confined within several rooms and a garden as Edward is. Albert is physically free to move about among his home, a railway coffee stall, Mr. King's house, The Girl's room. He is, nevertheless, just as trapped as Edward. He is trapped by his own insecurity, which makes him uncomfortable wherever he goes and sends him back to the confining atmosphere of mother's home. Moreover, the play opens familiarly in the kitchen with a scene between a domineering mother figure and an insecure son. The only difference is that it is dinner time, not breakfast; and Mrs. Stokes is actually Albert's mother, not his wife or his landlady. The visitors do not come to Albert; he goes to see them, but all of them do cause him great anxiety. The significant difference is, of course, that Albert's principal hostility is aimed at his mother, not his father. Unlike *The Room,* in this play murder is only a wish and a gesture. Unlike the protagonists of the other punishment plays, Albert does not meet a final destruction; he only continues as he was—a mother's boy.

Albert has been living, docile and repressed, with his widowed mother. She, like Meg and Flora, has smothering motherliness: there's a good boy; you're all I've got; you never tell me you love me; I cooked dinner specially for you; what am I going to do while you're out? She is also a nag: put a light bulb in grandma's room; eat your supper; don't muck about with girls; you look a disgrace; do you know what time it is? what would your father say? On the evening of the play, Albert persists in going out to an office party. Once there, he is taunted by the office bully, Gidney, for his failures in a recent office football game, for his shy manner, and for his uneasiness with girls. One of the office girls, Eileen, accuses Albert of touching her, taking a liberty. Gidney uses the incident to pick a fight. Out in the hall he pursues Albert with insults and threats. Finally, he calls Albert a "mother's boy"; Albert hits him, and they exchange blows. These people at the party perform the functions of Goldberg, McCann, and Lulu. They spotlight Albert's inner sense of inadequacy and his isolation from society. Albert returns home to be lectured by his mother for staying out late, leaving her alone, not giving her enough money to manage on. Albert picks up a clock and "violently raises it above his head."[14] She screams and the scene ends. The audience are not sure whether he has killed her or not. Once again out in the night, Albert is picked up by a prostitute —The Girl. Initially, The Girl seems to be the first example of a new character type that is to reappear in subsequent plays—

Sally in *Night School,* Sarah in *The Lover,* and, of course, Ruth in *The Homecoming.* All of these characters are young women split between whoredom and respectability. Despite her novelty, however, The Girl does have antecedents in the earlier plays. As a young woman, she is preceded by Lulu whose propriety was swept away by Goldberg at Stanley's birthday party. As a woman of emptiness and yearnings, she is a reflection of Meg and Flora. As a whore, she seems to be the promiscuous seductress, split off from all the other wives and mothers. Unfortunately, her pretensions to motherhood and her nagging remind Albert of his mother. His hostility erupts. He threatens her with an alarm clock just as he did his mother. This time, however, he drops the clock before he leaves the room. The audience are momentarily terrified. They suspect Albert has killed his mother and barely restrained himself from killing The Girl. In the next scene Albert enters the dark house, throws his clothes around, stretches himself, and smiles at the ceiling. Then the illusion is shattered by his mother's voice: "Albert!" Albert comes back to himself as "her reproach turns to solicitude" (p. 47). She moves in close, strokes his hand, forgives him, and purrs: "You're good, you're not bad, you're a good boy. . . .I know you are. . . .You are, aren't you?" (p. 47).

The realism of this play highlights its contrast to previously established expectations of Pinter. Usually, a realistic reading spawns a host of questions. Not so with *A Night Out!* Only Martin Esslin finds an unanswered question in this play: "not even the extreme act of violence to which he [Albert] resorted has been able to free him. Or has it?"[15] The remainder of the critics agree that Albert has not been freed. Perhaps John Russell Taylor says it best: "The final insult, . . . his mother's willingness. . .to forget everything. . .is the final demonstration that Albert does not count and nothing he can do really matters."[16] The question, however, is academic; it pertains to speculations about post-play behavior. Within the play there is no obscurity.

The lack of obscurity does not rule out the operation of the primary process mechanisms. They have done their work, but analysis of their dynamics is not made necessary by holes in the play's logic. Insight into these dynamics can, however, deepen the understanding of the play. For example, the dream mechanisms aid in the revelations of the inner life of the characters. The decorous prostitute emerges as a pitiable child whose fears are complemented by unfulfilled wishes. She once dreamed the oedipal fantasy of being wife to her father, and within the play she pretends to be mother to his daughter by claiming her own childhood photograph to be that of her daughter. Dream symbolism furnishes other evidence of her birth fantasies. Freud says that according to Carl Jung and Ernest Jones, the loss of a tooth, which means castration in a man's dream, signifies in women a parturition dream. The common element, he claims is that both castration and birth involve removing a part from the whole body.[17] Later, Freud equates traveling with sexual intercourse through the link of the "honeymoon journey."[18] The Girl tells Albert that she has had a tooth out. More revealing of her fantasy life, however, is the speech by the window: "Sometimes I wish the night would never end. I like sleeping. I could sleep. . .on and on. . . .Yes, you can see the station from here. All the trains go out, right through the night" (p. 40). Each night she takes a honeymoon journey to escape from the barrenness of her life. When she awakes, she continues her escape, this time from her shame, in the pose of "a respectable mother."

Mrs. Stokes's possessiveness and nagging emphasis on control suggest an anal fixation. Holland's explanation is appropriate: "The child is likely to feel that he is being forced to give up a treasured part of himself, perhaps even a living being like himself. He may confuse the process of defecation with that of giving birth. . . ."[19] As Mrs. Stokes once loved narcissistically that other externalized part of her body, her feces, she now loves Albert. He is part of her; he represents her: "You can't go out and disgrace me, Albert. If you've got to go out you've got to look nice" (p. 12). Her mothering concern also disguises its function of keeping him under tight control. She expects him to answer her calls, tell her his plans, fix the lights, set the table. Most of all, she expects him to stay home; he is her possession. Mrs. Stokes shows the same possessiveness toward the dead as to the living. She can not give them up. Grandma's been dead for ten years, but Mrs. Stokes still goes to sit in Grandma's room. What is more, she collects junk in it. Mr. Stokes is dead, but to her he still lives — in her breast, and the house is still *his* house. What is more, Albert can still upset him.

With such an anal mother, it is no wonder that Albert has problems. Lidz seems to be describing Albert's probable childhood when he says:

> The cardinal tasks of gaining a sense of initiative and of confidance in his own competence are likely to be countered by the manner in which the child is controlled, which can foster inhibition of action and lack of self-confidence. Some struggle between child and parents over control is almost inevitable and often focuses on bowel training or feeding. The child's overt compliance and conformity is often accompanied by suppressed anger, heightened ambivalence to parental figures, covert resistance, and stubbornness that can exert lasting influences upon the personality.[20]

Albert's lack of self-confidence, his shy manner, his secretiveness — all suggest this kind of struggle with his mother over control. Albert can only dream of being in control himself. He tells The Girl that he is a film director — one who controls fantasies. But even in his dream, he is only the assistant director. Albert also exhibits the neatness so characteristic of anality. He polishes his shoes, asks to have his tie pressed, and expresses concern about dirtying his shirt in the cellar. It is, however, the "overt compliance and conformity" coupled with suppressed anger that describes him best. Despite Mrs. Stokes's complaints, Albert has been a "good boy." He lives with mother, supports mother, usually minds mother, and stays home with mother. Indeed, he even loves mother. But his love is countered by a burning rage that fits the meaning of his name, Stokes—supplies a fire with fuel. In the oedipal period, he has apparently failed to achieve the autonomy from his mother that he should have. Since that time he has been tied to her apron strings—docile and hostile, willing and resentful. This crucial failure has exaggerated his sexual guilts. It is not surprising that he is uncomfortable with girls. A child's oedipal disappointments can only be increased by the mother's insistence that the father still lives within her. Albert displays this disappointment when he hisses at The Girl: "I've got as many qualifications as the next man" (p. 43). All of these unconscious disappointments lie behind Albert's feeling of inadequacy. They are also the fuel that stokes Albert's rage, causing it to erupt in the violent gesture toward his mother. But something stays his arm—his love, his guilt, his dependence. When the lava comes pouring out, it is displaced onto The Girl.

In addition to adding dimension to the characters, the primary processes explain Albert's choice of weapon—an alarm clock. The alarm is ringing that his rage is boiling over. For him, it's time to stop and let off steam. For mother and The Girl, it is time to stop talking and bossing; it is time to be alarmed. Furthermore, Albert's raising the alarm calls a temporary halt to the bad time he has been having. In brief, it is time for everyone to wake up. The Girl needs to stop sleeping and dreaming of honeymoon journeys as she listens to the trains go out. Mrs. Stokes needs to wake up and realize that time has advanced: Grandma and her husband are dead;

Albert is not a child. She needs to let him have a life of his own. And Albert needs to wake up to his blindness, to his self-destructive submissiveness, to his alarming need to get away from his mother. It is a sharply etched concretization.

Once again there is a montage of meaning condensed in the title. *A Night Out* is, of course, Albert's evening away from home—partying. *A Night Out* is also an evening when Albert is outside of himself—different, aggressive. The meaning of Albert's name—nobly bright, illustrious—couples with the title to add further meaning. This name was given Albert by his mother; he is her light—the only one she has left. There is no light in Grandma's room, no light in the cellar, only Albert's brightness. When he leaves for a night out, her light is out. Finally, the night out represents the darkness that Albert lives in, his blindness to his own needs. He, the light, is important to illuminate his own night—the alarming night from which he needs to awaken.

These illuminations of the title tie into the equally familiar Pinter technique of encapsulating the theme in an incident at the opening of the play. At the outset Mrs. Stokes sets up Albert's inadequacy and her own ignorant plight by complaining about the lack of light bulbs in Grandma's room and the cellar—the absence of light in her house. Albert highlights his own impotence by asking her for his tie—a dream symbol for the phallus.[21] Mrs. Stokes ignores Albert's question. She holds back his tie. She doesn't want to let him have it, even though she has pressed it flat—at his request.

The absence of obscurity in *A Night Out* reduces ambiguity, also. Nevertheless, its resemblance to earlier plays suggests alternative determinations. In many ways *A Night Out* is a remake of *The Birthday Party*. Like Stanley, Albert hides in the house of a potentially incestuous mother. Like Stanley, he attends a party where he watches the others play childish sex games. Like Stanley, he finds himself the center of a would-be sexual assault. The difference here points to the shift in emphasis. Stanley was the aggressor; he was asking for trouble, for punishment. Albert, on the other hand, feels too inadequate to get involved in trouble. He is trying to stay out of it; he wants to be a "good boy." Both Stanley and Albert express their ambivalence. Stanley tried to strangle Meg; Albert threatens to strike Mrs. Stokes. And both boys—men?—end up in the strait jackets they have briefly broken out of. Stanley, however, has been captured and castrated by fathers. The dreaded punishment has come. Albert was castrated long ago by mother. No one forces him back into her clutches. He returns of his own will—his unconscious will. He is not a bad boy; he is a good boy. He is not a bad boy, he is a good boy!

A Night Out can also be compared to *A Slight Ache*. Both Edward and Albert are trapped in situations they have not the initiative to break out of. Edward has welcomed the mothering that has emasculated him. So does Albert, even though both men resent it as well. As Edward's own impotence, externalized as the Matchseller, blocks his gateway to freedom, so do Albert's associates heighten his inadequacy and send him back to the security of mother's home. Both men suppress violence. Edward releases it on the wasp. Albert releases it by threats against his mother and her youthful counterpart—The Girl. Only the endings differ. Edward ends collapsed and abandoned by Flora. Albert ends forgiven by Mrs. Stokes and accepted back into the trap.

This discussion of *A Night Out* points clearly to its principal themes—ambivalence and inadequacy. Albert's ambivalence toward his mother is obvious. He loves her: only a deep affection could have prompted him to respond to her nagging in the opening scene by putting his arm around her and saying: "I won't be late. I don't want to go. I'd much rather stay with you" (p. 6). His hate needs no further comment than his violent gesture of readiness to kill her with the alarm clock. He spews upon the prostitute the reasons for his hate: "You're just a dead weight round my neck"; "Always something"; "I've got as many qualifications as the next man"; "I'm giving the orders here;" "Just keep your big mouth closed, for a start" (pp. 43-45). The unspoken reason for his hate is the vague, unrealized feeling deep inside him that she is the cause of his inadequacy. He shows this by always getting "a bit niggly when she's mentioned" (p. 14) — to quote Albert's friend Kedge.

Albert does not really understand his inadequacy. When Gidney says: "with my qualifications I could go anywhere. . . . Couldn't I, Stokes?" (p. 22), Albert fails to reassure him and replies instead: "So could I." Later he reasserts his qualifications to the prostitute. Yet, he always feels inadequate; that's why he would rather not go out. Besides, everyone else finds him inadequate — most of all, his mother. He lets the lights go out in the house; he leads an unclean life; he upsets his dead father; he is unable to make her happy.

The play also shows the interrelationship of ambivalence and impotence. *A Night Out* says that the suppressed rage of the impotent son takes only temporary relief. The other side of his ambivalence then leads him back into his plight. Indeed, ambivalence seems to bolster impotence; the guilt created by hateful actions paralyzes the impulse to flight. As Stanley's guilt led him back into the paths of his fathers, Albert's guilt leads him back to mother's will. He feels free and manly after his violent self-assertions. Yet, he returns to a docile, slumped figure at his mother's purr. His guilt blinds him to the change he has wrought in her. He relinquishes his opportunity to lead and readies himself to be her good little boy again. His alarm went off; his rage exploded, but his ambivalence caused him to turn off the alarm, to let her purr him back to sleep in the dark night he lives in. Blindness is indeed the accompaniment to impotence, as Pinter has so often shown. Blind ambivalence leads to impotence, and impotence permits a smothering maternal love that leads to blind ambivalence. Here is the repetition compulsion that Freud saw as the evidence of man's "inexplicable need to suffer."[22]

THE CARETAKER

A Night Out was first performed in a B.B.C. broadcast in March of 1960. The following month, April, *The Caretaker* opened in London. It was Pinter's first truly successful stage play. Its success was not measured by a long run, but by the critical approval it received. Because it was more realistic than the earlier stage plays, critics were able to accept it and to recognize the emotional power and the poetic appeal that is Pinter's. The realism of *The Caretaker,* however, can not be compared to that of *A Night Out. The Caretaker* is not totally without obscurities. In fact, the real challenge of this play lies in the poetic ambiguity that it couples with almost classic universality. Indeed, this is the play that may well be a masterpiece. And like all masterpieces, it allows for a multitude of differing interpretations from a variety of critical approaches. The range and scope of the criticism it has already attracted attest to this fact. Like a well-cut diamond, it attracts the light of understanding from many facets. Martin Esslin characterizes best this play's combination of realism and ambiguity: "*The Caretaker* is the first of Pinter's plays to have achieved this complete synthesis between utter realism in the external action and the poetic metaphor, the dream image of eternal archetypes, or the deeper — or higher — levels of impact."[23]

The Caretaker, written for the stage instead of radio, goes back to the familiar setting — a room. It is a closed room with only one window in the back wall, and it is cluttered with every conceivable kind of junk — even a kitchen sink. The room is the home of Aston, a slow, quiet man who likes to tinker and who was once given shock treatment in a mental institution. The room is situated on the upper floor of a large, empty, old house in great disrepair. The house itself is owned by Mick, Aston's brother. Mick is Aston's opposite: quick, intense, restless, ambitious, and menacing. Aston has assumed the task of renovating the old house, but shows no urgency whatever about accomplishing it. He has to build a shed in the garden first, but somehow he is never able to begin the shed. Into this situation, Aston brings Davies, an old tramp whom he has rescued from a brawl in a nearby cafe. Davies is suspicious, irascible, grasping, bigoted, selfish, and deluded. His identity is a mystery. He has two names, Davies and Jenkins; many insurance cards; and identification papers at Sidcup. He has been trying to get to Sidcup for his papers for about fifteen years but he never quite makes it. Usually the weather is bad, or he does not have the right shoes.

Aston shows his kind and trusting nature by befriending the old man. He gives him a bed, gets him a bag with some clothes, buys him some shoes; he even gives him a few bob for spending money. But the old tramp is never satisfied. The bed is in a draught, the shirts are not striped the way he likes them, and the shoes have no laces. Mick treats the old man with hostility. He forces him to the floor; he tongue-lashes him; he takes his pants; he threatens to carry him off to the police.

This three-way relationship continues briefly. Aston offers to let Davies be caretaker of the house, but Davies is reluctant. "They" might get him if he answered the doorbell. At the next encounter with Mick, the tone of their relationship changes. Mick makes uncertain overtures to Davies. He gives him a sandwich, asks his advice, complains of Aston's slowness, and finally offers Davies the job of caretaker. Aston continues to give the old man his confidence. As he trusted Davies with the key to the house, he trusts him with the story of his mental illness. Davies tries to ingratiate himself with Mick, whom he sees as the more profitable man to know. He assumes he is "in" with Mick enough to begin pushing Aston out. He rejects the shoes Aston brings him; he even taunts Aston about his illness: "They can put the pincers on your head again, man!"[24] Then he pulls his knife on Aston. Aston responds by quietly suggesting that Davies find another place to live. He offers to give Davies a few bob to get down to Sidcup. Davies reveals his craftiness by shouting back: "You build your shed first!" (p. 68). Finally, Davies goes to Mick with the hope of dispossessing Aston, but he goes too far. Mick turns on him. He accuses Davies of misrepresenting himself as an interior decorator, and pays him off for his caretaking by flicking him a coin. Then in a rage Mick hurls Aston's Buddha against the gas stove. Aston comes in, he and Mick smile faintly at one another, and Mick leaves. Now Davies makes a last desperate effort to renew his friendship with Aston. He offers to keep his old bed, to help Aston put up his shed; he even says he thinks the shoes Aston gave him are working out all right. Aston does not reply. He remains still with his back turned to Davies. Davies's protestations drift off into silence — a long silence.

Pinter insists on a realistic determination of this play. For that reason Clive Donner's 1962 film version of *The Caretaker* pleased Pinter very much. Kathleen Burkman explains: "The transfer of the play to the screen enabled Pinter to make an important point about the entire body of his work: he envisions his characters realistically living in actual places, not operating in a void."[25] Pinter's response to Terrence Rattigan makes the same point. Rattigan interpreted the play as "an allegory about the God of the Old Testament, the God of the New Testament, and Humanity." Pinter's reply was that "the play was about a caretaker and two brothers."[26] There is no wish here to contradict Mr. Pinter. This play is about Davies, Mac Davies alias Bernard Jenkins, and his confrontation with the two brothers, Aston and Mick. Nevertheless, as others have pointed out, archetypal images do rise out of and transcend these three real people, so also does the dream-work associate unconscious childhood memories with these three real people. These unconscious associations lend power and classic depth to Pinter's play for the very reason that they are not private and individual like Davies, Mick, and Aston: they lend this power and depth because they are universal aspects of everyman's human experience.

The Caretaker is a montage of images or determinations. The overlying image of the montage is Davies, the old tramp. Impotence swaddles him. The only superiority he can claim is by accident of birth; he is not Black, Indian, Greek, or Polish. Yet "they" do not realize his superiority; "they" have taken all the chairs at the cafe and left him to stand. Even this one claim to superiority, his identity, is not satisfying or secure. He can not remember where he was born. He has had to change his name. A remote person in Sidcup holds the papers that prove who he is, and Sidcup is unreachable. He claims to have been married. If so, he was unable to maintain his marriage, and he has been unable to hold a job. He has never been able to make a place for himself in the world; he has been constantly on the move. Consequently, one of his principal cares in life has come to be finding a good pair of shoes. He says to Aston: "Shoes? It's life and death to me" (p. 14). Davies's impotence is, in fact, so great he can not face it. He continually defends himself by rationalization. He finds excuses for his failures by displacing them onto other causes: he left his wife because she kept her dirty underwear in the vegetable pot; he does not have a good pair of shoes because the monk at the monastery told him to "piss off." Then, of course, there is the lifeline of his inadequacy: "If only the weather would break! Then I'd be able to get down to Sidcup!" (p. 19).

In its broadest sense, ambivalence means the coexistence of contradictory feelings toward a person, a thing, or an action. The controlling contradiction in Davies's life is his ambivalence about the act of caretaking itself. Davies loves to accept care but not to give it. He wants the care Aston takes of him—the bed, the clothes, the shoes; but he does not want to take care of Aston. He does not thank him for his generosity; he does not return his trust. He even betrays Aston's friendship and would have dispossessed him if Mick had allowed it. The spark of Davies's friendship with Mick is the prospect of more luxurious care from this more ambitious brother. Throughout the play Davies shows his love of care as he reveals his grasping and selfish nature. He shows his dislike of giving care in his reactions to the job both brothers offer him. Aston offers it first: "You could be. . .caretaker here, if you liked" (p. 42). Davies's reply is more honest than he intends: "Well, I. . .I never done caretaking before, you know. . .I mean to say. . .I never. . .what I mean to say is. . .I never been a caretaker before" (p. 42). When he learns that the job would entail answering the front doorbell, he is more uncertain than before, and his reason is ironic: "I got to be a bit careful" (p. 43). Later Mick asks Davies if he would like to be caretaker, and the reply is similar: "I ain't never done no caretaking before" (p. 50). Only when he understands that there will be no real responsibility other than "keeping an eye on things" and not letting anyone "mess him about," does he accept the job.

On the realistic level, Aston's impotence is as clear as Davies's. Aston blames his impotence on the shock treatment he received in the mental institution years ago. Since then, he claims, he has been unable to think clearly or get his thoughts together. He never goes to the café anymore because he can no longer talk to people. He is not able to accomplish anything either. Mick calls Aston "work shy." And Aston, like Davies, has an ever-ready rationalization for this inadequacy. His plans for renovating the house wait on his building a shed in the garden, and building the shed waits on finding the proper saw.

Every time he goes out after a saw, it is, for some reason, gone when he gets there. Aston thinks often of going back to the café to find the man who started the lie that sent him to the hospital and brought on his impotence. But he never gets around to it. He wants to do something first — build that shed. Again, he is like Davies who can not get back to Sidcup to find the man who has his papers. It is, undoubtedly, this identification with Davies that prompts Aston's sympathetic effort to take care of him. When he saw Davies being knocked about, he probably remembered his own struggle with the doctors and attendants at the hospital. He also understands Davies's petty pride. When Davies offers excuses for having no money, Aston tries to protect the old man's pride by speaking of his own unwillingness to drink Guinness from a thick mug. Each recognizes the other's rationalizations. Mention of Sidcup frequently stirs mention of Aston's shed and vice versa. Aston, however, is a caretaker. His understanding and identification prompt him to bring Davies home, give him a bed, a key to the apartment, clothes, shoes, and friendship. He also takes care, initially, to protect the old man's feelings. When Davies phrases his reluctance to be caretaker with the words: "But it'd be a matter. . .wouldn't it. . .it'd be a matter of a broom. . .isn't it?" (p. 43), Aston raises the prestige of the position: "I could fit a bell at the bottom, outside the front door, with 'Caretaker' on it. And you could answer any queries." Not until the end does Aston admit he needs the window open because Davies stinks. But when Aston does make this admission, he reveals his ambivalence. He tells Davies he has been stinking the place out for days. A backward glance gives evidence that Aston's discomfort has been living with his generosity toward the old man for some time. He brings Davies a pair of shoes, provides him with laces, and then walks out refusing to listen to the old man's mutterings. In the following scene he reacts irritably to the old man's nighttime groans. He shakes Davies and says: "Hey, stop it, will you? I can't sleep" (p. 66). Aston's final rejection of the old man may also indicate some repressed hostility to Mick. When the old man is in Aston's care, his friend, his fellow outcast, Aston tolerates his noises, his odors, and his bad manners. He is able to smile down on the old man while he sleeps. But when Davies assumes the role of Mick's friend, Mick's fellow landlord and commander, Aston is no longer willing to be understanding and tolerant. He requests the old man to move. Aston's self-interest comes to the fore.

Mick's impotence is less easily detected than Aston's and Davies's. He assumes such a frightening and commanding aspect that he appears masterful and successful, but closer inspection reveals that his appearance is a masquerade. To gain a sense of power he has to resort to terrifying an ignorant old man by chasing him in the dark with an Electrolux or by snatching his bag and playing the childish game of "keep-away" with it. It is impossible to know how much of his boasting is false, but his need to boast betrays his sense of inadequacy. Yet, he is a caretaker. He has, apparently, set Aston up in this old house and given him the purpose of renovating it. He also seems to be leading Davies into the self-revelation that will bring about Aston's rejection. In this way, Mick shows some wish to protect Aston from Davies's selfishness. On the other hand, Mick is also concerned with protecting his property, keeping it from becoming a catch-all for vagrants as well as a catch-all for old junk. By this dual concern, Mick displays ambivalence. His most forceful show of ambivalence contains this same complexity and mingles it with impotence. It is the speech he makes when he hurls Aston's Buddha against the gas stove. His words express his pent-up frustration at being unable to take care of the house and Aston: "Anyone would think this house was all I got to worry about. I got plenty of other things I can worry about. I've got other things." But he also expresses hostility over the care and concern Aston causes him: "I've got my own business to build up, haven't I? I got to think about expanding. . .in all directions." Then he shows contempt for Aston's condition: "I don't stand still. I'm moving about, all the time. I'm moving . . .all the time." Then he reverts to concern: "I've got to think about the future." Finally, he shows frustration over not being able to have his own way with Aston and the house: "I'm not worried about this house. I'm not interested. My brother can worry about it. He can do it up, he can decorate it, he can do what he likes with it. I'm not bothered. I thought I was doing him a favour, letting him live here. He's got his own ideas. Let him have them. I'm going to chuck it in" (p. 74). The prelude to this speech has already revealed the root of Mick's and every caretaker's ambivalence toward his ward. While smashing Aston's Buddha, Mick has shouted: "THAT'S WHAT I WANT!" John Russell Brown cites these words as the "revelation of Mick's intense concern with himself."[27]

This first determination then is a complex one of three overlapping images. It contains, as Pinter insists, a caretaker and two brothers—all real people. But the images they reflect are of three would-be caretakers whose self-interests have ended their responsibilities to others. This tripartite image must be perceived as a circle of translucent glass, for it transmits light from a second circle of images that lies beneath it. The images in this lower circle of glass correspond to those above, but they are not as sharply defined. They take their outline and shape from the upper pictures, but these lower ones provide the dimension and the depth. These lower images, of course, are the latent content of the play, and the characters there are those familiar ghosts that people the unconscious—the family. They provide a second determination about a father and two sons. The sons are, of course, Aston and Mick; they project their father images onto Davies, the caretaker.

This image of father and sons is complicated by the sons' differing views of the father. One son identifies with an ignorant but gentle and accepting father; the other son has identified with a crafty, violent, rejecting one. Aston is, of course, the gentle son. He remembers only the inadequate, gentle old father. He has repressed the memories of the other side. The fears became more than he could handle, so he displaced all the betrayal and neglect onto the mother. It was she who allowed the father figures to deprive him of mental potency—to castrate him. He has relinquished all claims to mother and identified with father. At the outset he gives Davies the key to the room. He is, thereby, no longer in danger of the father's wrath. He has disconnected himself from memories of mother's nurturing womb; this is the meaning of the discarded stove and sink in Aston's life. He has given up the defiance of the anal stage and is satisfied with collecting junk that he can piddle with and keep. Aston shows many signs of problems in the phallic and oedipal stages of development. The phallic phase is a time of learning to get pleasure from the genitals. Holland explains that in the context of onanism "anything that keeps the hands busy, playing cards, for example, or a camera or tools can be defensive substitutes for a phallus."[28] Aston's hands are constantly busy with his plug—the electrical plug he is forever mending and probing. Moreover, he admits on several occasions: "I like. . .working with my hands" (p. 18). Probably when he was small, he would lie in bed smiling to himself as he enjoyed this pleasure. But father would lift the blanket, discover his busy hands, and scold him with dire warnings of the insanity that was sure to follow. These memories need now to remain repressed, so Aston defends against them by reversal. Father Davies is the one in bed under the blanket, and he spies on the smiling Aston through the hole in his covers. It is part of Aston's defense to disguise memories of what he once learned, what he once saw and heard. He once saw things very clearly, had hallucinations; these phrases suggest that Aston witnessed the primal scene. When he made the mistake of talking about it, "they" silenced him. "They" carried him away and gave him a mental shock that left him unable to think and unwilling to talk. Aston has to disguise the identity of those castrators. To remember that it was the father is too fearful. Whether some fiendish prank was played on the child to frighten him or whether he only fantasized one in his anxiety, the effect was the same — Aston was silenced, mentally destroyed, castrated. He is still disturbed by night noises. He is unable to sleep when Davies breathes heavily. The image of father Davies spying from under the blanket is a reversal that also protects Aston from the terrifying memories of primal-scene watching. Aston's whole primal-scene experience is symbolized by his favorite object — the Buddha. Buddha is wise and enlightened as Aston once imagined himself to be when he saw so clearly. Buddha is also silent and inscrutable as Aston has become. The electric plug that Aston is forever probing is also symbolic of his experience. The shock treatment or the fiendish prank, real or imagined, is connected in his mind with electricity — pincers, like the prongs of a plug, on either side of his head. Aston is forever trying to mend this plug, make it work again, undo the damage that was done. Among the mechanisms of defense is one called *undoing*. Holland says it is akin to reversal and is used by some neurotics "to wipe out an event or impulse by some ritual action."[29]

Mick's memories of his father are entirely different. Mick projects onto Davies all the unpleasant aspects of father. The first thing he does is put him down literally by throwing him to the floor and holding him there with his foot. Immediately afterward Mick makes the first of two long speeches that reveal his unconscious contempt for father. Consciously, he is talking nonsense to disorient and intimidate Davies, but the thread of unconscious hostility runs throughout. He begins by refusing even to acknowledge the word *father*. He tells Davies: "You remind me of my uncle's brother" (p. 31). Martin Esslin was the first to comment on this interesting verbal feint; Esslin asks: "Who is one's uncle's brother? Another uncle—or one's father. As Mick's mother never called Sid his uncle, it follows that the man of whom Davies reminds Mick was Mick's father."[30] The picture that Mick paints is of a deserter and a philanderer. "He was always on the move" and he "had an eye for the girls" (p. 31). The constant search for shoes, therefore, takes on a second meaning; he was always looking for a shoe to put his foot into, a girl to make. He says he wore out many a pair. His desertion is represented by references to the foreign parts he visited, but these same references indicate father played around with women of other races, other colors: "there was a bit of the Red Indian in him" and he "married a Chinaman." These guilts join his racial prejudices in accounting for his fears of Blacks and Indians and foreigners. At the end of this first speech to Davies, Mick's mind is still on his father's infidelity and his own oedipal feelings. He asks Davies what bed he slept in last night and how he likes his (Mick's) room. Then Mick launches into his second diatribe against his father, but he still refuses to call him that. This time Davies reminds him of "a bloke I once knew in Shoreditch" (p. 32). The rest of the speech indicates the illegitimacy of the "bloke's" birth and the promiscuity of his mother: "His old mum was still living at the Angel. All the buses passed right by her door." The images of the bloke's mother and wife blend here and become inseparable, and the hint of incest is repeated by Mick's recollection: "I used to leave my bike in her garden. . ." (p. 32). A bike, like a stairway, calls for the legs and feet to go up and down and symbolizes copulation. Mick admits: "Yes, it was a curious affair." Clearly Mick is greatly troubled by the fears associated with oedipal fantasies. He constantly questions Davies about where he sleeps, in which bed. He calls him an "old robber" and tells him: "Keep your hands off my old mum" (p. 35). Mick defends against his fears in a different way than Aston. Mick has reversed the roles of attacker and attacked. Anna Freud describes this transformation in relation to a little boy whose aggression "was turned against the actual person from whom he expected aggression. . . ."[31] Mick will not let the old man dispossess and castrate him, he will dispossess and castrate the old man first. The real-estate jargon of Mick's long speech, in which he taunts Davies with offers to rent him a suite of rooms, contains the imagery of dispossession. He knows the old man can not pay. Insinuated there is also the imagery of a brothel: Mick is a renter of rooms; these are unfurnished flats, not homes; he can get a taker tomorrow at seven quid a week. The speech ends with the suggestion of castration: "Of course we'd need a signed declaration from your personal medical attendant as assurance that you possess the requisite fitness to carry the can, won't we?" (p. 36). In another castrating gesture, Mick takes away the old man's pants. Later he keeps away the old man's bag; Freud confirms Stekel's belief that "luggage often turns out to be an unmistakable symbol of the dreamer's own genitals."[32] Here the image has dual meaning; Mick is castrating the old man and refusing to let the old man castrate him. Mick also turns primal-scene imagery against Davies, the father. Usually, it is the child who is frightened by vague shapes moving noisily in the dark and by the fantasies this scene prompts in his mind. But as Davies stumbles in the dark, trying to light matches, and unable to find the "bloody box," Mick frightens him by chasing him with the Electrolux.

Mick recognizes in the old man the worst in himself. He spits it all out in one of his last speeches to Davies:

> Most of what you say is lies. You're violent, you're erratic, you're just completely unpredictable. You're nothing else but a wild

animal, when you come down to it. You're a barbarian. And to put the old tin lid on it, you stink from arse-hole to breakfast time. (p. 73-74)

Mick and the old man are both liars. Mick's successful business ventures are no more certainly true than Davies's distorted stories of his lost job at the café or his mistreatment at the monastery. Mick has displayed his violence in his first encounter with Davies, and Davies pulls out his knife at the merest provocation. In this way both show their fears; Lidz says: "Aggression and hostility are. . .clearly defensive and protective drives or affects. . . ."[33] Both men show themselves erratic by their shifting loyalties. Mick hates his father and hates himself for hating his father, so he thinks they both stink. Earlier he has recognized the old man's crafty manipulation of people; Mick demonstrates this same ability by pretending to be Davies's friend in order to trick him into being rejected by Aston. (There may be traces of sibling rivalry here as well. After all, at the first meeting, Mick cites his uncle's brother's "penchant for nuts.") One final similarity exists between Mick and the father image he projects on Davies. As Sid, the uncle's brother, had deserted his family, so would Mick like to desert his heritage. He too is always on the move, he says, in his van. There is also in Mick a guilty wish to desert Aston. Like his father, Mick does not like to be a caretaker. He shows this wish to be rid of Aston when he smashes Aston's Buddha at the same time that he dispossesses Davies. "THAT'S WHAT I WANT," he says; he wants to be rid of them both.

The overdetermination of *The Caretaker* contains a third image that creates a third circle of translucent glass underlying the other two. The lowermost position of this third image bears witness to its closer relation to the unconscious. The light rays that emanate from it are also stronger because they must penetrate and illuminate all the top layers of glass. This third image is the dominant one; it highlights the theme of ambivalence by showing Mick and Aston as two halves of the same person. They are one son, split into love and hate. They are the good boy and the bad boy that live inside one psyche. Martin Esslin also sees Mick and Aston as "different sides of the same personality": Mick as the worldly side, Aston as the emotional aspect; Mick as the actor, Aston as poet.[34] Lois Gordon lends further authority to the brothers as "two halves of a single personality": Mick schemes to build new things and Aston devotes himself "to repairing old, broken ones."[35] The large outlines of the play, however, reveal another function of the split. They are the two halves of the son's ambivalence. In alternating scenes they confront the father figure first with gentleness and then with hostility. In *A Night Out* Albert puts his arm around his mother and confesses he would rather stay home with her than go to the office party. A few scenes later he raises the alarm clock over his head in a violent gesture. So it is with Aston and Mick. The structure of the play lends further credence to this theory. The brothers play only one scene together with the old man. Always one brother leaves as another enters. Only when Aston brings the suitcase of clothes to Davies do the brothers act together with the father image. The sequence of events in this scene also suggests the split. As usual, when Aston enters Mick ceases his hostility. The stage directions say: *"Aston comes in. Mick turns and drops the trousers"* (p. 36). Mick has been taunting the old man by refusing to give him his pants. The brothers exchange glances — which is another ritual that occurs each time Aston enters — and Mick ceases his hostility. It is as though the glances, the meeting of the eyes, symbolizes the transformation of one into the other. Aston then offers the bag to Davies, but Mick snatches it saying it is his bag. Aston insists that Mick give the bag to Davies. Then the bag rotates among them: Mick grabbing it from Davies, Aston taking it from Mick and giving it back to Davies, Mick grabbing it again, and so on. Here is the same alternation of feelings that is established in the overall sequence of scenes — generosity and then hostility. Moreover, if the bag is seen in its phallic symbolism, the concretization is sharpened. The bag can represent the male genitalia, in which case Mick reverses castration fear by attacking the father; then Aston alternates this defense by identifying with the aggressor. He submits for the sake of protection and returns the stolen bag. On the other hand, the bag can represent the verbal expression for an old woman. The effect is the same. Ambivalently the son alternates between trying to rob his father of his mother and renouncing his oedipal strivings by returning her. At the end of this scene, a drip sounds in the bucket hanging overhead under the leak in the roof. The son has proven the father's insignificance once more. The concretized moment of intense ambivalence is over, so Mick exits.

The striking contrasts the other critics have pointed out show that in every way Mick and Ashton are alternating opposites indicating alternating moods: Mick is active and restless while Aston is passive and apathetic; Mick is talkative and outgoing while Aston is quiet and reserved. Furthermore, Mick's vacuum-cleaner trick and Aston's account of his shock treatment are emotionally colored by castration fantasies — one active, the other passive. Mick, the angry side of the son, habitually reverses the father's aggressiveness, and he is doing so again when he chases Davies with the Electrolux. Davies, the father, is stumbling around in the dark looking for his "bloody box." Someone kicks it. Davies shouts: "Who's this? Who's this got my box?" After a pause, he adds: "I got a knife here. I'm ready" (p. 45). The latent meanings are clear. He has found someone else in bed with his wife. The scene continues. Davies is on the floor. The Electrolux starts after him. Davies falls, breathlessly and screams: "Ah, ah, ah, ah, ah, ah,! Get away-y-y-y-y!" Then the Electrolux stops. The figure removes the Electrolux plug from the light socket, puts in the bulb, and the lights go on. Davies is flattened against the wall, his knife in his hand. Mick stands on the bed, holding the plug (p. 45). It is not difficult to imagine this scene in reverse. When the father discovers that the usurper of his bed is his son, he throws him out upon the floor, chases him with a vacuum cleaner, and . . . .Each member of the audience must supply this part of the fantasy for himself. What did the father do to the child with this Electrolux and its plug? The end of the scene, the child up against the wall with pincers on its head, is provided by Aston's tale of his electric-shock treatment. After it Aston could not walk or talk or think. He was only sure his spine was not damaged. He laid everything out in his room; he felt he should have died. He does not try to find the man who did it, but he thinks often of finding him. Mick is the side that thinks of finding him and attacking the aggressor who had once attacked him.

The final scene of the play also becomes more meaningful in this light. Mick says; "THAT'S WHAT I WANT," as he smashes the Buddha, symbol of his gentle side. What he wants is an end to this conflict within him over the father. He wants the father punished, rejected, dispossessed by both sides of his self. And it has been accomplished. When Aston returns, they exchange glances and faint smiles of understanding. Mick exits. Aston shows no regret at the broken Buddha. He too is glad to be one with his other half. He proves it by firmly rejecting the father. He remains silent and unrelenting through all of Davies's pleas. Pinter's own comment about this play seems most in tune with this last determination. Pinter's words are:

> At the end of *The Caretaker,* there are two people alone in a room, and one of them must go in such a way as to produce a sense of complete separation and finality. I thought originally that the play must end with the violent death of one at the hands of the other. But then I realised, when I got to the point, that the characters as they had grown could never act in this way.[36]

Pinter does not speak of three characters remaining, yet Mick wants Davies to go as much as Aston does. True, Mick is literally offstage, but if there were any likelihood of a violent death, only Mick could have done it; so Mick is surely not excluded here. The answer lies in the oneness of Mick and Aston, even in Pinter's mind. In the final sentence, he speaks of them in the plural again—the characters, but indicates the growth that brought them together and quelled the violent side of their nature. Mick and Aston are one again, alone in the room with Davies, their father, who must go. Therefore, Mick/Aston can send him away with finality.

The dense texture of this play also includes a concretization of the psyche such as there was in *The Room*. The old dilapidated house with a leaky roof is the neglected, damaged psyche of the son. The downstairs is "closed up. Needs seeing to. . ." (p. 12). In other words, the subconscious needs probing in order to help put the upstairs in order. The upstairs is "out of commission" (p. 12). It not only has a leaky roof, it is filled with junk—an old sink, an old stove, a ladder, an Electrolux, a broken plug. All are remnants of a disastrous past—broken relationships, traumatic events. Aston and Mick—love and hate, trust and suspicion, peace and violence—live there together. One is sitting tenant; the other is landlord. Together they have introjected the father's traits, and he is stinking up the place. They would like to kick him out and clean up the house, redecorate it. Once they have thrown out the rotten memories, they will no longer be in conflict. They can live together in peace, no longer split. By reliving all these old fantasies, getting to the bottom of them, they do just that. They throw out the rubbish in their mind when they throw out the tramp.

Again the beginning of the play reflects its theme. When the play opens, Aston has rescued Davies from a commotion. Davies had been dispossessed for refusing to carry out a bucket of rubbish. In the play Davies is the bucket of rubbish that is thrown out. The split son must resolve his ambivalence before he can do it. But the outcome is prophesied from the moment Aston rescues Davies, for rescue fantasies express a wish to be one's own father. Holland explains: "the child by rescuing his father proves his innocence of any wish to kill him and at the same time by paying a life back, as it were, he owns his own life free and clear of any father. . . ."[37] Mick in his first speeches shows the same wish to banish the father by speaking of his father's confused, illegitimate origins. Again Holland explains: "A related group of fantasies [related to the rescue fantasies] are those of poor or obscure birth: 'My father is so insignificant he is nonexistent.' "[38]

The measure of this play's intuitive strength is in the thematic synchronization of its overdetermination. Every interpretation reinforces the same themes. Davies, the would-be caretaker, has been rejected by those who would have taken care of him because he, Davies, did not care about taking care of their house, because he did not take proper care in the game he played with them, because he did not care about anyone's needs but his own. Mick, because he cared for Aston, took care that Aston would join him in a mutual refusal to continue caring for Davies. The rejection of Davies was necessary if they were to take care of themselves. Stated less cryptically, care-taking is a mutal responsibility, involving proliferating needs for protection, concern, caution, and affection. But sooner or later, each individual puts his own self-care before all these other cares, and betrayal and rejection result. Thus, ironically, is the universal desire to be cared for frustrated. This inter-action between care and rejection interlocks with feelings of adequacy and inadequacy. One feels adequate when he cares and is cared for; one feels inadequate when he betrays and is rejected. The consequence of it all is love and hate, ambiva-lence. The interrelationship of ambivalence and impotence has a new aspect. In *A Night Out*, Albert resumed his impotence when he resumed his submissive slump at the sound of his mother's voice. He did not need to hit her violently; he only needed to wake up to the alarm. It was time to let the angry side of his feelings help him toward independence and manliness. In *The Caretaker* the split son, Mick/Aston, is able to become one man because he does let self-concern end caretaking. He rejects the infantile father who would have taken his free life in exchange for his own comfort. He rejects the vagrant father who has never become responsible enough to be a caretaker. Caretaking is needed by the child, but the child must dispossess the caretaker when it is time to be a man.

NIGHT SCHOOL

Pinter followed *The Caretaker* with a play written for television, *Night School*. It was performed on Associated-Rediffusion Television in July of 1960, but Pinter would not allow it to be published until he had rewritten it for radio in 1966. In Pinter's blunt words: "It so happens that this was the worst thing I have written."[39] Many of his critics agree— however politely. Alrene Sykes says: "It would perhaps be unduly harsh to suggest that Pinter's earlier decision not to publish *Night School* was the right one, but even in its revised form the play does not come anywhere near his best."[40] John Russell Taylor says that the play demonstrates "that Pinter can, like anyone else, make his mistakes. . . ."[41] Other critics give greater offense by withholding all mention of the play.

Indeed, like *A Night Out*, this play is minor Pinter, but certainly Pinter. Because television filming does not demand unity of place, there are several set changes. Physical confinement is missing, but the mothering female is present in the aunts, Annie and Millie. The insecure son is present in Wally.

The visiting usurper is, of course, Sally, whose double life associates her with The Girl. Like the others, this play has its unique variation of the Pinter situation. Wally comes to want Sally, but Mr. Solto, a father figure reminiscent of Goldberg and McCann, somehow spirits her away. The oedipal struggle then takes place over Sally rather than over the mother figure. The manifest content of the play suggests the wish to be rid of someone by the absence of an actual mother or father, by the use of surrogate parents, and by the reversal of the wish in Wally's feeling that everybody wants to be rid of him.

The play takes place in the home of Annie and Millie Billet, maiden aunts to Walter Street. Wally, as he is called, has just been released from prison. He is a forger of post-office savings books, but not a very good forger. This is the third time he has been in jail. While he has been gone, the aunts have rented his room to Sally Gibbs because they needed the money. In their eyes she is an ambitious young schoolteacher who is also studying foreign languages at night school. What is more, she pays the rent promptly and helps with the dusting on Saturdays. Their not-so-secret scheme is to promote marriage between Wally and Sally. Wally is more concerned with repossessing his room. He discovers a photo of Sally, revealing that she is, in fact, a dance girl in a night club. Wally gives the photo to Mr. Solto, a small-time entrepreneur with exaggerated visions of himself and his adventures. Wally wants Mr. Solto to locate Sally and her night club. Soon after these events, Wally visits Sally in her room. They have some brandy together, swap tall stories about their identities, and form a mutual interest in one another.

Meanwhile Mr. Solto does find Sally and the night club where she works. In her dressing room, Sally speaks of a man she has lost her attraction for. On the dance floor, Solto shows his fancy for her and tells her that Wally is a forger and a petty thief. Subsequently, Solto and Wally try to convince one another the girl does not exist. Each seems to want to keep her for himself. The next morning, however, Sally is gone. She has left a note and another photo. In this photo she is with a group of schoolgirls holding a netball (a combination soccer and basketball). Annie says: "I never knew she was the games mistress. She never told us." Millie says: "It looks as though she's gone for good." Walter says: "Yes. *Pause*. That's what it looks like" (p. 88). The fade marks the end of the play.

Some critics find this play simple and straightforward. John Russell Taylor says that "all the ambiguities are resolved in a way which offers no surprises."[42] Esslin, with his usual perception, points to one obviously obscure scene—the one in Sally's bedroom. He wonders whether or not "Sally actually does the actions she is ordered to perform" and whether "Walter's exercise of his authority is the prelude to lovemaking or merely the expression of his impotent infantile sadism."[43] A second question needs to be added: why does Sally leave at the end of the play? Most critics say she leaves because she can not face up to the lie she has told. This is certainly a valid interpretation. However, Taylor's judgment notwithstanding, the play is ambiguous on this point. A second determination of Sally's motive can be made merely by interpreting the manifest content of the play. Presuming that Wally's performance in the bedroom was "impotent infantile sadism," Sally may have become disenchanted by the end of the evening. Wally, then, may be the man Sally says she no longer finds attractive. Shortly afterward she learns from Mr. Solto that Wally is also a petty thief. This information can only diminish his desirability. Furthermore, she may be drawn to Mr. Solto as a father figure. She may also dislike facing up to her deception, but would this be very difficult when she knows Wally lied about himself, too? She may be acknowledging both deceptions and having the last word when she leaves the games-mistress photo. She may be saying, "It was all a game, and I won. I found you out, but you only think you found me out. I *am* a teacher as well as a night club hostess."

This alternate interpretation of the ending demonstrates that there is some small ambiguity in this play despite its realism. Perhaps Hinchliffe's comment provides the proper insight. He says: "*Night School* was intended to be the first of a new kind of Pinter play—light comedy with new realism. Its failure stems from the fact that no author can put old wine in new bottles."[44] Except for *A Night Out* and *Night School,* Pinter's works up to this point have been highly intuitive. In these two plays he has exerted more conscious control. In *A Night Out* he has resolved all obscurity and ambiguity; in *Night School* the few remaining enigmas seem to be contrived mysteries rather than natural outgrowths of the dreamlife of the play. This is reason enough for calling these plays *minor* Pinter.

Nevertheless, this play, like all plays, does have some latent content and more than one interpretation. The play can be viewed as a reversal of its group partner, *A Night Out.* Wally's petty criminality is the reverse of Albert's earnestness. The aunts can be viewed as mother, split in two. Thus, they become Mrs. Stokes's counterpart. The split mother wants to promote a marriage between Sally and Wally and thereby relieve herself of a responsibility. Mrs. Stokes wishes to keep Albert for herself and protests his "mucking about" with girls. Wally's feelings for Sally change from strong rejection to active acceptance. Albert, on the other hand, accepts The Girl's invitation and then experiences a growing repugnance for her. Mrs. Stokes sets up the dead father as Albert's rival by constantly insisting that it is still his house. In dream symbolism, of course, she is herself the house. Wally's rival is a live man and a surrogate father, Mr. Solto. Finally, Mrs. Stokes wins Albert; he returns to her. Sally, on the other hand, walks out on Wally. Here the pattern of reversal ceases. Both men appear to be losers. Albert is left to be stifled by his mother, and Wally loses his chance for a somewhat more mature role than a mother's boy.

Consistent with the focus of group two, this determination also reverses the direction of the wish to be rid of someone. Albert wished to be rid of his mother, of the taunting people at the party, and of The Girl. He raised his hand in violence against his mother and the prostitute, and he walked out on the party. In *Night School,* everyone else wishes to be rid of Wally. The mothering aunts are growing old and wish to shift Wally's care to Sally. Mr. Solto rids himself of responsibility for Wally by refusing to lend him money. Then, he tries to slough Wally off in order to keep Sally. Sally rids herself of Wally by her vanishing act at the end. Sally's rejection of Wally is the most punishing, since he has ultimately decided he would prefer her to the room. In the total picture of Pinter's work, this is the first time a young girl has been the young man's object choice, and it is also the first time he seems to choose her over her symbolic representation—the room. Consequently, Sally's riddance gesture to Wally takes on added significance. Even the world seems to wish riddance of Wally: periodically it puts him away in jail. Thus, the wish to be rid of someone here appears as its mirror image—the wish to be rid of oneself—in a reminiscence of the masochistic punishment plays.

Pursuing the relationship of this play to the rest of Pinter's works, it seems that in *Night School* Pinter is playing with the character splits and personality dimensions that grow out of ambivalence and identity problems. Thus, Pinter continues the theme of ambivalence, prominent in the last two plays, and highlights the problem of identity that has been present but unstressed until *Night School.* Stanley Webber, Edward, Albert, Mick/Aston—all struggle with identity problems, usually linked to their ambivalence. But these problems have not been the primary focus of those plays. *Night School* begins a shift of emphasis to that theme.

All of the characters in *Night School* show some difficulty with identity, which is evident in their role playing and splitting. By these methods they link their identity problems to the softened wish to kill. These characters show a wish to be someone else that is an indirect way of wishing to be rid of parents.

Unlike the contrived enigmas of this play, the characters have the breath and breadth of life itself. Sally, of course, displays splitting most prominently. She has two separate lives, if one accepts the identity of the second photo. Like Ben and Gus, Mick and Aston, she is the good child and the bad child, but this time Pinter has given her only one body. She is the victim of the split that results from the defiance-submission polarity of the anal period. The good girl is a demure school-teacher; the bad girl is a high-stepping dance hostess. She shows her anality by her excessive cleanliness, too. Her bathing and decorating and dusting are all results of reaction formation. Mack and Semrad define reaction formation as a defense that "enables the individual to express an unacceptable impulse by transforming it into its opposite."[45] Sally's wish to be dirty is transformed into compulsive cleanliness. Her two identities are similarly linked. As Katina, the night-club hostess, she wishes to break all the rules introjected from her parents. So she plays games with dirty old men. The demands of her superego to submit to the values of her parents are expressed in the schoolteacher. Thus, she displays both her ambivalence and her identity crisis. She also shows her similarity to The Girl in *A Night Out*.

Walter's personality is, of course, predominantly oral. He has lived as an infant in the nursery of Millie and Annie. They have suckled and swaddled him in the clean airy room usurped by Sally. Whenever he has put his foot out the door, he has been arrested and put in jail. The life of petty thieving and forging takes adult effort, so Walter prefers to fail. Then he can be put back into the dark womb of the prison cell where he is treated "very well. Very well" (p. 53). This time he has been in the dark womb of prison exactly as long as a fetus: "I been away nine months, I come home for a bit of peace and quiet to recuperate" (p. 55). He looks forward to time in the nursery again: "I'll come back here. . .I'll lie on my bed. . .I'll see the curtains blowing by the window. . .I'll have a good rest, eh?" (p. 52). The opposite of this passivity is activity, the polarity connected with the oral phase. Wally indulges the active side of this polarity by his fantasies. He tells Sally: "The boys used to come here [to this room], though. This is where we used to plan our armed robberies" (p. 73). No mention is made of Walter's father; even Mr. Solto comes to the house rarely. Walter has had then no strong male figure to identify with. Consequently, the night-club hostess might be a threatening character to him. In his infantilism, he probably feels safer with a prudish schoolteacher. The aunties seemed to know this when they made their secret marriage scheme. Solto seems to know it when he says: "That's your mark. Someone with an education" (p. 87). Perhaps Walter's sexual fantasies go no farther than ordering girls about, telling them when to sit down, when to cross their legs. Walter is not a complete split like Sally, but he is a strange combination of opposites—a child and a criminal. He reminds one of Stanley, who in his guilt over refusing to grow up commits wrongs that will insure his punishment. He reminds one of Ben/Gus who have also translated this infantile wish for punishment into a life of crime. In both cases there is an ambivalence toward parental law. There is disrespect for it in violating it; there is respect for it in demanding to be punished.

The aunts are as delightful and as funny as any characters Pinter has created. This play is worth publishing just for them.

They represent the other kind of split, a split into two separate bodies. In every way they are each other's opposites. Annie is the active, busy one, while Millie is the passive, lazy one; yet Millie dominates and Annie obeys her orders. Millie's pleasure is in being dominant and being waited on; Annie's pleasure is in being the one standing up, which gives her the right to complain. Together they constitute Meg's childish mothering, Flora's business about the house, and Mrs. Stokes's nagging ambivalence.

Mr. Solto is two-faced, too; he is a hypocrite. He has money but pretends to the tax collector that he is broke. He is a landlord who pretends to family friendship until he is asked for a loan. This tightfistedness with money shows he is an anal hypocrite. He is an old lecher who plots to keep Sally/Katina for himself when he has promised as a friend to find her for Wally. He is also an old man who pretends to great youthful adventures. Keeping Sally is further evidence of the residue of anal possessiveness within him, but it also couples with his adventure tales to demonstrate the phallic assertiveness of a young boy. He still prefers poking around and investigating to settling down with responsibility. He is at the same time like-able and unlikable. The audience likes him because he is humorous and human; they dislike him because he is unprincipled and selfish. In his many images he is reminiscent of Goldberg/McCann; in his humorous but selfish disregard for others, he is like Davies/Jenkins.

The play is also a link and transition between the plays that stress punishment and ambivalence and those that stress identity and deception. All these themes are basic to the people in *Night School,* but Pinter lays stress on them by his opening clues. When Walter first arrives home from prison, Annie shows her ambivalence by welcoming him with cake she bought around the corner. She did not bake it for him herself. Next Pinter introduces identity and deception by symbolic reference to curtains. Annie and Millie have had a dispute about the proper way to hang the curtains. Walter has looked forward to watching the curtains blow as he rests in his room. He knows the wind brings change. The curtains flutter in the wind, changing their contour and the patterns of light they let through. The windblown curtains inspire a world of fantasy where identities shift and pretenses take on empty shape. A closing clue from Pinter highlights the theme of deception. In the school photo Sally is holding a netball. The netball symbolizes the concept of life as a game. The object of the game is to keep the ball going over the net, never to let it get caught in the web of lies and deceit that stand between the opposing teams. If the ball gets caught in the net, the game is over.

The plot of this play centers on a battle for possession of a room and a girl. However, the real focus of the play is on the characters as individuals. The title is the clue. These characters are like a school of fish—feeding and migrating together in the dark night of ignorance, trying to avoid the nets of deception set out to ensnare them. Like the difference between the herring and the pilchard that Millie and Annie dispute, these characters are basically alike in their ambivalence and pretensions; only their names and shapes are different. They belong to that school of obscurity wrought by language differences. Sally's language as a teacher is foreign to the tongue Katina speaks. And these differing languages reflect changing identities, as do the names of the fish in *Night School*. Perhaps night will always reign in this school—life's school—because of the deceptions people practice. In the last line of the play Wally bears this out. He conceals his response and diffuses Sally's actions when he says: "That's what it looks like" (p. 88). So the lights fade and the curtains close on the shifting identities in *Night School*.

THE DWARFS

Shifting identity continues as the focus of the next play, *The Dwarfs. The Dwarfs* is the fourth and last play of group two. Written for radio and produced on the B.B.C. in 1960, it has also been produced on the stage. The first time Pinter himself directed, but the play is too abstruse to command any kind of public acceptance or even unqualified critical approval. Pinter himself admits this in a comment on that first stage performance in 1963: "Apparently ninety-nine people out of a hundred feel it's a waste of time, and the audience hated it."[46] Pinter, and all of the critics, too, are quick to explain that *The Dwarfs* was based on an unpublihsed novel written between 1953 and 1957. The novel is, at least partially, autobiographical. Consequently, this "terribly sparse" play — to borrow Pinter's words — is "very clear" only to him.[47]

These two factors need to be remembered in any assessment of this play. Having been written for radio, it is very verbal imagery. Pinter could not rely on sophisticated camera logues in stream of consciousness style. The play is also full of verbal imagery. Pinter could not rely on sophisticaed camera techniques, or even facial expression and physical movement, to show mental aberration. He has instead created verbal pictures of striking character and detail that impart the mental states of his characters. Consequently, viewed on the stage where the audience are used to movement and action, the play seems static. Moreover, the beautiful poetic monologues demand concentrated listening. On radio attention can be funneled to the single voice. Each whisper and nuance can be made to capture its full moment. On the stage, even in a single spot the actor seems too removed, too embodied to create this same hold on the spectator. Clearly, this play loses much of its artistic effect when it is transferred from its intended medium.

Second, the play is about a private world. Pinter says: "I know all the things that aren't said, and the way the characters actually look at each other, and what they mean by looking at each other."[48] Consequently, Pinter has forgotten, consciously or unconsciously, to supply much logical overlay. This play is almost pure dream-distortion. After *The Caretaker* with its almost perfect balance between realism and dream and *Night School* with its strong conscious control, *The Dwarfs* swings to the other extreme. Much of it can only be interpreted by the dreamer. Some of the associations seem obscure to the playgoer because undoubtedly they are more personal than universal. However, there is also a great deal of universality in the play — in its symbols, in its characters, in its themes. And those parts that relate to everyman can be interpreted. What is more, the language and imagery of the play are so strikingly beautiful, and the revelations of the tortured, suffering inner man are so genuine and sincere, that this play should never be called a waste of time.

Perhaps the only thing *The Dwarfs* shares with the light comic realism of *Night School* is the basic Pinter situation. It opens with two men in a room. They discuss food and await the arrival of a third person. It is difficult to call him a *visitor* because he is awaited in his own apartment. These three men are supposed to be friends, but actually they menace one another. There is no mother here, as there is not in *The Dumb Waiter* or *The Caretaker*. In fact, Len and Pete are not unlike Gus and Ben in their opening scene. Len talks and stirs about looking for food, much as Gus does. Pete is more quiet and more dominant. He also reads. As the play progresses Len takes on the prepsychotic character of Stanley and Edward, while Pete takes on the violence and hostility of Bert and Mick. Mark seems, in some ways, to be a new emanation, but on closer examination he is a combination of Goldberg's hollowness, Edward's vanity, and that dash of individuality with which Pinter invests all of his characters. At the end of the play all of these people have dispossessed one another.

If the play must be interpreted realistically, it is about three friends who are drifting apart, who have lost their common bond, who no longer really like each other. Len is introverted, observant, talkative, insecure, and dependent. He is also ill. Pete says if Len doesn't pull himself together he will be ready for the loony bin."[49] Mark is elegant, material, quiet, self-composed, and aloof. Pete says he is a "man of weeds," "an attitude" (p. 93). Pete is critical, disdainful, practical, and aggressive. Len sees him as cruel, too; he tells him: "You're a homicidal maniac" (p. 87). Later, Len characterizes Pete as a gull, "a slicing gull" (p. 100). Len sees Mark, on the other hand, as a spider who sits and waits for his victims to be trapped in his web.

These friends visit back and forth, either in Len's solid old apartment or in Mark's modern, fancy one; they are never in Pete's house. Their encounters are never supportive or generous of spirit. They criticize each other; they ignore each other; they give harsh advice. They undercut each other. Mark and Pete each warn Len not to see too much of the other. Each claims the other is not good for Len. Len cuts Mark by telling him Pete thinks he is a fool.

Len begins having hallucinations. He sees dwarfs who watch him, prey on him, litter his yard with garbage, wash their veins in his sink. Ultimately Len ends up in the hospital. At Pete's suggestion, Mark and Pete visit Len in the hospital, but they have almost nothing to say to him. They treat him with indifference, and Len orders them off his bed. When Len comes out of the hospital, he has been deserted by Mark and Pete and by the dwarfs as well. He is alone in his clean yard where a shrub and a flower grow.

Pinter says this is "a play about betrayal and distrust."[50] And indeed this sparse logical version does display these ideas. The play seems to be about mutual dispossession. Two friends, Pete and Mark, dispossess Len of their friendship. Len, then, dispossesses himself of all memory of them. Even the most casual playgoer must admit, nevertheless, that this thematic extraction, however satisfying in itself, rests on a very simplistic view of the play. It springs from the tissue-thin surface of the play's manifest content. The remaining obscurities are too numerous to be catalogued by a few questions. If this play is approached as a dream, its heart can be seen to throb below the thin surface with an intensity that rends the tissue and exposes the nerves of the suffering soul beneath it. The suffering soul is Len in a desperate search for his identity.

In this second determination Len speaks his problem to Mark in the longest monologue of the play: "The point is, who are you?" (p. 104). Len is not elastic enough to contain the burgeoning facets of himself. As Pete says: "By elastic I mean being prepared for your own deviations. You don't know where you're going to come out next at the moment. You're like a rotten old shirt" (pp. 92-93). Len is indeed "like a rotten old shirt," disintegrating into a three-way split. Len is the core, the real self. Mark and Pete are the projections of his conflicting selves. Martin Esslin gives tacit agreement when he comments that Pete and Mark are seen from Len's point of view.[51] John Russel Taylor speaks a similar sense of the play when he notes that Pinter has taken the audience inside Len's mind. [52]

Len's mind is a sick mind. He suffers from the same illness that plagued Stanley and Edward and Mick/Aston. Each of these characters is shown in some stage of schizophrenic transformation. Len has moved into the delusional world that is dominated by projection — "a returning or giving back to the external, interpersonal world of something which originated in that world." [53] That something is the low regard of significant adults that the sick person has introjected and taken as his own. It has become his sense of inadequacy, his low self-esteem, his self-reproach. Now in his illness the patient tries to "maintain a tolerable sense of self" by projecting to "the external world the evaluation of the self that he now rejects."[54] Mark and Pete are the unacceptable selves that Len is projecting outward. As Len speaks to Mark near the end of the play, he confirms that Mark is only an emanation:

> It's not important then that it's conspiracy or hallucination. What you are, or appear to be to me, or appear to be to you, changes so quickly, so horrifyingly, I certainly can't keep up with it and I'm damn sure you can't either. But who you are I can't even begin to recognize, and sometimes I recognize it so wholly, so forcibly, I can't look, and how can I be certain of what I see? (pp. 104-105).

Nevertheless, at the outset Len sees Mark as his outer shell, the external body, the self that faces the world, the pose that the real man hides behind. Len is afraid to let Mark bend over to pick up the toasting fork. If Mark bends, the hollow, dry shell might break. Mark's profession fits his facet of the self; he is an actor. Mark has chosen the modern flat he lives in; Mark has selected the suit with no "turn-ups" and a "zip at the hips," which Len/Mark admire by turns. As Len describes Mark sitting by the fire, he clearly describes himself. Mark is seen in that speech from the vantage point of his own eyes, but it is Len who sees through those eyes:

> Mark sits by the fireside. Crosses his legs. His fingers wear a ring. The finger poised. Mark regards his finger. He regards his legs. He regards the fireside. Outside the door is the black bossom. He combs his hair with an ebony comb, he sits, he lies, he lowers his eyelashes, raises them, sees no change in the posture of the room, lights a cigarette, watches his hand clasp the lighter, watches the flame, sees his mouth go forward, sees the con-

sumation, is satisfied. Pleased, sees the smoke in the lamp, pleased with the lamp and the smoke and his bulk, pleased with his legs and his hand and his body in the lamp. Sees himself speaking, the words arranged on his lips, sees himself with pleasure silent. (p. 102)

Len is distanced from his Mark/self. He sees the narcissim of his Mark/self and finds it as despicable as a spider. Len's ambivalence is turned upon himself.

In Pete, Len perceives the harsh, aggressive, violent side of himself. He hands out harsh advice when he talks back and forth with himself: "Buck your ideas up," "nourish the power of assessment" (p. 93). As Pete, Len could pull himself together; he could tell the difference between what he smells and what he thinks. As Pete, Len could gamble on an "efficient idea" and win. He did it when he "went to work in the city"; he fought them on their own ground. He thinks it time to quit "wasting away down there. The time has come to act" (p. 97). But Len abhors the cruelty that accompanies this efficiency. After hearing his Pete/self speak thus, Len pictures a squashed insect on a plate, feels his hand in the body of a dead bird. Len sees the hurt his Pete/self inflicts so he characterizes him as a gull—a "slicing gull": "Gull pads. Gull probes. Gull stamps his feet. Gull shinnies up. Gull screams, tears, Pete, tears, digs, Pete cuts, breaks, Pete stretches the corpse . . ." (pp. 100-101). Even the dream that Len's Pete/self describes reflects a combination of Len's illness and Pete's violence. People are panicked in Pete's dream; their faces are coming off in slabs; their skin is "sizzling on the electric rails" (p. 93). The falling apart, the disintegration is Len; the tearing, searing manifestation of it is Pete.

Sometimes Len hides from his projected selves by returning to the old family home, Len's house. There he observes his table, his chair, his bowl of fruit, his curtains. Arieti explains that the schizophrenic suffers from "aholism," the inability to see wholes. He divides "wholes into smaller unities"; instead of seeing a door, he sees "only the knob or the keyhole."[55] So with Len. Moreover, he observes those elements of his room that can lend him security. His psyche is not capable of sustaining an abstract idea, however; so he transforms it into concrete representation.[56] He sees security in terms of dream symbols: mother is table; father is his chair. His bowl of fruit, Freud would equate with mother's breasts.[57] His curtains are the cover that hides him from the world. "There is no wind" (p. 88). Therefore, his curtains are still. "It is past night and before morning" (p. 88); he is safe in the dark of his family room—the womb. Here he says: "There are no voices. They make no hole in my side" (p. 89). Having projected his self-hate to the outside of himself, the sick man feels accused, martyred.[58] At one point Len tells Mark: "Both of you bastards, you've made a hole in my side, I can't plug it! *Pause.* I've lost a kingdom" (p. 99). But hiding in his womb-room, he has a temporary feeling of safety; they can make no hole in his side; they can not crucify him. Len's moment of security is brief, however; his distorted perception combines with his need to concretize abstract ideas; his room begins to change shape. He "can't tell the limits, the boundaries," which he has "been led to believe are natural" (p. 91). Later Len can not see himself in the mirror; he can only see through the mirror to the other side. In other words, he is losing the sense of himself as "an entity, a person, a center of consciousness"; Arieti describes this as occurring in advanced schizophrenia.[59]

Presiding over all these manifestations of his illness, Len perceives the dwarfs. Many critics have, like Alrene Sykes, asked the question: who are the dwarfs? Sykes denies those critical interpretations that see the dwarfs as "financial barons," "poetic imagination," and "unseen rulers of the world." He views the dwarfs as "the miseries, jealousies, and ignobleness of the dissolving relationship . . . ."[60] R. F. Storch sees the dwarfs as the embodiment of Len's "infantile fears and obsessions."[61] Sykes and Storch are only a few steps away from the opinion held here: the dwarfs are concretizations of Len's feelings of inadequacy. These feelings introjected from the attitudes of significant adults in his life have become unbearable inside, so Len has externalized them. In so doing he has given them a concrete form that corresponds to the abstract idea. A dwarf is small, ugly, and insignificant — an excellent concretization of the way Len's inadequacy makes him feel — insignificant and stunted. Dwarfs also suggest busy little people, and Len's dwarfs are always on the job; they keep an eye on proceedings; they "clock in early"; "they don't stop work until the job in hand is ended, one way or another" (p. 94). If Len is to take stock of himself, he must watch the "rate of exchange," "the rise and fall of the market" (p. 94). The dwarfs have a distorted resemblance to all those who have criticized Len and who expect at any moment his disintegration and collapse. "They stumble in the gutters and produce their pocket watches"; they scrub and spruce and preen to be dressed for the dirty occasion; "Time is kept to a T"; they celebrate the occasion with food, and chuckle with anticipation while they await the event (p. 96). The dwarfs like to eat so well they sometimes go on picnics. So does Len's low self-esteem eat away at his insides, at his sense of well-being. If the dwarfs leave Len alone awhile, "in come the rats" (p. 98) with their connotations of betrayal and gnawing guilt. Len's betrayal of his friends gnaws at him just as his inadequacy eats him up. Len's hallucinations include the leavings of the dwarfs and the rats, the remnants of his own insides that the dwarfs gobble and spew. These uneaten morsels mix with the piles of excrement left by Len and the dwarfs. Len is not equal to cleaning up the mess. He tries. When the dwarfs return, he tells them he has "slaved like a martyr" (p. 98), but the dwarfs will not grant him a tip or a bonus. "They yawn, they show the blood stuck between their teeth, they plan their scratching game, they tongue their chops. . ." (p. 98). Len begs them to notice his attempts to kill the rat in himself: "What about the job in hand? After all my devotion. What about the rats I dealt with? . . . I tried all ways to please you?" (p. 98). But the dwarfs ignore him. They engage in sex play among themselves: "squatting and bending, dipping their wicks in the custard" (p. 100). As Len watches he stands "wafted by odours" (p. 100). Thus, he concretizes his extreme inadequacy. Arieti explains: "a patient who believes that he is a 'rotten person' develops the olfactory hallucination that a bad odor emanates from his body. The rotten personality becomes concretized in the 'rotten body which smells.' "[62] So Len applauds the dwarfs' efficiency. They have reduced him to a whiff. But when Len emerges from the hospital, his confidence and adequacy have apparently been restored. Pete and Mark, the manifestations of his split personality, have deserted him. The dwarfs have packed up and gone. Len's yard is usually littered with the dwarfs' leavings—"scraps of cat's meat, pig hollocks, tin cans, bird brains, spare parts of all the little animals . . ." (p. 110). Such images of mutilation suggest the ultimate male inadequacy—castration. But at the end of the play, the dwarfs and their litter are gone: "all is bare. All is clean" (p. 110). In the clean yard, there is growth—a shrub, a flower.

This second interpretation, then, focuses on the deterioration of a man's personality. Only when the deterioration is complete can the man be salvaged. There is here a sharp memory of Stanley and Edward. Stanley took on the images his fathers forced on him because his own guilts would not allow him to do otherwise. Edward felt like an impostor and collapsed under the weight of a false self. Len deteriorates under such burdens until he is cleansed of them.

The powerful throb of this play gains its final resonance from a third determination. Buried even deeper in the latent content of this play is the birth fantasy Len's cleansing demands. Perhaps it could more aptly be called a *rebirth* fantasy. The inadequate personality and its ugliness are purged and new, clean life is born. R. F. Storch recognizes the purging imagery and suggests that about the time Pete remarks on Len's lack of elasticity, the "situation becomes more clearly an anal fantasy."[63] There certainly is an anal fantasy here, but it is only one phase of the whole rebirth. Freud's explanation of the "cloaca theory" clarifies this point: "In childhood the female genitals and the anus are regarded as a single area — the 'bottom' . . . ; and it is not until later that the discovery is made that this region of the body comprises two separate cavities and orifices."[64] In other words, the child envisions fetus and feces emerging through the same passage — the anal passage. This is the kind of fantasy hidden in the imagery of this play.

Len consistently speaks of himself in the womb. He says he works at Paddington station, and the station is "an oven" (p. 87). All he does there is sleep; he curls up in the corner and reads the timetables. The image is of the fetus awaiting the moment in time when it will be born. A railroad station also suggests a journey — the birth journey. Later in his womb-room at the family home, he speaks of the journey: "This is a journey and no ambush. This is the deep grass I keep to. This is the thicket in the center of the night and the morning" (p. 88). At the beginning of the speech he expects to be ambushed at birth, but his birth is halted. He remains at the mouth of the birth canal between the dark night and the womb and the morning of birth. He elaborates: "I have my compartment. I am wedged" (p. 89). Shortly after he complains to Mark that his room opens and shuts; it changes shape, so that he can not tell its boundaries, its limits. He is beginning to feel forced to separate from the womb. This event, Len's dreaded expulsion from the security of the womb, is one of the events the dwarfs wait and watch for. Len perceives the dwarfs preparing to assist in the delivery. "They collect at the back step," "under the kitchen window" (p. 96). In other words, they are ready at the place of birth. Like the doctor, they "scrub their veins at the running sink," and they are "gorged in the sud" (p. 96). They expect to eat the fetus once they have delivered it. In anticipation they begin to chew before they have eaten. At the next hallucination, the image of the dwarfs has undergone a transformation. Pinter prepares the listener for it. He lets Len describe the schizophrenic's transformation of the remains of a squashed insect into a large fluff that becomes the body of a dead bird. Similarly the image of the dwarfs awaiting a fetus to eat is transformed into dwarfs feasting on excrement. Pile mixes with pile. Len has had a clearance. The dwarfs gobble and spew. But they also wait; they bring nets and webs and traps for their innocent catch. As Len's anxiety grows, he feels the very womb he hides in has been invaded: "You're all in my corner" (p. 99). He can hide nothing from them, put nothing aside. Now it is the corner that waits to devour him: "it waits, it eats, it's voracious . . ." (p. 99). As his listener, Mark, vanishes and the lights fade, the dwarfs are again waiting and watching. They play while they wait—squatting, bending, wick dipping; occasionally they sniff at their expected prey and a "lick of flame screws up their nostrils" (p. 100). With a shift of light, another transformation—"Pete walks by the river"; he stops under the woodyard wall while the night ticks. Rivers and all waters are, of course, representative of uterine waters, and wood represents woman, as signified fittingly by a Portugese word association. Freud says: " 'Wood' seems, from its linguistic connections, to stand in general for female 'material.' The name of the Island of

'Madeira' means 'wood' in Portuguese."[65] Pete, the gull, stops
where the "wood hangs" and he probes, tears, digs, pulls. The
river jolts. The dwarfs collect by the shoreside. They wear
raincoats. They watch as "Pete tugs, he tugs, he's tugging, he
kills, he's killing, the rat's head, with a snap the cloth of the
rat's head tears" (p. 101). The imagery is clear. Pete has been
midwife to the birth of the sneaky, verminous self, while
the dwarfs watched, dressed for the flood of birth waters.
The image quickly shifts. Len is ill of diarrhea; he "couldn't
stop shivering" and he "couldn't stop squatting" (p. 101).
Again the images are clear; there has been a purging birth.
All the evil and the bile are outside of Len now. His need
to project the unwanted in himself has been concretized.
Later, Len worries to Mark: What have I seen, the scum or
the essence?", and, "What happens to the scum?" (p. 105).
He wonders if it is sucked back. But when Len emerges from
the hospital, the dwarfs have stopped eating. They are "chock-
full," but they are packed to go. They have eaten up all that
was purged. Even their leavings are gone. All is bare and clean.
A shrub and a flower grow. A new life is born. But Len looks
warily at his new world. In its sterility he feels naked. All
his crutches are gone with the dwarfs and his other selves.
"They've cut me off without a penny," he says (p. 109). If he
is to continue, he must go it alone.

The thematic messages of these determinations are as
meaningful as the play is obscure and ambiguous. The realistic
reading of the play does support Pinter's declared theme —
betrayal and distrust. As friends, Pete, Mark, and Len do distrust each other. Pete and Mark expect Len to fall apart, to go
to the "loony bin," to be unequal to relationships. Len reveals
his distrust of Pete and Mark by characterizing them as gull
and spider, respectively. Pete and Mark show a mutual
antagonism, Pete thinks Mark is no more than an attitude;
Mark calls Pete an infection. In the hospital scene Pete tells

Len that he and Mark have "been walking up the road back to back" (p. 108). They are together, but they do not see each other; they do not even perceive from the same point of view. Their antagonism culminates in Pete's threat to Mark: "All I've got to do to destroy you is to leave you as you wish to be" (p. 109). This three-way distrust and antagonism can only end in betrayal, and they do betray each other. Mark and Pete desert Len completely—before, during, and after his illness. They both see Len's breakdown approaching, but they withhold the emotional support he needs from their friendship. They actually increase the threat to his security by their warnings and advice. Their one visit to the hospital seems so cold as to be an empty ritual. They prophesy their future desertion of Len as they leave his hospital room. Each in turn says: "Give me a call," but neither responds to Len's loaded question: "How do I know you'll be in?" (p. 108). Having thus betrayed Len's need, they return to Mark's apartment for their betrayal of each other. Mark accuses Pete of having wasted his time for years, of having thought him a fool. Pete's reply is final: "You are a fool" (p. 109). After his threat to abandon Mark, Pete does just that: "He walks out of the room" (p. 109). Mark makes no move. He remains behind, staring. Their betrayal of each other has been spoken and acted out. Each has been content to perceive the other as unworthy. Each has been unwilling to care for the other's needs, as together they have been uncaring of Len's needs. There are no caretakers here, only traitors to friendship. Thus, the play echoes one of the major themes of *The Caretaker*.

The second determination focuses on man's attempt to understand the many facets of himself. Each part despises the other part. Pete and Mark perceive Len as weak; Len perceives Mark as empty and Pete as cruel. Thus, betrayal and distrust finally apply to the self. Man's distrust is seen to extend even to the dimensions of his own personality. He betrays himself by rejecting his own inadequacies and submitting to their external punishment. When he digs deeper into himself looking for a secure identity, he reaches back to his parental beginnings; this is represented in the play by Len's return to the parental home with his table and chair. Here the dwarfs, his sense of inadequacy, eat him up. Here it becomes clear that the real betrayal comes early. It comes from the figures who first implant the feeling of inadequacy in the child, for he is never able to escape it. Len screams this pain: "it never dies, it's never dead. I feed it, it's fed well. Things that at one time seem to me of value I have no resource but to give it to eat and what was of value turns into pus" (p. 99). Another dimension has also been added to the play—the search for identity means the struggle to be one man. Len says of Mark and Pete: "You're still both of you standing behind my curtains, moving my curtains in my room" (p. 105). Len, like everyman, wants to be one man with self-respect: "What have I seen, the scum or the essence?" (p. 105). His question points to the difficulty of knowing what is perceived. In this play Pinter verbalizes man's inability to verify who and what he is. The many faces of one man, his relativity in time and space, his inadequacy to deal with it all—these are the factors that dwarf man and his potential to know.

The rebirth fantasy adds new meaning still: to be reborn man must suffer a painful purge. The violence in himself must be turned upon himself to tear out the unwanted. But then the reborn must endure the loneliness of a new sterile world. The idea of purging the ugly, the inadequate, the vile, the unwanted, recalls *The Caretaker*. There, too, the bucket of rubbish was the psyche, torn between love and hate, and its conflict could only be settled when the unwanted tramp was dispossessed. He was the object of dispute. Once gone the split in the psyche was mended; the roof no longer leaked. So in this play, the sick man is split until he is purged. Then he can begin to grow again in his clean, sterile yard.

This image of rebirth, the new growth in the clean yard, is matched by Pinter's usual thematic images at the openings of the play. The first full sentence of the play is Len's: "What's the matter with this recorder?" As he speaks, *"he pulls recorder in half, looks down, blows, taps."* Then he adds: "There's something wrong with this recorder" (p. 83). The brain is a recorder, too. It records all the sights and sounds and experiences of life and plays them back. This recorder has not been working properly: "The sound is fragmentary" (p. 83). So like his own mind and personality, Len pulls it in half. Then Pinter shows the audience that Mark's icebox is empty and the milk is hard in the bottle. Mark's house can not nourish all of his psyche; the core of his self, Len, is hungry and there is nothing to eat. Without food, man's growth is stunted, and so the relevance of the title is brought into focus as it was by the new growth symbols at the close of the play. Len and Mark and Pete are dwarfs, stunted by the inadequancy and impotence bred in them from birth. This nourishment by hardened milk is the great betrayal.

A unique feature of this play is the recurrence of symbols and images used in previous plays. Symbols that seemed somehow vague in earlier plays reappear in *The Dwarfs* and become clear. In other cases, reuse merely reaffirms their meaning. The "bullock"—the full-grown, castrated ox—that once represented Edward's projected impotence in *A Slight Ache*, serves the same purpose for Len/Mark. The image of the Billet sisters gaining substitute sexual pleasure by running up and down stairs in between eating is repeated by Len. He explains it to Pete as "the only thing you can do in the night" (p. 86). Len speaks of the curtains in his womb-room as does Wally in *Night School*, but Len's curtains conceal Mark and Pete, while Wally's merely blow in the wind. Len notices Pete's shoes; he wants to know where he got them and how long he has had them. Later he notices there are shoes on his own feet. Thus, he is reminiscent of Davies who was forever seeking a good pair of shoes. When Len speaks of the "hundred-watt bulb like a dagger" (p. 88) in his room, the absence of bulbs in Albert Stokes's house comes to mind. Grandma's room and the cellar were in darkness because all the bulbs were, like Albert's father, dead—or buried in the cellar. The wasp Edward scalded and then squashed on a plate in *A Slight Ache* reappears in *The Dwarfs* as an insect squashed on a plate by Len. The landscapes—yards, grasses, flowers—(which Freud has equated with body imagery)[66] appear in *The Dwarfs* as they do in *A Slight Ache* and *The Caretaker*. Then, of course, there is the room—the womb-room—that appears and reappears in each of Pinter's plays.

From this room someone is always dispossessed—dwarfs, girlfriends, old tramps. In this case Len dispossesses himself of his unwanted selves and the parents who created them. He dispossesses himself of his past, his heritage. He is rid of them all. This series of dreams has accomplished its aim. In *A Night Out*, Albert wishes to kill Mrs. Stokes and her counterpart, The Girl; but he does not. In *The Caretaker*, Mick/Aston softens the wish to kill. He only wishes to throw out Davies/father—to be rid of him. In *Night School,* Wally is almost rid of parents; he has only a substitute mother and father. Also in this play the dream-censor displaces the riddance wish onto Wally himself. This punishment is preparation for the final wish fulfillment—the total purge of *The Dwarfs*. In *The Dwarfs* a new man is born into an unlittered life. The new life promises to be empty of dark old houses without the light bulbs. The new life is bright. It promises to be empty of leaky old houses filled with junk. The new life is renovated. The new life is empty of fathers and mothers. It is bare and alone.

4

Anxiety Dreams: The Wish To Have Mother

The relationship between the plays that center on riddance and the next five plays that center on wanting mother recalls the dream work's disregard for opposites. From *A Night Out* through *The Caretaker* and *Night School* to *The Dwarfs*, there is a progressive fulfillment of the wish to be rid of both parents—a softened version of the wish to kill. At the end of *The Dwarfs*, Len seems to have achieved the final exorcism of parental ghosts and their attendant inferiorities. Nevertheless, he is suspicious, and even a little wistful, that the dwarfs might return. He feels "left in the lurch," and he remembers when they "told old tales by suntime," but he smells a rat p. 109). These vague contradictory feelings, in a sense, herald and prophesy the plays of group three. *The Collection*, *The Lover*, *Tea Party*, *The Homecoming*, and *The Basement* represent the progressive fulfillment of the wish to have mother. In other words, the struggle to purge her, along with father, is reversed into a struggle to possess her. However, mother is disguised, recognizable only in the latent content.

On the surface she is a girlfriend or a wife, but the male who would possess her transfers to her the attitudes and inadequacies associated with mother. Thus, ambivalence creeps in, and the relationship is colored by a wish to have a change of lover.

In *The Homecoming* the parallel between Ruth and mother is clearly drawn, and here wish fulfillment is most complete. Thus, the final play of the group, *The Basement*, takes on the appearance of a backward step in that Jane's identification with mother is slight. However, Martin Esslin points out that *The Basement* actually dates back to about 1963 when it appeared "under the title *The Compartment*, in the manuscript for a composite film planned by Grove Press. . . ."[1] The play, then, takes a chronological position between *The Lover* (1963) and *Tea Party* (1965). *The Homecoming* (later in 1965) then becomes the culmination of this group. Thus, the progressive development of the wish fulfillment follows a pattern similar to that of the previous group.

Another progression also needs noting. The plays of group one move steadily away from the violent finale of *The Room* until in the transition piece, *A Slight Ache,* violence is done only on a wasp; Edward's punishment is collapse and rejection. Group two carries on with rejections and riddances, softenings of the violent wish. Group three concentrates on adaptation, adjustment, and acceptance. In *The Collection* there is an incident with a knife, and some dissatisfactions are expressed. The two couples are, however, finally reunited with the prospect of having to make new adjustments to one another. *The Lover* is a study in adaptations as Richard and Sarah change their game to meet each other's changing needs. *The Basement* has perhaps more violence than any other play in this group. Law and Stott battle it out, but their violence lacks a serious tone. It has rather the spirit of a game as does their shifting relationship to Jane, which demands constant adjustments and readjustments. Even the punishment play, *Tea Party*, does not present any clear case of rejection. Disson's betrayals are seen through his own vision, distorted by illness. Their reality remains in question. Finally, in *The Homecoming* the most awesome alterations in relationships are accepted as though they were commonplace.

This shift into adjustment and acceptance of change highlights the thematic developments of group three. These plays focus on the ever-changing qualilty of individual character in response to shifting interpersonal relationships and perceptions. Or do the relationships shift in response to the changes in character? In either event, women move about among the roles of mother, wife, and whore, while men shift among the roles of father, husband, son, and lover. This thematic focus seems to spring out of the role playing and splitting that dominated group two. In this regard, *Night School* is the transition piece between these two groups of plays, for it features role playing and shifts in personal relationships. There, for the first time in Pinter's plays, a man struggles to possess a young woman. There, also for the first time, the would-be lovers play games with each other. Both of these factors are dominant in the plays of group three.

Night School is a transition piece in another sense as well. *The Collection* and *The Lover* are, if not minor Pinter, a new kind of Pinter. The newness is twofold. First, they repeat the tendency to comic realism begun in *Night School*. John Russell Taylor says that *The Collection* amuses rather than terrifies,[2] and perhaps that is an accurate description of all three of these plays. Second, these plays seem more intellectual than intuitive; they show a greater conscious control in their structure. Simon Trussler seems to have the same opinion when he says that *The Collection* and *The Lover* are "mannered." He adds: "Human behavior reduces itself to a sequence of chessboard maneuvers, and the plays shrink into dramatised chess problems."[3] *The Basement* has The same light comic tone and the same conscious control, but it lacks the move toward realism. *Tea Party* begins on a light-hearted note but ends in a total collapse that can hardly be called funny. It also lacks the realism of the other plays. However, the conscious control remains a constant factor. Ronald Hayman comments on this factor while speaking of the mystification inherent in Pinter's lack of verification. Hayman says: "After *The Lover*, . . . what had been a means becomes an end, and the quality of the work suffers."[4] Hayman is speaking about *Tea Party* and *The Basement,* but *Night School, The Collection,* and *The Lover* should also be included in the criticism. In the earlier plays, the absence of verification was a natural by-product of the dreamlike quality of the plays. It was there because the plays sprang so spontaneously from Pinter's extraordinary access to the unconscious. It was there because the plays were dominated by the primary processes and their disregard for logic and chronology. In these later plays Pinter has tried to reproduce this effect consciously, and a different, if not less effective, style results. *The Homecoming* returns to the earlier style, although it, too, shows some slight self-consciousness. More obviously it resembles *The Caretaker,* giving an outward impression of realism but, nevertheless, vibrating with resonance from latent content. The light comic tone is also gone. If this play does not terrify, it certainly horrifies.

The plays of this group are a mixed bag. Some of them represent a new style. They vary in the degree of their displacement into realism, and they vary in tone from light and teasing to heavy and horrifying. Yet they can all be called *anxiety dreams* because they all contain distress. Even *The Lover* and *The Collection* contain signs of insecure relationships that signal hidden distress. Moreover, they are all unified in their concern with one central wish—to have mother.

THE COLLECTION

The first play of this group, *The Collection*, was written for television and presented by Associated-Rediffusion Television in May of 1961. The freedom of movement that television allows does not, however, remove the play from the Pinter pattern. Instead it doubles it. In this play there are two rooms and two couples who are menaced by an intruding visitor. James's and Stella's visitor, Bill, is initially discussed rather than seen. He visited Stella in Leeds. Later Stella is visited also by Harry. The other couple, Harry and Bill, are threatened by a visit from James. With the exception of Stella, all of these characters seem relatively new. Until now Edward has been the only upper-middle-class male character in Pinter's repertory. And even Edward's position smacks of pretension and veneer. Harry, James, and even Bill—who Harry contends is only a "slum slug"—display a sophistication and an acceptance of affluence that has been lacking heretofore. They move about easily in Harry's elegant house and Stella's tasteful flat. Perhaps Mark was acquiring this ease, but he, like Edward, still seemed unaccustomed to it. Furthermore, Bill is the first Pinter character to be blatantly effeminate and homosexual. Harry has the sadistic forcefulness of Pete, but it is combined with a confident sense of social superiority that would not have concerned Pete. James resembles Wally Street a little in that each begins confidently with plans to rectify his situation and ends in naive bewilderment. Stella, of course, is a development of The Girl and Sally. She is youthful and two-sided. She is also a dreamer who seems willing to compromise her respectability with extramarital affairs. The opening situation of the play echoes *Night School* where Wally's relationship with the girl in his room, Sally, is threatened by her meeting in another locality, the night club, with another man, Mr. Solto. In *The Collection* James's relationship with his wife, Stella, is threatened by her recent meeting with Bill at Leeds.

A realistic reading of the play provides a picture of James and Stella living in a tasteful flat on one side of the stage and Harry and Bill living in an elegant house on the other side of the stage. All four of these people are in the dress business. James and Stella own a boutique nearby. Harry is a wholesale clothier, and Bill is his young designer. Clearly, Harry and Bill have a homosexual relationship. As the play opens, it is four o'clock in the morning. Harry is returning home from a party, and the telephone is ringing. Answering it, Harry discovers that an unidentified person wishes to speak to Bill. The unidentified caller is James, who is using the telephone booth situated on a promontory in the center of the stage between the two apartments. The audience soon learns that Stella and Bill have met at Leeds where the season's dress collection was being shown. Stella has reported to James that she was unfaithful with Bill that night in Leeds. After two unsuccessful tries, James meets Bill at his elegant house and confronts him with Stella's tale of near rape. Bill claims the story is only half true—that Stella was the aggressor. Meanwhile, Harry is upset by this new alliance of Bill's. He goes to visit Stella, and she denies the whole story, claiming James has imagined it all. In the meantime, James develops an interest in Bill that he taunts Stella with. He tells her that by accident she has "opened up a whole new world" for him.[5] On the next visit to Bill's, James and he have a very ambivalent encounter. While they recognize their mutual attraction, they also theaten each other with knives. James, in fact, actually throws a knife at Bill's face. As Bill catches it, he cuts his hand. Harry arrives home in time to witness, unseen, the end of the encounter. After noting the budding attraction between Bill and James, Harry is doubly upset. He tells them both of Stella's denial of the Leeds affair. But he alters the story. Harry explains that Stella has admitted the whole event to be her own inexplicable fabrication. Then he lashes out at Bill by revealing his origin in the slums. James, uncomfortable, apologizes to them both and prepares to leave. Bill confesses that he and Stella had merely sat in the lounge and talked. James returns home to Stella, repeats Bill's latest story, and asks, "That's the truth . . . isn't it?" (p. 80). She smiles enigmatically, but neither confirms nor denies. The lights fade on both couples sitting in their apartments.

The audience, of course, realizes that the truth will never be known. Stella and Bill know, but each has told so many stories that no one will ever know which to believe. Nor will anyone ever know for certain what caused these two to behave as they did and say what they did. Nor will anyone ever be able to assess the effect of the whole affair on the relationships within and between these two couples. The truth is unverifiable.

The audience have been amused and delighted with the subtle interconnecting relationships and deceptions. They can even go away pondering the effect of James's self-discovery on his marriage to Stella. The audience have not, however, been gripped. They have not been menaced. Their emotions have been only minimally involved. They do not even feel puzzled. They feel they understand very well what the play has said and how it was said. Pinter has given them something new, a charming comedy based firmly in theatrical realism. The uncertainties are there, but they are charming and understandable not frightening and puzzling. The audience feel intellectually adequate and satisfied.

Yet, there is a hidden dream life here. It is so deeply buried that its reverberations are not consciously felt. Norman Holland explains that "virtually all the familiar entities of literature—plot, character, and form—serve at least partly as defensive modifications of unconscious content."[6] As the dream-work uses displacement, so the secondary processes use these literary entities as a defense against the exposure of the buried wishes and dreams the primary processes reveal. That is what has occurred in *The Collection*; the intellectual manipulations of the plot have managed the unconscious material so well that it presents no threat at all.

Nevertheless, a knowledge of dream dynamics does increase the understanding of this play in which a collection of ironies spins the characters back and forth between oral, phallic, and oedipal fantasies. It all begins with Stella; she is, therefore, the star. Stella is one of those dual personalities. On the one hand, she possesses male assertiveness: she is a capable, independent career woman who goes out to her job each day and attends out-of-town conventions. On the other hand, she is an oral, passive person. This is the picture she presents as she curls on her couch silently stroking and nuzzling her kitten. Her position is almost that of the fetus and her baby kitten, purring as it is fondled, symbolizes her own self-image—or desire. She likes to be stroked and fondled. Lidz seems to be describing a woman not unlike Stella when he says:

> Anxieties concerning sexual adequacy can lead to a marriage undertaken primarily to assure the self of one's adequacy as a man or woman, or occasionally simply to conceal impotence or homosexuality from the world. A young woman who has considerable guilt over masturbation and who has some intermittent concerns that she might be homosexual because she recognizes her competitiveness with men and her jealousy of their friendships with each other, starts having casual affairs.[7]

Stella shows her competitiveness by her job, her masturbatory leanings by the kitten she strokes, and her feeling of sexual inadequacy by the casual affair she alleges she has had with Bill. The undertone of marital distance and neglect in the opening scene between Stella and Bill indicates the loss of excitement in this relationship and emphasizes Stella's need to act out or fantasize an affair with Bill. She reemphasizes her need by telling James about it. James responds with oral anxiety. Stated in Holland's words, he fears that "a source of comfort or power (his mother) will be taken away by a rival."[8] This revelation of James's insecurity—she calls him Jimmy—suggests that Lidz's description is applicable to James as well as to Stella. Lidz says a marriage may be undertaken to assure adequacy as a "man or woman." Furthermore, Lidz goes on to say, about a female of this type, that she seduces into marriage a passive young man whom she can dominate. "She does not recognize that he seeks to marry her because of his need to find a boyish girl in order to feel aroused, and soon after marriage she resents being treated as a boy rather than a girl."[9] James and Stella can be fit very easily into these roles. Her resentment at his husbandly neglect has prompted her to punish him with the threatening story of her infidelity. In his struggle against inadequacy he acts out the fantasy of phallic assertiveness. He goes out in quest of the truth. Holland supports this with: "Phallic fantasies can become stories of poking or prying into things, particularly in a fearful or helpless way. . . ."[10] Holland gives as illustrations "medieval tales of quest, ordeal, or trial." Once James assumes this phallic quest, his oral anxiety blends into oedipal strivings. Holland explains that "the oedipus complex itself is an outgrowth of earlier phases. Even in early infancy, the child has longed for the exclusive possession of his mother. . . ."[11] Ironically, this quest for the culprit who has attempted to frustrate his wish to have mother leads James to a homosexual nest.

Harry's elegant house, his possessive attitude toward Bill, and his insistent control of the situation reveal his anal personality. Also he has taken possession of a "slum boy" with a "slum mind." He thereby indulges the anal fantasy of playing with something dirty. Bill, on the other hand, has apparently been so frightened by his oedipal feelings for his mother and his castration fears from his father that he has accepted a feminine role to avoid the conflicts. He tends Harry's house, fixes his food, and in return receives Harry's fatherly/husbandly protection. There is a blend here with regression to an oral state that predates oedipal conflicts.

It is ironic then that James's presumed culprit is too frightened of oedipal feelings to have indulged in intercourse with Stella or any woman. Thus, the latent content sheds some light on the truth. The irony is doubled when Bill arouses James's latent homosexuality. Stella, in her attempt to win attention, has sent James into the possibility of a new attachment. To all of James's accusatory attacks, Bill responds jokingly but truthfully at first. He says he was nowhere near James's wife: "I'm quite sure of that apart from that, I . . . just don't do such things. Not in my book" (p. 54). Then he tries to explain his status, still jokingly: "I'm going to be Minister for Home Affairs" (p. 54). James, caught between the conflicts of his own latent homosexuality and his intended phallic assertiveness, finally relaxes and applauds Bill's wit: "You're a wag, aren't you? I never thought you'd be such a wag. You've really got a sense of fun . . ." (p. 56). Later, however, Bill trips and falls over the pouf. James then is left towering over him. The image arouses Bill's castration fears. James takes on the figure of the angry father about to punish the incestuous son. In terror, Bill confesses but defensively makes Stella the aggressor.

Harry, meanwhile, feels James to be a threat to his possession and mastery of Bill. He recognizes a phallic design on his boy/wife. He questions Bill about James: "I've got a funny feeling he wore a mask. . . . He didn't dance here last night, did he, or do any gymnastics" (p. 63). Commenting on special representations of sexual intercourse, Freud says: "Rhythmical activities such as *dancing, riding,* and *climbing* must be mentioned here. . . ."[12] Therefore, in dream language Harry is expressing suspicions of sexual relations between Bill and James. Then he warns Bill: "I don't like strangers coming into my house without an invitation" (p. 63). Bill recognizes the irony—the threatening master is threatened. He retreats tauntingly with the noncommittal response: "Will you excuse me? I really think it's time I was dressed, don't you?" (p. 63).

James, meanwhile, is aware, he thinks, of Stella's game; so he retaliates by taunting her. He first lets her know what he thinks he knows:

> You know what men are. I reminded him that you'd resisted, that you'd hated the whole thing, but that you'd been—how can we say—somehow hypnotized by him, it happens sometimes. He agreed it can happen sometimes. He told me he'd been hypnotized once by a cat. Wouldn't go into any more details though. (p. 66)

Then he punishes her further by admitting his homosexual attraction. He does it cryptically at first by explaining Bill's resemblance to a bloke at school named Hawkins: "Hawkins was an opera fan, too. So's whatsisname. I'm a bit of an opera fan myself. Always kept it a dead secret" (p. 67). Then he is more blatant: "After two years of marriage it looks as though, by accident, you've opened up a whole new world for me" (p. 67). His fear of sexual inadequacy has turned into fear of maternal engulfment, and he fights against it.

Harry finds himself in the position that James was in initially. He has been threatened with loss of his boy/wife/ mother. He fights to regain control. He repeats James's performance. He calls Stella on the telephone and then goes to visit. He lets her know how ridiculous her story is by making it clear Bill is homosexual: "I gave him a roof, gave him a job, and he came up trumps. We've been close friends for years" (p. 70). Then he threatens her; he says James has been bothering Bill. A complete ironic reversal of the original situation has occurred. The male partner, Harry, is now at James's house threatening James's female partner just as James was earlier in Harry's house threatening Bill. Stella responds as Bill did by saying what Harry wants to hear, but she also defends herself. She tells Harry that James made it all up. Then Harry turns the tables on James by making romantic overtures toward Stella. He indicates it by addressing his attention to her self-image, the kitten: "Oh, what a beautiful kitten, what a really beautiful kitten. Kitty, kitty, kitty, what do you call her, come here, kitty, kitty" (p. 72). This appears to be the prelude to lovemaking, either actual or fantasied. The stage directions say: "Harry sits next to Stella and proceeds to pet and nuzzle the kitten" (p. 72).

Meanwhile, Bill and James tempt each other, but again the sexual assaults are fantasies in dream language. Bill asks James to admire and handle his knife—to "grasp it firmly up to the hilt" (p. 73). But James refuses to touch it. He is frightened. Bill enjoys his advantage and teases: "Youre a chap who's been married for two years, aren't you, happily? There's a bond of iron between you and your wife. It can't be corroded by a trivial thing like this. I've apologized, she's apologized. Honestly, what more can you want?" (p. 74). The long pause and lingering look followed by Bill's smile reveals the double entendre of all that has been said. James rallies. He picks up a knife—a fruit knife—and challenges

Bill to a mock duel. Then Bill reneges. He puts down his knife. James picks it up and confesses he has a third. Bill asks: "What do you do, swallow them?" James replies: "Do you?" Then James shouts invitingly: "Go on! Swallow it!" (p. 75). As he speaks he throws his knife at Bill, and Bill is cut; his hand bleeds. The fantasy of sexual assault is complete.

In the meantime, this whole scene has been played before the hidden eyes of Harry. He has come in unnoticed and watched from the hall. Since he sees Bill as a female figure, this sexual battle with its bloody finish takes on the aura of a primal scene to him. Like the child who sees or imagines the primal scene, Harry is angry that the mother figure is so promiscuous, and all his anger at women is aroused. He makes his presence known, he chastises Bill for not ducking the knife, and announces his possible transgression with Stella: "By the way, I've just seen your wife, what a beautiful kitten she has, you should see it, Bill, it's all white. . ." (p. 76). Thus, he punishes both James and Bill with the knowledge that each has been betrayed by his partner's infidelity. He tells James his wife has confessed to having made up the whole story about her and Bill. Then he suggests that James "knock her over the head with a sauce pan" (p. 77). Next Harry tongue-whips Bill. In so doing he reveals the sadism that usually accompanies anality. As he hurls the hurtful, belittling words at Bill, he discloses as much about himself as he does about Bill:

he's a slum slug, there's nothing wrong with slum slugs in their place, but this one won't keep his place, he crawls all over the walls of nice houses, leaving slime, don't you boy? He confirms stupid sordid little stories just to amuse himself, while everyone else has to run around in circles to get to the root of the matter and smooth the whole thing out. All he can do is sit and suck his bloody hand and decompose like the filthy slum slug he is. . . . (p. 78)

Most of the imagery here should be clear except perhaps that " 'smooth' walls are men," according to Freud.[13] Harry himself is the wall he accuses Bill of dirtying. Harry defends himself by projection. While he smears Bill with dirty words, he accuses Bill of smearing him. Bill becomes again the threatened one. The knife thrown at his hand can be construed as a castration attempt as well as a homosexual assault. Bill's fears before the angry father figure activate all these unpleasant associations. He confesses that he never touched Stella. They had only talked and spun fantasies together. James leaves with apologies. Harry has beaten him at his own game; Harry has theatened James's nest. Moreover, Harry has reclaimed mastery of his own nest. James, who had once left home in an aggressive phallic quest for the truth, now returns with his tail between his legs to beg the truth of his silent wife. Ironically, his question, "That's the truth . . . isn't it?" (p. 80), has become more pregnant than before. Now he needs to know if she was unfaithful with Bill, if she was unfaithful with Harry, if indeed his own homosexual advance to Bill was miscalculated. Like Harry, Stella has regained the upper hand. She knows all, and she can taunt James best with her silence.

This second reading of the play, utilizing the symbolism of dreams, points up the play as a collection of ironies as well as a collection of insecure characters who have been shuffled with a collection of lies, fantasies, deceptions, and stratagems. The purpose of these collections seems to have been to drive home Pinter's point about the impossibility of verification. Pinter has so determinedly insisted on the realism of his earlier plays that it is not difficult to imagine this one as a deliberate attempt to demonstrate the realistic honesty of his refusal to identify characters and verify their motivations and actions. In his early plays the gaps in the logical overlay had left audiences puzzled. They wanted to know who Riley was, what Stanley had done, who had sent Goldberg and McCann, who was ordering food through the dumbwaiter. Besieged by such questions, Pinter had included an explanatory note in the program for the Royal Court Theatre's production of *The Room* and *The Dumb Waiter* in March 1960. A portion of this note read:

> The desire for verification is understandable but cannot always be satisfied. There are no hard distinctions between what is real and what is unreal, nor between what is true and what is false. The thing is not necessarily either true or false: it can be both true and false. The assumption that to verify what has happened and what is happening presents few problems I take to be inaccurate. A character on the stage who can present no convincing argument or information as to his past experience, his present behaviour, or his aspirations, nor give a comprehensive analysis of his motives is as legitimate and as worthy of attention as one who, alarmingly, can do all these things. The more acute the experience, the less articulate its expression.[14]

In *The Collection* Pinter pointedly demonstrates that there are "no hard distinctions" between "what is true and what is false." By the end of the play, the characters and the audience are convinced of the impossibility of verification. The clues in the opening scene also indicate that this is a principal thematic concern of the play. It begins with an unidentified telephone call, thus setting up the unknowability of people and events.

Thematically, then, *The Collection* carries on the idea of identity and its attendant uncertainties that is so prominent in *The Caretaker, Night School,* and *The Dwarfs.* It picks up the idea of deception and pretense that runs through most of Pinter's plays and emerges fullblown in *Night School.* Its prime focus, however, is on the impossibility of verification due to the ever-changing character of human personality. James is a truth seeker who will never know Stella's secret—or Harry's—or Bill's.

The Collection also etches sharply the conscious side of fantasy life, as does *Night School.* This later play, however, adds a new reason for spinning yarns—boredom. Life seems to have gone stale for all these characters. The estrangement between Stella and James is clear in their first scene together. She hesitantly inquires if he will be home that night. He gives no answer. Instead he reaches for an ashtray and regards it. Harry and Bill seem no better off. Harry has been to a party, but Bill has been left at home. Harry has come to treat Bill as a dirty plaything—a "slum slug." So all of these people relieve their boredom with sex fantasies. Stella begins it with her story about Bill; Bill continues it with his story about Stella. James joins in by picturing Bill as an appealing and elegant collector of fine objects. Even Harry spins one about a pure, clean, white Stella. The play says that present relationships go stale; therefore, men must fill their empty lives with new or imagined alliances. Freud confirms the truth of this assertion:

> Something in the nature of the sexual instinct itself is unfavorable to the realization of complete satisfaction. . .First, as a result of the diphasic onset of object-choice, and the interposition of the barrier against incest, the final object of the sexual instinct is never any longer the original object but only a surrogate for it. Psychoanalysis has shown us that when the original object of a wishful impulse has been lost as a result of repression, it is frequently represented by an endless series of substitutive objects none of which, however, brings full satisfaction. This may explain the inconstancy in object-choice, the 'craving for stimulation' which is so often a feature of the love of adults.[15]

Lurking within this play also is the familiar Pinter theme of dispossesion that, intentionally or not, is highlighted by the names, Harry and James. Harry means "ruler of the house," and James is the English form of Jacob, which means "supplanter, one who overthrows." James tries to overthrow Harry, just as he imagined Bill was trying to overthrow him. No one, however, is physically dispossessed. Harry keeps his mother/wife figure, and James keeps his, each in the knowledge of the adjustments made necessary by recent events. The theme of inadequacy is also still here. Each of these characters suffers from the distress of inferiority and self-dissatisfaction. Ronald Hayman makes this point very well:

> The value of the incident in Leeds, whatever it was, is that its consequences illuminate all the insecurities that the characters have about themselves and each other. Harry doesn't trust Bill, James doesn't trust Stella, and neither Bill nor Stella, obviously, are finding fulfillment in their lives with their partners.[16]

The inadequacy overlaps with distrust and fear of betrayal.

THE LOVER

The Lover first appeared in 1963, two years after The Collection. Since then the two plays frequently appear on a double bill, and they do make a good pair. Both were originally television plays, but both have been successfully adapted for the stage. However, the essence of their partnership is in the similarity of their materials. Each takes a different look at the same idea. The Lover shows an alternative course of action for couples in stale relationships. The people in The Collection weave private fantasies and threaten each other with substitute alliances; the people in The Lover attempt to be all things to one another. They have communicated their longings to one another. Walter Kerr, in his study of the existentialism in Pinter's plays, says that The Lover shows that man is "what he is next."[17] Thus, Kerr capsules the why of one of the principal ideas that these plays share — the unknowability of man.

It is a tribute to Pinter's ingenuity that this play like all the others is a unique variation of the same basic pattern. Richard and Sarah are two people in a room expecting a visitor. The visitor is, of course, Richard in his other role, Max.

Max is not a menace, however, because Richard and Sarah do not repress their erotic feelings; they accept them and act them out. The play's opening scene is a teaser; it sets up false expectations for the audience. Richard inquires "amiably" of Sarah, "Is your lover coming today?"[18] They appear to be that rarity of the real world — a thoroughly domesticated couple who are totally accepting of each other's lovers. Another false lead follows when the milkman arrives at the door, but he turns out not to be Sarah's lover after all. The trick explodes in the audience's surprise at discovering Richard is himself the lover. For this role he wears a new costume and a new name — Max. Sarah, too, wears different clothes — high heels and a sexier dress — for her role of mistress. Max and Sarah act out a series of interconnecting sexual fantasies. Their conversation reveals the seriousness of their games. Each pretends to be two utterly separate people, marriage partner and illicit lover. There are signals, however, that Richard is beginning to feel some dissatisfaction. When he returns home from work in his role of husband, he tells Sarah, his wife, that he is tired of his mistress. She is too bony. He would prefer a plump whore. He also insists that Sarah give up her lover and threatens to do Max violence if he shows up on the premises again. Sarah is both startled and pained. She has been quite satisfied with the game as it is, but Richard in his need for a change begins their ritual at a new time on this day. As the game progresses, he forces upon her the new role his need demands. As the play ends, she acquiesces and he whispers with satisfaction: "You lovely whore" (p. 40).

The play seems to be little more than a bit of froth designed for a theatrical surprise. Simon Trussler verbalizes this feeling: "But *The Lover* shares a fault which always distinguishes a 'good' minor play of Pinter's from his major work. It is anecdotal, and once one knows the punch line of the anecdote there's not a lot of interest left."[19] However, if this play is approached as a dream, it joins its partner *The Collection* in revealing a psychological truth about adult relationships that inspires lively interest beyond the punch line.

Like *The Collection*, *The Lover* deals with a relationship that has gone stale, but Richard and Sarah are making desperate efforts to keep it vital. To borrow Freud's words again, they have "the 'craving for stimulation' which is so often a feature of the love of adults."[20] They satisfy this craving by acting out their fantasies. Thus, the dream life that normally lies buried is exposed in this play; it becomes part of the manifest content. However, the motivations for these dreams remain hidden even from Richard and Sarah. They are part of that unconscious control that creates a conscious confusion and causes people to be unknowable. Richard is a precise example of the psychically impotent male whom Freud describes. To restore his potency, he must debase his sexual object: "As soon as the condition of debasement is fulfilled, sensuality can be freely expressed, and important sexual capacities and a high degree of pleasure can develop."[21] Freud explains that such psychical impotence springs out of "an incestuous fixation on mother or sister, which has never been surmounted. . . ."[22] This is the latent content of *The Lover* as a dream. In the dream Sarah becomes Richard's mother, and he becomes a child with oedipal desires. Freud explains that the child develops a strong current of affection for his mother, which is nourished by the loving attention the parent gives to the child. At puberty this affection-ate current is joined by a "sensual current" that runs up against the incest barrier. Consequently, it attempts to find its way to some other object with whom a real sex life can be carried on. If this attempt is frustrated or if the original attachment to mother is too powerful to be relinquished, the child becomes fixated to unconscious incestuous fantasies. As a result, the sensual current "seeks only objects which do not recall the incestuous figures forbidden to it. . . ."[23] The affectionate current, however, seeks an object as much like the original one as possible. Freud's own words explain most clearly the resulting dichotomy:

> The whole sphere of love in such people remains divided in the two directions personified in art as sacred and profane (or animal) love. Where they love they do not desire and where they desire they cannot love.[24]

This situation is further complicated by a tendency to perverse sexual aims. The man thus afflicted feels a serious loss of pleasure if these aims are not met, but he can only demand them from a "debased and despised sexual object."[25]

Richard clearly fits this pattern. Clearly his affectionate current attaches to Sarah, his housewife/mother. He tells her he finds her very beautiful and that he has great pride in being seen with her. His very words are: "And to know you are my wife. It's a source of a profound satisfaction to me" (p. 31). It is for this reason that Sarah is so surprised at his desire for a whore. She says: "It's just not possible. You have such taste. You care so much for grace and elegance in women" (p. 12). He consents and adds "and wit." Then to her persistent "why?" he answers:

> Why? I wasn't looking for your double, was I? I wasn't looking for a woman I could respect, as you, whom I could admire and love, as I do you. Was I? All I wanted was. . .how shall I put it. . .someone who could express and engender lust with all lust's cunning. Nothing more. (p. 13)

Apparently, Sarah's role of mistress was originally a sufficient debasement, but it no longer suffices. Richard's impotence is returning. When the play opens, he is not anxioius to come as her lover that afternoon. He says: "I thought you wanted to go to that exhibition" (p. 5). Then in the evening when he returns, he indicates that he had been an ineffective lover in the afternoon. He says his long meeting of the afternoon was "rather inconclusive." He also comments that their living room must have been stiflingly hot and blindingly sunlit that afternoon. The stifling heat recalls Edward's near suffocation in Flora's garden. Moreover, Sarah states that her lover is "not all that interested" in gardening. In dream symbolism this is a blunt statement of his absent sexual response, and the blinding indicates mental castration. The next evening when Richard returns, Sarah says apologetically of her lover: "We all have our off days" (p. 30). Richard's reply presents his conscious reason for wishing to change the game so that Sarah is his whore instead of his mistress:

> He, too? I thought the whole point of being a lover is that one didn't. I mean if I, for instance, were called upon to fulfill the function of a lover and felt disposed, shall we say, to accept the job, well, I'd as soon give it up as be found incapable of executing its proper and consistent obligation. (p. 30)

Subsequently, he orders her to cease her "debauchery." He threatens to kick Max's teeth out. In dream language, it will be remembered, losing a tooth stands for castration. He tells her to take Max out to a "ditch" or a "slag heap." Thus, he indicates his wish for a more debased object. Then, at the end he is still ordering her to meet his developing need as he says: "Change. *Pause.* Change. *Pause.* Change your clothes. *Pause.* You lovely whore" (p. 40).

Beneath the adult image of Sarah, there is in the latent content of the dream a little girl who compensated for the sexual restrictions placed on her life by indulging in fantasies. Freud says of such females:

> But their long holding back from sexuality and the lingering of their sensuality in phantasy has another important consequence

for them. They are subsequently often unable to undo the connection between sensual activity and the prohibition, and prove to be psychically impotent, that is, frigid, when such activity is at last allowed them. This is the origin of the endeavour made by many women to keep even legitimate relations secret for awhile; and of the capacity of other women for normal sensation as soon as the condition of prohibition is reestablished by a secret love affair; unfaithful to their husband[s], they are able to keep a second order of faith with their lover[s].[26]

The little girl in Sarah clings to fantasy as the proper outlet for sexual feelings. It was she who first invented the game. When Richard reminds her of this, she at first denies it and then gives silent assent by looking at him "with a slight smile" (p. 14). She has been very happy with the arrangement ever since. She tells Richard: "I think things are beautifully balanced" (p. 17). He has come to her any afternoon she has chosen and played the role of Max, her lover. When he threatens to change the game, she reveals in her anger that her fantasy life has not stopped there. She has had private fantasies on the afternoons that Richard has not come:

Do you think he's the only one who comes! Do you? Do you think he's the only one I entertain? Mmmmm? Don't be silly. I have other visitors, all the time, I receive all the time. Other afternoons, all the time. When neither of you know, neither of you. I give them strawberries in season. With cream. Strangers, total strangers. But not to me, not while they're here. They come to see the hollyhocks. And then they stay for tea. Always. Always. (p. 37)

It will be remembered that in dream language fruit represents the female breasts and flowers represent the female genitalia. Even Sarah's tea table has sexual significance. Tables represent women, and this one wears a long velvet cover (p. 5). Freud says of a dreamer's associations with *"velvet* and *moss"* that they "were a clear indication of a reference to pubic hair."[27] Sarah's lover retreats underneath this table at the climax of their fantasy. Appropriately, after this revelation of her promiscuity, Richard begins their sex ritual. Her self-debasement has met his need.

One other facet of Freud's discussion of psychical impotence is present in the sexual fantasies of Richard and Sarah. Freud says:

> It can easily be shown that the psychical value of erotic needs is reduced as soon as their satisfaction becomes easy. An obstacle is required in order to heighten libido; and where natural resistances to satisfaction have not been sufficient, men have at all times erected conventional ones so as to be able to enjoy love.[28]

The fantasies Richard and Sarah create are actually built around the setting up of obstacles. To his early overtures for a light, she gives rebuffs. She tells him to go away. Then she calls up the larger obstacle of her marriage; she is waiting for her husband. Then when he has won her over, he sets up obstacles. He retreats, speaks of his wife. In her aggressiveness, she becomes cheap, debased. Then he is aroused. He locks her in. She is trapped, unable to get out. Her wish to escape is another obstacle. At this point he calls: "It's teatime, Mary," and he "disappears under the velvet cloth" (p. 23). Suddenly the title of this play takes on an acute irony. The lover is a near-impotent male castrated by an incestuous wish that requires constant props and spurs to keep his desire alive. His insistent cry, at the end of the play, for change, change, change, underlines this point.

This little play may be minor Pinter, but along with its partner, *The Collection*, it demonstrates that even minor Pinter presents truth. These plays show the temporary nature of marital excitement and the cause of man's infidelity, real or fantasied, as built-in products of his oedipal guilts. Freud himself testifies to the universality of this theme: "Psychical impotence is much more widespread than is supposed, and. . .a certain amount of this behaviour does in fact characterize the love of civilized man."[29] Of course, the play also repeats *The Collection*'s theme of the unknowability of man. His constant need for change coexists with his own continuing development; he is, therefore, "what he is next," to repeat Walter Kerr's phrase.

An overview of both these plays prompts notice of another theme — the overemphasis on an unending physical satisfaction that is unattainable and the emptiness of mind and spirit that it entails. Because their physical desires have gone stale, the relationships of James and Stella, Harry and Bill are empty. If man's knowledge of himself were sufficient, might not knowing his unalterable limitations salve his feeling of inadequacy and dissatisfaction? Richard and Sarah, for the moment, succeed in keeping their relationship vital, but how long can it last? Can Sarah continue to debase herself for her lover while maintaining her dignity for her husband? What is left to nourish the mind and spirit when such a total effort is committed to the body? Perhaps the answer lies in Edward's total collapse in the presence of his silent, unknown fear. The ignorance of the conscious mind about its unconscious control is in the forefront again.

THE BASEMENT

After two plays in which the wish to have mother is disguised as a wish to keep a wife and a wish to change a wife to suit sexual needs, *The Basement* seems to be a more blatant display of the oedipal wish. Law and Stott wish to kill each other in combat, and the prize seems to be Jane. Alternately Law and Stott experience fulfillment of the wish to have Jane, but she is in Law's possession at the end of the play. At the start, she is with Stott. Thus, this play presents that variation of the Pinter situation in which people exchange places. The first of this variation was *A Slight Ache* where Edward loses wife and home to the Matchseller. Another variation was in *Night School*, where Wally loses Sally. However, there is a more equitable split in *The Basement*: Law loses his apartment and gains Jane; Stott loses Jane and gains the apartment. The struggle for possession rages over woman and her symbolic representation — the room.

Despite these Pinter characteristics, however, the play represents a complete change of style. The light comic tone of *The Collection* and *The Lover* remain, but realism is gone. Like the two preceding plays, this one makes conscious and deliberate use of lack of verification, and it also makes conscious and deliberate use of ambiguity. Moreover, it retreats from dialogue and relies almost entirely on pictures. Since it was originally created as a film script, this is understandable. Nevertheless, the diminished dialogue adds to the ambiguity. This play is a true enigma. Alrene Sykes describes it as "pictorial rather than verbal, like most people's real-life dreams."[30] Indeed it is dreamlike, but not in the same intuitive, spontaneous way that *The Room* and *The Birthday Party* are. This play is more like a consciously structured dream.

It unfolds in a sequence of fast-moving images. The first image is Stott, dressed in a raincoat, standing outside Law's basement flat on a rainy winter night. Behind him, leaning against a wall, is Jane. The next image is the interior of Law's comfortable apartment. He sits by the fire reading an illustrated Persian love manual. In the next series of images, Stott is welcomed warmly into the house — a long-lost friend. Then at Stott's request Jane, too, comes inside. They immediately undress and make audible love in Law's bed while he continues to read by the fire. From here the scenes shift from the room, to the beach, to a cave; and the seasons alternate as rapidly as the places. Jane discusses Stott with Law; she smiles at Law as she lies in bed with Stott. Then Stott and Law discuss Jane. A shift to the beach finds Jane caressing Law. Back at the apartment the decor begins changing. This time it is Scandinavian. Jane still sleeps with Stott, who begins making demands for a record to be played on the hi-fi. Next there is a brief scene in a bar after which there is a winter race between Stott and Law. Law stumbles while Stott makes no effort to run at all. In the following scene Stott sees Law and Jane clenched together in the cold. Next is the backyard and Law suggests that Stott move out. He reneges. In the next scene Jane is in Stott's lap. Stott demands a record. Law angrily breaks several records against the wall. The room then returns to its original furnishings, and Jane is once again in bed with Stott while Law is once again in his chair by the fire. In the following scene, however, Jane avoids Stott's touch. Next, in the cave with Law, she urges him to ask Stott to go. She speaks as if she and Law have lived together for some time. Then in the backyard again Law tells Stott that Jane is betraying him. Back inside Stott lies in the bed as if dying while Jane and Law discuss him. The image changes to Jane and Law cuddling in a corner. Stott closes the curtains, the the room has become refurnished in Italian Renaissance. Stott assaults Law by throwing marbles at him. A fish tank is broken, and Law is hit in the forehead with a marble. Next the room is completely bare. Stott and Law threaten each other with broken bottles while a Debussy record plays. Then Law and Jane are seen standing outside the flat. Law wears the same raincoat Stott had worn. Stott is inside reading by the fire. He opens the door and greets Law like a long-lost friend.

This summary makes clear that although *The Basement* was produced on B.B.C. Television in 1967, it is less a play than Pinter's other television pieces. *Film* seems somehow a more appropriate classification, and that was, of course, Pinter's intention when he wrote it in 1963. It was to be one of a three-part series planned by the Grove Press; the other two films were by Samuel Beckett and Eugene Ionesco. Only Beckett's *Film* was actually produced.[31] Pinter's was laid aside for four years until the B.B.C. Television production. This bit of history explains *The Basement*'s weakness as literature without detracting unnecessarily from its author. Like *The Dwarfs, The Basement* suffers when transferred from its own medium. Pinter intended it for the eye primarily. Apparently the actual pictures communicate much that words on a page omit. Hinchliffe comments that in the B.B.C.'s 1967 production "the rapid changes in the weather and the furnishings of the flat reflected not merely the passage of time but also the changing emotional relationships of the three characters."[32]

If the reader tries to imagine the visual effect of this play as it would be on film, he realizes that it does communicate a realistic determination. It paints in a kaleidoscope of images the story of a struggle between Tim Law and Charles Stott. Tim Law is a God-fearing (as his first name implies), law-abiding (as his last name implies) man. Charles Stott is strong and vigorous (as his first name implies) and very much the carnivorous weasel (as his last name implies when its similarity to *stoat* is recognized). Charles is invited into Tim's apartment. He brings Jane with him and soon begins to take over the place. He takes Tim's bed. He makes love to Jane in the presence of lonely Tim. He redecorates the apartment. He demands that records be played. Tim tolerates it all until he begins to feel an affection for Jane. Then, he begins to wish to be rid of Stott. He asks him to leave. When Stott refuses, Tim tries to best him at a fair challenge, but Stott refuses to race. Stott becomes ill, but he is too contrary even to die. As Jane begins to show preference for Tim, Stott begins to get vicious: he throws marbles at Law, and he challenges him to a murderous fight with broken bottles. Finally, the fair-minded, law-abiding Tim is turned into a primitive man fighting for his woman and his house. In keeping with realism, Stott must surely win. Tim is, therefore, evicted, but Jane chooses to leave with him. After a little while out in the cold, Tim is ready to challenge Stott again to win back his shelter.

Considered in the context of *The Lover*, which was written in the same year, *The Basement* emerges as a game. True, it is a very elaborate game, but not much more so than the game played by Richard and Sarah. This game always begins with one man and a girl outside in the cold asking refuge from one man inside, warm and cozy. The inside man is titillated by the lovemaking of the outsiders. Then, both men increase the vitality of their desire by setting up obstacles to the winning of the girl. They challenge each other to games. The winner gets the girl, and the loser gets the apartment. Sometimes they get truly angry during the games; other times they actually wish each other dead. Whoever is put out must come back so that the game can repeat itself endlessly. The sequence of images reveals differing portions of the annual cycle. By the end of the play, the complete sequence of the game's events has been shown but with bits and pieces from successive games in successive years. Fragments of evidence support this determination. First of all, the play ends as it begins, except that the male roles have been reversed. At Stott's first arrival, Tim comments that his old friend has got a new raincoat. At the end of the play, Tim is wearing this same raincoat. Also, Law and Stott discuss other challenges in other times—cricket, squash; they discuss each other's former skills at these games. Stott says: "Your style was deceptive"; Law says: "You were unbeatable."[33] On another occasion, Jane speaks as though there was once a time when she and Law had lived together without Stott: "Tell him to go. It's your place. Then we could be happy again. Like we used to. Like we used to. In our first blush of love" (p. 105). This view of the play as a continuing game coincides with Ronald Hayman's judgment. "The whole play is a game in which one game creates the next."[34]

Third, the play can be construed as a conscious daydream. Esslin,[35] Trussler,[36] and Sykes[37] all offer and seem to prefer this interpretation. The opening of the play does suggest a fantasy. Law sits by the fire perusing a "Persian love manual, with illustrations" (p. 92)—what better stimulus for erotic reverie. Law imagines himself as the earnest, square-shooting adversary fighting against an uncivilized, grasping opponent for the love of a fair maiden. His love is so great that when he realizes he can not win both the house and the girl, he sacrifices the material possessions for love. Then he begins to fantasize all over again, this time to imagine how he would protect his love from the thieving Stott if he were forced to beg shelter in Stott's apartment.

Finally, the latent content of this daydream can be examined. Beneath the manifest content, then, will appear the old oedipal fantasy. Tim becomes the son fighting against his father for a promiscuous mother who casts her favors on both contenders. Tim's taking Stott in becomes then a rescue fantasy such as Aston had about Davies. Perhaps Holland's explanation needs repeating here: "The child by rescuing his father proves his innocence of any wish to kill him and at the same time by paying a life back, as it were, he owns his own life free and clear of any father. . . ."[38] Law, the son, can, therefore, oppose Stott, the father, as an equal. In the Freudian dream world, the scene of Jane and Stott making love while Tim sits by the fireside listening becomes a primal scene. Stott's dominance represents the powerful father who has control of the situation at all times. Stott's near-fatal illness becomes the child's wish to kill the father almost realized by animism. Ultimately, of course, the child wins; he has been ousted by father but he has won mother. This final interpretation features some concretizations created by the primary processes. The concept of the play's taking place in a basement apartment suggests once again a concretization of the psyche. The basement, the lower depths of the house, is where lust lives in the unconscious. The upper house, the conscious mind, is dark, asleep. Thus, the setting and the title provide the hint that this play is truly a dream, a dream of lust. In similar fashion Jane points to the fanciful nature of Law's tales about Stott's background — his chateaux and his cars. As Law spins this yarn, Jame builds castles in the sand. Later Stott opens the window, and Jane and Law are seen clenching each other as they shiver with cold. Thus, Stott's attempt to freeze them out is concretized. The record that Stott demands to be played over and over concretizes the cyclical nature of this oedipal dream; it recurs again and again and again, just as the record goes round and round playing the same old song. Near the end of the play a Bacchanalian revelry is enacted. The room is furnished in Florentine splendor with rich tapestries, golden chairs, lush carpet, and marble pillars. Law plays the flute while Jane serves grapes. Stott chooses a grape, bites into it, and then "tosses the bowl of fruit across the room" (p. 107). Remembering Freud's equations of fruit and bowl with the feminine anatomy makes clear that Stott, the vicious weasel, attacks Jane and then hostilely flings her away. Earlier in the backyard, he has attempted to touch her breast, and she has moved away. Shortly after, Jane has been pleading with Law to ask Stott to go. Then Stott has been ill. When he recovers, Jane and Law are "snuffing each other" in a corner. Stott's hostility, therefore, erupts at that time. Having flung Jane away, he attacks Law with marbles. In other words, he assaults him with his masculinity. The breaking of the fish tank can be viewed as a concretization of the bursting of the men's emotional limits. The waters spilling across the marble floor are washing away the men's civilized veneer. Thus, in the next scene they crouch opposite each other primitively, holding weapons of broken glass. Then the camera swings back and forth between them and Jane. Images of the contenders' advances and their weapons alternate with images of Jane pouring sugar, milk, and coffee into cups. These flashing pictures bring into sharp relief the child's vision of the oedipal conflict—father and son engaged in mortal conflict for the nourishing mother. Then the camera shows the broken bottles smashing together; the conflict is over. The record is turning on the turntable; the theme of repetition-compulsion is concretized. The next picture is of Jane and Law together outside the flat. Law, the son, has won mother from Stott, the father. When Stott admits them to the apartment, the conflict will begin again.

Thematically, this play itself suggests a repetition compulsion in that it repeats old themes. The familiar oral theme, fear of being dispossessed, and the familiar anal theme, the struggle for dominance, are present here as they are in all of Pinter's plays. By now they are too familiar to need explanation. Like the oedipal wish, they are a constant factor in Pinter's work—tailored, almost, to the basic Pinter situation. This play also restresses one of *The Collection*'s themes: love is disruptive and ever-changing. The affections and loyalties of Stott, Law, and Jane are constantly shifting. The men greet each other as old friends in the beginning and in the end, but in between they seem bent on murdering each other. Jane allies herself to one and then the other. Her shifts of affection spur their hostilities, and their hostilities bring about altered perceptions of each other. In fact, the overriding message of the realistic determination of this play is that love, or the subconscious desire to have mother, can turn law-abiding, gentle men into primitive cave men. Thus, ambivalence appears in a new dress. In the determination that it is all a game, the old Pinter theme of impotence recurs. It strikes the new chord, however, hit by *The Lover;* it is psychical impotence. Law and Stott, if they are indeed playing an elaborate game, can only be doing so to be rid of boredom. Like Sarah's Richard, they must create roles and obstacles to bolster their declining sexual capabilities. In this connection the title of the play can become a corny but meaningful pun — "de-basement." When the play is viewed as a conscious fantasy, it reveals man's strange dissatisfaction with peace and quiet. Law has both of these, but he dreams of excitement — love and danger. Law's fantasy shows again the contrast between man's outer appearance and his inner self. Beneath man's calm, civilized exterior dwells the animal whom he tries to keep leashed. Finally, the latent content of the dream reveals again that this unruly animal is really a child unable to disentangle himself from the trauma of his early desires. Therefore, he repeats his struggle to kill a father and marry a mother again and again and again. This is repetition-compulsion: "The tendency of individuals to repeat past behavior. . .even if such behavior had proved to be ill-advised."[39]

TEA PARTY

As *The Basement* was created for film several years before it was produced as a television show, so was *Tea Party* created as a short story before it was adapted for television. The short story was read by Pinter himself on a 1964 radio broadcast; later it was published in *Playboy* magazine.[40] The television version was undertaken for the European Broadcasting Union, an organization of sixteen countries that was preparing a series called *The Largest Theatre in the World.* Under these auspices, *Tea Party* was first presented by B.B.C. Television on 25 March 1965.

Tea Party resembles *The Basement* in style as well as genesis. These two plays are truly companion pieces in that both require a film presentation. *Tea Party* is dependent upon camera techniques. The distorted vision that reveals Disson's illness can not be concretized effectively in any other way. Moreover, this play has the light comic tone (at least until the end) and the dreamlike character of *The Basement*. As *The Basement* takes spectators into Law's dreams, *Tea Party* takes them into Disson's sick mind. The camera gives spectators pictures of actual events and then Disson's perception of those events. Thus, the external realism of *The Collection* and *The Lover* is gone.

A third resemblance to *The Basement* is *Tea Party's* opening variation of the basic Pinter situation. In both plays one man is alone on stage at the start. In *Tea Party*, that man is Disson. However, for the first time in Pinter's dramatic repertory, the opening scene is in an office, not a house. In the slick, sleek office of Disson's sanitary-ware manufacturing company, Disson receives his visitor—Wendy. It quickly becomes apparent that Wendy is the promiscuous but proper female, by now so familiar. In this case, however, she is also an efficient secretary, if one can trust Disson's judgment. The other female, Diana, bears a resemblance to Stella and Sarah. She is career oriented like Stella, and she is an admired wife like Sarah. Disson, as many critics have noted, is very much like Edward in *A Slight Ache*. Both are stuffy and insecure; both, like Oedipus Rex himself, push on blindly toward their own defeats. Edward, however, was rescued from hardship and maintained in comfort by Flora. Disson, on the other hand, is a self-made man at the pinnacle of success. Nevertheless, both are sick men who end up in total collapse. This play also resembles *The Birthday Party* and *A Night Out* in that all three have a party scene involving large (for Pinter, that is) numbers of people and a climactic scene of sexual assault that hastens the principal character's mental aberration. Moreover, in all three cases, the mental aberration stems from oedipal guilts.

Disson suffers from the incestuous wish to have mother.

Since *The Collection*, this wish has been becoming more and more open. In *The Collection* James has a wife in whom he is temporarily uninterested. In *The Lover*, Richard plays games with a wife who is already very much his. In *The Basement*, the intensity of the wish to have mother finally emerges. Law fights primitively for Jane. Yet in all three of these plays the women can only be associated with mother in the latent content. In *Tea Party*, Diana and Wendy are also young women in the manifest content. However, the incestuous nature of Disson's feelings is made explicit by the pictures of his distorted perceptions. The incestuous relationship that he suspects between Diana and Willy is undoubtedly a projection of his own repressed wish. Thus, if these plays are approached as dreams, they are producing wish fulfillment in separate stages.

In fact, put very simply, this play is about a man, Disson, who has fulfilled every wish but the incest wish. He has risen to great financial success in the business world. The halls of his expensive office suite are lined with alcoves containing *"individually designed wash basins, water closets, and bidets, all lit by hooded spotlights."*[41] Disson heads a company of the "most advanced sanitary engineers in the country" (p. 44). He has risen to great social success by winning Diana Torrance of Sunderley as his bride. The play opens on the eve of his wedding. On this day Wendy rides up in the elevator to Disson's office. She becomes his "personal assistant," his "very private secretary" (p. 44). From the moment he hires her, he begins a losing battle with his lust for her. Meanwhile, he hires Diana's brother, Willy, to be his "second-in-command." Willy, in turn, hires Diana for his secretary. As Disson's lust for Wendy becomes more and more uncontrollable, he develops eye trouble. He sees two balls when he plays ping pong with Willy. He becomes irritable with his sons and loses his skill at carpentry. He begins to suspect Willy of making sexual advances to both Diana and Wendy. He goes to see his friend, Disley, an eye doctor, about his troubled vision; But Disley can find nothing whatsoever wrong with Disson's eyes. Finally, Disson resorts to having his eyes bandaged—first with Wendy's chiffon scarf and then with a proper bandage applied by Disley himself. Finally, on the first anniversary of his wedding, he collapses at the tea party he has given in his office. Everyone is there: mother, father, sons, friends, Wendy, Diana, and Willy. The camera shows these people in conversational groups chatting, then in conspiratorial groups from Disson's point of view. Ultimately, Disson perceives Wendy and Diana stretched out head to toe on a desk while Willy caresses the face of first one and then the other. Disson falls to the floor. With great effort, Disley and Willy set his chair upright, but they are unable to remove Disson from the chair. He is paralyzed. Willy says: "Anyone would think he was chained to it!" (p. 87). Diana kneels beside him and speaks insistently: "Can you hear me? *Pause*. Robert, can you see me? *Pause*. It's me. It's me, darling. *Slight pause*. It's your wife" (p. 88). The camera dollies in for a close-up of Disson's face, then his eyes. They are wide open.

A realistic approach to this play leaves several questions in the spectator's mind. Alrene Sykes verbalizes one of them: "Has Disson gone mad, or very close to it?"[42] Ronald Hayman phrases another declaratively: "But there is a puzzling scene in which Willy gets Diana and Wendy to lie down on Wendy's desk." He goes on to say that the camera never shows whatever is going on here. Then he adds: "The enigmatic end comes when a shoe drops to the floor at the base of Wendy's desk."[43] Esslin asks another: "Is it [blindness] Disson's punishment for having aspired to the bed of the chaste, madonnalike Diana?"[44] Undoubtedly a variety of approaches to these questions are possible, but Freudian psychoanalysis and the language of dreams does certainly provide one set of very viable answers.

From a purely objective stance outside the play, Disson can be seen as a nearly perfect example of the condition Freud describes in a paper called "Those Wrecked by Success."[45] Freud begins by explaining how bewildering it must seem when a person falls ill as soon as he has achieved fulfillment of long-cherished wishes. He cites as an example a young girl of fallen virtue (in Victorian eyes). Eventually she became the faithful companion of an artist. After many years together, he succeeded in gaining his family's acceptance of her, and they were legally married.

> At that moment she began to go to pieces. She neglected the house of which she was now about to become the rightful mistress, imagined herself persecuted by his relatives, who wanted to take her into the family, debarred her lover, through her senseless jealousy, from all social intercourse, hindered him in his artistic work, and soon succumbed to an incurable mental illness.[46]

The likeness to Disson is plain. As this play begins, Disson has achieved all his goals. He is a successful business man with the attendant rewards of money and respect. He has just acquired an attractive and highly recommended new secretary. He has completed his climb up the social ladder by his marriage into the Torrance family. He has also won for his wife a woman of grace and beauty whom he has undoubtedly idealized. He says at his wedding: "This is the happiest day of my life" (p. 50). Then he begins to go to pieces. He can no longer function well in any of his former skills. He imagines himself the victim of a conspiracy among his wife, his brother-in-law, and his secretary. He finally succumbs to a mental illness that first affects his eyes and then paralyzes his whole body.

Freud explains that such cases can be understood when a distinction is made between "an *external* and an *internal* frustration." External frustration results when a desired object in the real world is withheld. Internal frustration results when a desired object in the fantasy world is withheld. Only when the one frustration is joined to the other does trouble arise:

It is not at all unusual for the ego to tolerate a wish as harmless so long as it exists in fantasy alone and seems remote from fulfillment, whereas the ego will defend itself hotly against such a wish as soon as it approaches fulfillment and threatens to become a reality. The distinction between this and familiar situations in neurosis-formation is merely that ordinarily it is internal intensifications of the libidinal cathexis that turn the fantasy, which has hitherto been thought little of and tolerated, into a dreaded opponent; while in these cases of ours the signal for the outbreak of conflict is given by a real external change.

Analytic work has no difficulty in showing us that it is forces of conscience which forbid the subject to gain the long hoped-for advantage from the fortunate change in reality.[47]

Later Freud adds that the forces of conscience that operate here are closely connected with the oedipus complex.[48]

In other words, Disson, like Richard in *The Lover*, has never overcome his incestuous wish for his mother. For years he has sublimated this wish by working hard to succeed in business. He tells Wendy: "We manufacture more bidets than anyone else in England. *He laughs.* It's almost by way of being a mission" (p. 44). He then transfers his energy to winning Diana. Her name likens her to the chaste moon goddess who punishes all violations of chastity. Her social position adds to her seeming unattainability. An external frustration and an internal frustration are thus joined. When Disson wins Diana, his conscience will not allow him to enjoy her as his wife. Like Richard, he needs a debased woman for his sex object, so he takes Wendy. To indulge his lust for Wendy, however, is a violation of his moral code. He becomes ill with frustration and guilt. He projects his own frustrated wishes onto Willy. The incestuous wish that Disson associates with Diana is externalized in his suspicions about the brother-sister relationship between Willy and Diana. The lust Disson feels for Wendy is externalized in fear that Willy has sexual designs on Wendy, also. Finally, Disson can only blind himself so as not to see what he dare not see; he can only paralyze himself so as not to do what he dare not do.

This psychoanalytic view of Disson deepens the insight into the play as a dream. Approached as a dream, the play opens with Disson's rising lust. Wendy rising in the office elevator concretizes the coming into consciousness of Disson's repressed erotic feelings. Wendy, the new secretary, is a rising feeling coming to the successful man at the top. Freud reveals that if there is an elevator in a dream, "we shall be reminded of the English word 'to lift,' that is 'to lift one's clothes.' "[49] Disson will wish for Wendy to lift her clothes and satisfy his lust. Yet Disson's office corridor reflects his reaction formation: the defense mechanism that transforms unacceptable impulses into their opposites. Disson has transformed his wish to be a "dirty old man" into an assembly line of sanitation equipment. Wendy emerges into a world of clean toilets — middle-class respectability. As she walks down the corridor of spotlighted toilets and bidets, Wendy seems like Alice in Anal-land. Holland's words seem to resound off the cold, clean walls:

> Anal fantasies tend to stress laws and rules, particularly meticulous, precise, petty behavior, which deals especially with collecting or excessive cleanliness or rituals. Control, either by oneself or by another, is an important theme.[50]

This expensive, scrupulously clean, well-ordered building could only result from the tight control of an acquisitive businessman and his precise and proper board of directors.

Disson's whole life is ordered and sanitized. His children behave like automatons, doing and saying exactly what Disson expects them to do and say. In John's words, they are "very good at making adjustments" (p. 55). When Diana tells them that they mean a great deal to their father, John wonders what " 'a great deal' means," and Tom wonders what " 'mean' means" (p. 55). Emotion has been wiped clean from Disson's life. He says so to Willy: "I never waste my energies in any kind of timorous expectation. Neither do I ask to be loved" (p. 53).

What is more he dislikes fraternization with office personnel. Even with his second-in-command, he meets only "by strict arrangement" (p. 52).

The chaste and beautiful Diana seems ideally suited to his way of life. She has been reared as an object of beauty to be admired but not touched. Mother and brother stood together and listened and watched while Diana played Brahms. Father's "one great solace from the busy world" was to watch Diana "ply her needle" (p. 48). Diana was reared to be "a woman of taste, discernment, sensibility, and imagination" (p. 49). Nothing about her is earthy, warm, or sensual. In fact, she would appear to be narcissistic; judging from the dream symbolism of her activities, she supplies her own caresses. Freud says: "Satisfaction obtained from a person's own genitals is indicated by all kinds of *playing*, including *piano-playing*."[51] Holland explains that anything which keeps the hands busy — in this case it is needle-work — can signify onanism.[52] She also seems incapable of love. When Disson asks why she married him, she replies: "I found you admirable in your clarity of mind, your surety of purpose, your will, the strength your achievements had given you" (p. 75). When Disson marries this vision of purity and beauty, he develops a great need for a debased love object, Wendy. If he feels any physical attraction for Diana, his dread of incest is aroused. Diana expresses this when she tries to explain his wish that she give up her job at the office. She says: "You mean I'm so near and yet so far?" (p. 62). Literally, this is the crux of Disson's problem. His wish fulfillment is so near and yet so far away. His mother figure is beside him in his marital bed, but his guilts forbid his taking her. Wendy, then, becomes the object of his lust. Her buttocks loom up before his eyes, signifying their total capture of his attention. He longs to touch her, but he dare not. The game he initiates with Wendy is really a sex fantasy. It begins when he puts up his hands to keep at bay the enormous vision of her buttocks; he accidentally knocks his lighter off the desk. Since cigarettes are phallic symbols, the cigarette lighter takes on the significance of a sexual spark. He kicks it toward her, and invites her to tackle him. His words are: "Tackle me. Get the ball." They move toward each other, elude each other, grasp arms; finally, she calls to him to tackle her. Then he sinks to the floor. Freud's citing of playing of all kinds as a masturbation symbol now makes a mental connection with his statement that "rhythmical activities such as *dancing*, *riding*, and *climbing*" are "representations of sexual intercourse."[53] The two together indicate Disson's wish to touch and be touched in some kind of mutual sex play. Wendy seems to participate in this wish, but he must refuse her invitation because of his guilts; he falls to the floor. On another occasion she places her chiffon around his eyes as she purrs invitingly: "No—you musn't touch me, if you're not wearing your chiffon" (p. 79). Moments before he has reached out and touched her; now, at her invitation, he "tumbles" and lets the chiffon flutter to the floor. He denies his wish again.

The constant denial of his erotic wishes causes his paranoic suspicions and projections. His protestations about his happiness and his wife's love reveal his doubt of them both. The children's whispering upsets him. He kneels on the floor to peep through the keyhole when Wendy goes into Willy's office. Finally, the tea party brings all the warring elements of his life together. Mother and father are there. They note his new mirror; his new self-image. It is an expensive mirror; he is no longer a cheap man. Disley and Lois are there. Disley is Disson's best man; he has known Disson a lifetime but can not recognize the nature of Disson's illness. Such is the sterility of Disson's friendships. Disson's sons are there. They exchange trite conversation with their grandparents, revealing that their inability to establish any real rapport extends beyond the parental sphere. Two elderly ladies are there to serve the tea and cakes. The nourishment of this family has come from outsiders; it has been impersonal.

Willy and Diana and Wendy are there. Disson's wish is finally externalized as he sees Diana and Wendy stretched out head to toe on the desk. Willy caresses each girl's face in turn. This vision is, of course, a symbolic rape scene. Willy's caressing the girls' faces is displacement upward. In Disson's fevered fantasy, Willy's caresses are sexual approaches. In each close-up of Willy caressing one of the girl's faces, the stage dirctions note that the other girl's shoes are in the background. Freud's words come back to the mind: "Shoes and slippers are female genitals."[54] The face and genitals juxtaposed become one in Disson's mind. Willy rapes first one girl and then the other. Thus, in Disson's fantasy, Willy fulfills the incestuous wish for the body of Diana/mother and also his lustful wish for the body of Wendy. In fantasy Willy has acted out Disson's repressions. The fantasy ends as "a shoe drops to the floor"; the last thing Disson sees is the symbol of the female genitalia. Then he falls over in his chair. He is stuck in this symbol of fatherhood and male authority. He is wedded impotently to it — a frozen image. He is symbolically castrated — dead. He has become blind, deaf, and paralyzed. He can not see, hear, or do evil. The purpose his illness serves is underlined by the final words of the play. Diana says: "Robert. *Pause.* Can you hear me? *Pause.* Robert, can you see me? *Pause.* It's me. It's me, darling. *Slight pause.* It's your wife" (p. 88). She is very near but of necessity the toilet magnate has made her very far away. Disson's wish to have mother has been simultaneously fulfilled and thwarted. He is thwarted by his own inner conflicts that also bring about his own self-punishment.

Pulling back for an overview makes clear that this play, like *The Room*, concretizes the return of the repressed wish. But there is a difference. In *The Room*, the case is simpler: Riley, the repressed erotic feeling, comes up from the basement, the subconscious, into Rose's room, the conscious mind. Here he is killed by Bert and denied by Rose; thus, the wish is relegated to repression again. In *Tea Party*, the repressed erotic feelings,

Wendy, ride up in the elevator to the sterile world of success, which has been the sublimating effort that has made repression possible. In this play, however, the business tycoon fights mightily to continue repression and is himself destroyed by the effort. Disson is not able to continue his repression. His lust and fear of incest war with each other and destroy him. In the process, the defense of reaction-formation is concretized and dramatized. First of all, the sterile, well-lighted toilets concretize the total transformation of the dark and dirty anal impulses. Then Disson's dropping of Wendy's chiffon to indicate his refusal to touch her dramatizes the transformation of his lust into its opposite action. His reaching hand that then trembles and moves toward the telephone instead of toward Wendy has revealed his true desire. In still another instance, Disson pushes back his growing distrust for Willy and oscillates to the other extreme by inviting him to become a partner in the firm. Disson's aching eyes concretize his refusal to see the titillating body of Wendy that he longs to watch. He bandages his eyes to struggle further against this desire. With the blindfold he symbolically castrates himself in opposition to his lustful wish. Ultimately, he paralyzes himself to prevent himself from performing the incestuous, lustful acts that he projects outside himself onto Willy.

These concretizations and dramatizations emphasize the great Pinter theme of man's conscious confusion and his unconscious control. Disson, the man who believes in assessing one's own powers, can not carry out his own inner desires. His unconscious fears and guilts forbid him even to know what he wishes. He is made to believe they are someone else's wishes. All the while he moves blindly toward his own defeat.

This play is also, in one sense, a sequel to *The Dwarfs*. There Len purges himself of his heritage, and begins a new clean life. Here in *Tea Party*, Disson comes to the catastrophe brought on by that sterile life. Disson's family are all shadowy figures, empty of intimacy and personal feeling. They are hollow voices, speaking hollow clichés. Disson has risen to a new life, reflected by his new, expensive mirror. This new life is the ultimate success he has longed for. Here Disson picks up resonance from Mick in that Disson can now reupholster his armchair in "oatmeal tweed" and buy a new table in "afromosia teak veneer." But success proves to be sterile and unrewarding. Disson is uncomfortable and insecure in this expensive new world. He is haunted by guilts that refuse him any pleasure or joy in his achievements. *Tea Party* says that when man gives up his own heritage, he gains emptiness and insecurity; when he climbs the ladder of success, he reaches toward self-destruction. The play also repeats the universal message of *The Lover* that Freud states so well: "Anyone who is to be really free and happy in love must have surmounted his respect for women and have come to terms with the idea of incest with his mother or sister."[55] Out of this message emerges the irony of the title. A tea party carries connotations of prim, proper, civilized behavior; and these characters have gathered in Disson's clean, expensive office with no other expectations. But the hidden thoughts of the creator of all this sterility and sanitation transform the harmless tea party into a scene of carnal appetite and mental collapse.

THE HOMECOMING

The final play of this third group, *The Homecoming*, is also a party or celebration; and, like all of Pinter's parties, it also features carnal appetite. *The Homecoming*, however, reverses the pattern of *Tea Party*. Instead of the lust of one man projecting a carnal image over the propriety and decorum of a family group, the lust of a family group substitutes carnal behavior for the restraint and nostalgia of one man. Ted's sentimental expectations are met with primitive activity. This antithesis is matched by the range of critical response to *The Homecoming* since its London debut in 1965. For a sample, Simon Trussler damns it with such descriptive phrases as "modishly, intellectualized melodrama" and "unmotivated oppugnancy."[56] John Lahr, on the other hand, calls it a "triumph of craftsmanship and artistic intention."[57]

Regardless of the judgment, the play bears Pinter's stamp. This time a whole family is in a room that has been made larger by removing a wall. Into this room come two visitors — Ted and Ruth. Ruth's presence causes old feelings to rise up in all the men of the family — Max, Sam, Lenny, and Joey. They act out their feelings by wresting Ruth from her husband, Ted. All of these characters are familiar. Not one of them is a replica or exact duplicate of any previous character, but each one is a different configuration of traits and idiosyncrasies that have belonged to similar characters in earlier plays. Max has Goldberg's domineering presence and Davies's insistent self-concern. Sam has Mr. Kidd's meekness and Petey's preference for watching from the sidelines. Lenny resembles Mick and Pete in his violent conversation, his tearing, searing intensity. Joey has an open concern with the physical that is reminiscent of Gus; in other ways, he seems like a younger version of McCann, the muscle man. Ted has the detachment of Mark with the sterility and success of Disson. He also has the basic insecurity and fear of impotence that all Pinter's male characters bear; Teddy, however, defends against it in a different way — with intellectualism. Ruth, of course, is the whore/wife/mother that appears and reappears in Pinter's repertory. She lacks the ignorance and poignancy of the mother figures like Rose and Meg and Mrs. Stokes. She lacks the lightheartedness of Stella and Sarah and Jane. She has a strength and will to power that only Flora has approached until this play, but Flora's dominance was more casual because it met so little resistance from Edward.

Ruth is a match for any man, even Lenny. She challenges his threats to her authority and emerges the victor—mistress of the family.

Her victory, however, is the family's victory, for her maternal enthronement is the fulfillment of their desire. As Arthur Ganz states: "Her position as a desired sexual object gives Ruth. . .her triumphant status at the end of the play."[58] From the moment they recognize her likeness to Jessie, their dead mother, the family displays overtly their wish to have her. They move unabashedly to take her from Teddy. They offer her a proposition; she will be their mother and their whore. She accepts. She is theirs. Their wish is fulfilled. Unlike James and Richard, they have not had her all along; they win her during the play. Unlike Law, they don't trade her for their home. Unlike Disson, they do not collapse when their prize is won. She is theirs, and they group around her to receive satisfaction for their needs.

Stylistically, this play appears to be as realistic as *Night School* or *The Collection*; but if it is realism, it is a bizarre realism that audiences find impossible to recognize or identify with. Bert O. States says: "The reaction one has to the play comes nowhere near Pity and Fear, . . .but is better described as *astonishment at the elaboration.*"[59] Margaret Croyden, in an article entitled, "Pinter's Hideous Comedy," calls the play a blend of "primitive ritual" and "comedy of manners."[60] Another explanation is that Pinter has put dream-world behavior and events into a background of precise realism. Clearly, this play has a dense ambiguity. Such ambiguity must find, for its point of departure, a concrete image—a realistic reading of the play.

The play is about the strange events that occur when Teddy, with his wife Ruth, returns home to see his family again. Teddy is a professor of philosophy at an American university. He and Ruth have three sons. Teddy has not seen his family in many years; they do not even know he is married. Since Ruth's childhood home was in the same neighborhood, it is safe to assume that Teddy's estrangement from his family predates the American job. Ted's London family consists of a father, an uncle, and two brothers who live together in a womanless home. The atmosphere in this home is more than just masculine, it is bestial, as the animal imagery of the lines makes clear. The animals are all in bed when Ted and Ruth arrive; their visit is unexpected. Ted seems nostalgic and Ruth seems uncomfortable at first. They both seem unsure of each other. When they are confronted by the family, change begins to occur. Ted's nostalgia turns to anger and then withdrawal; Ruth's discomfort vanishes into conquest; the family's bestiality is intensified by desire. A battle ensues. When the play has run its course, Ruth feels at home in her accepted role of whore and mother to Teddy's father and brothers. Teddy's uncle, Sam, has collapsed under the emotional pain of seeing adultery repeat itself. Teddy has rejected wife and family by submitting calmly to Ruth's decision to remain. He leaves with a casual, "It's been wonderful to see you" thrown in before his "bye-bye's."[61] She retorts: "Don't become a stranger" (p. 80). Then she relaxes into her new life. She sits in the patriarchal chair. Joey takes a position at her feet, his head in her lap. Lenny stands close by. Max begins to crawl around her chair begging for the share of her affection he fears he will not receive.

As the curtain closes, the audience's shock is matched by their bewilderment. Their overwhelming concern, like that of the critics, is with motivation. Why did Ruth give up her children, her husband, and her university life to become a whore to a bunch of animals? Why did Teddy accept it so passively? Needless to say, critical writings supply numbers of interesting and valid answers that add further evidence of the play's rich ambiguity.

This play is, indeed, so ambiguous that it allows multiple

interpretations even on the realistic level. One, of course, is Martin Esslin's explanation that the family has always been in the business of prostitution. Jessie was a whore, Max was a pimp, and Sam was a driver for prostitutes. Consequently, their serious proposition to Ruth is natural for them and unsurprising to Teddy. Ruth's casual acceptance of the offer is equally understandable because she too was a whore before her marriage, and has, therefore, found university life barren and uncomfortable.[62] Another beautifully realistic perception of the play emerges from the film version directed by Peter Hall for The American Film Theatre. The film script seems totally unaltered except for a few brief shots of the exterior of the house and one of the kitchen. However, Peter Hall treats the events of the play as a vicious family game. Hall explains his interpretation in an interview printed in the cinebill. The family members are competing with one another for supremacy, and they willfully destroy one another in the process. The rules of this game, however, forbid letting anyone know that he is being put on or mocked. Then Hall explains the crux of the play:

> The mainspring of the play. . .is that the entire family put on the elder brother to see if he'll crack. They suggest keeping his wife in order to try and crack him. He is actually the biggest bastard in a lot of bastards, and he won't be cracked. He would sooner see the destruction of his own wife, and of his own marriage, which, in a sense he does, except you could argue that where the woman ends up at the end is where she's always been and where she wants to be.[63]

Thus, Hall's interpretation ameliorates the shock of the play's amorality. Since the proposition to Ruth is really a game intended to crack Teddy, the family's actual sexual intentions toward Ruth are in doubt. Or, at least, they are deemphasized.

When the play is approached as a dream, there is no need to ameliorate or deemphasize the shocking events. Bizarre behavior is natural to dreams, as is the dense overdetermination of this play. These various determinations of *The Homecoming* are interconnected like a chain of linked rings so that it is difficult to know where to break the chain and begin. Perhaps an arbitrary commencement can be made by viewing the play as Teddy's anxiety dream. As such the play bears a strong resemblance to *A Slight Ache*. Edward externalized his growing fear of impotence into the Matchseller at the gate. Then, as his fear continued to grow, he hastened its realization by inviting the Matchseller into his house and transforming him into a vision of youth and virility that could take over his wife and home. So it is with Teddy. He fears impotence, concretized in the loss of his wife. The cause of his fear goes back to childhood. Teddy must have had strong oedipal feelings as a child, for Sam explains that Teddy had been mother's favorite: "She told me. It's true. You were always the. . .you were always the main object of her love" (p. 63). But mother had betrayed him by bestowing her affections on other more powerful men, like father and MacGregors. Teddy, consequently, retreated into intellectualism. Anna Freud explains that intellectualism is a frequently used defense against instinctual danger—libidinal feelings that threaten to overpower the ego. "The aim of intellectualism," she says, "is to link up instinctual processes closely with ideational contents so to render them accessible to consciousness and amenable to control."[64] Moreover, this defense allowed Teddy to withdraw from the competition for mother and not lose face. He could establish his superiority in another area; he could be mentally superior to compensate for the physical inferiority he felt. And it is no wonder that Teddy felt physically inferior—castrated—for his father is a butcher who threatens his sons with, "I'll chop your spine off" (p. 9). Furthermore, he reminds them that he knows how to "carve a carcass" (p. 40), for he has worked all his life using the "chopper and slab" (p. 47). As a child, Teddy's castration fears must have been so great that he dared not entertain his oedipal strivings for mother. With these built-

in fears of his own erotic feelings, Teddy's marriage was fore-
doomed, especially since he married a girl so like his mother. To
love her was to be unable to desire her. As this psychical
impotence has grown, Teddy's fear of losing Ruth has grown.
As he once lost his mother to more virile men, he fears losing his
wife to more virile men. The play is the nightmare in which
those fears come true. Teddy shows his uneasiness and concern
from the moment he arrives. He arrives at night when all are
asleep, and he is fearful lest they should awaken. He prefers not
to face them till morning. He wishes to hurry Ruth to the safety
of his room. When she insists on a walk outside, he watches from
the window chewing his knuckles uneasily. After she leaves,
Teddy has his encounter with Lenny. The realization of Teddy's
fears has begun. Teddy has precipitated his own crisis by bringing Ruth home. When Lenny enters the room, Teddy seems to
keep his distance and brings their encounter to a quick end.
Then Lenny has his meeting with Ruth; and when he learns she
is Teddy's wife, his appetite for her is whetted. To win her from
Teddy would settle a score with the favorite son who had once
edged his brothers out with mother. He begins immediately to
move toward his goal by addressing Ruth in conversation replete
with sexual innuendoes. He suggests that Ruth is the ticking
object that has awakened him—one of those objects which are
"commonplace" in the daytime but which tick in the night. He
offers her water apparently as a remedy for aridity. Then he
makes her aware of his youthfulness. He tells her if he had been
a soldier in World War II, he would probably have gone through
Venice, but he had been too young to serve. Then he asks to touch
her hand, a displacement from one body extremity to another.
But Ruth rejects him; instead of responding to his invitation,
she gives him a cold, "Why?" (p. 30). Her rejection associates
in his mind with early rejections from mother. The hostile side
of his ambivalence is aroused, and he lets Ruth know the contempt he feels for women and the harshness he can treat them

to. He tells her the story of his near murder of a diseased prostitute under an arch by the docks. Ruth shows no fright; she merely questions how he knew the girl was diseased. Lenny takes this response as another rebuke. He lets Ruth know this by discussing his "sensitivity to atmosphere." Then, he tries to threaten her again with a new story about last Christmas. This story seems to parallel his encounter with Ruth. In both instances he began in good spirits. In the Christmas story he had enjoyed the bite of the winter cold. Lenny likes antagonism, even from the weather. He had jumped on the lorry with his shovel; and once at his destination, he had gone "deep into the December snow." Then he had an encounter with an old lady—in the December of life. She wanted him to move an iron mangle that her brother-in-law had left in the living room. It belonged in the back room. The mangle was immovable, however, just as Ruth, a sister-in-law left in the living room of his home, is immovable. So Lenny told the old lady her mangle was out-of-date and "gave her a short-arm jab to the belly" (p. 33). After this threat, he propositions Ruth again by suggesting that he move the ashtray by her side. An ashtray is a receptacle for burned-out cigarette stubs. In dream language, Lenny has suggested that he get rid of the impotent male who lives at her side. Next he declares suggestively that he will relieve her of the glass. But Ruth refuses to let him have her glass. Instead she counterthreatens: "Why don't I just take you?" (p. 34). Then she becomes the aggressive one and challenges him to have a sip from her glass. As she retires to her room, Lenny calls after her: "What was that supposed to be? Some kind of proposal?" (p. 35). This scene has set in motion the realization of Ted's fear. Lenny and Ruth have come to understand one another. Their future is prophesied. Ruth is to become a whore again like her mother-in-law before her. She has tried to be what Teddy wants; she has repressed her old way of life, but the new life in America is barren: "It's all rock. And sand. It stretches. . .so far. . .

everywhere you look. And there's lots of insects there. *Pause.* And there's lots of insects there" (p. 53). Ruth not only objects to the sterile, dry life with Teddy but also to her pregnancies and her children. Freud says: "Small animals and vermin represent small children—for instance, undesired brothers and sisters. Being plagued with vermin is often a sign of pregnancy."[65] Lenny the pimp, can take her away from all these unpleasantries. When the family makes their formal proposal, she accepts. Leaving Teddy and the children and the life in America mean nothing to her. Teddy can only stand by wide-eyed and helpless as his nightmare unfolds. He is like the man in a dream who is about to be murdered but can not cry out for help—his voice will not come, nor can he run—his legs will not move. Teddy can only watch and accept.

As Teddy leaves, the play as his nightmare links with a second determination—the play as a multiple wish-fulfillment dream. This family of men needs a woman. As Hugh Nelson points out: "The first act is crucial in allowing us to see the motherless, wifeless, sexless family in operation. . ."[66] The stage setting itself concretizes this womanless house. The back wall of the room has been removed, making the hall one with the living room. Freud comments on the dream symbolism of such renovations:

> We find an interesting link with the sexual researches of childhood when a dreamer dreams of two rooms which were originally one, or when he sees a familiar room divided into two in the dream or vice versa. In childhood the female genitals and the anus are regarded as a single area—the 'bottom' (in accordance with the infantile 'cloaca theory'); and it is not until later that the discovery is made that this region of the body comprises two separate cavities and orifices.[67]

Changing two rooms into one seems then to indicate a return to a body that must utilize the same orifice for both birth and defecation—a male body. Max has taken Jessie's place as mother of the household. Teddy's explanation to Ruth supports this interpretation. He explains the alteration in the room and adds: "We knocked it [the wall] down. . .years ago. . .to make an open living area. The structure wasn't affected, you see. My mother was dead" (p. 21). What other reason could there be for connecting this renovation with his mother's death? After this renovation, these animals no longer live in the *bosom* of the family. The house reflects its absence of a nurturing mother. In the opening scene various members of the family— Lenny, Sam, and Joey—speak of their hunger, and Max states their problem bluntly to Joey: "Go and find yourself a mother" (p. 16). Max and his two sons revile women, refer to them all as whores and tarts; but this debasement bespeaks their desire. Even Sam looks back fondly on the time when Jessie was among them. He remembers escorting her in his cab: "They were some of the most delightful evenings I've ever had. Used to just drive her about. It was my pleasure" (p. 16). Sam never aspired to more. He, like Petey before him, has always used the defense mechanism Anna Freud calls *restriction of the ego*. Rather than be outdone, he has always withdrawn and watched. Anna Freud says this kind of behavior in children is related to their pasts:

> The sight of another person's superior achievement signifies the sight of genitals larger than their own, and these they envy. Again, when they are encouraged to emulate their fellows, it suggests the hopeless rivalry of the oedipus phase or the disagreeable realization of the difference between the sexes.[68]

Sam's present lack of desire for women is also an indicator of the strong wish he once had to have mother.

When Ruth arrives, they all recognize her as Jessie's counterpart, their long-lost mother, wife, and whore. When Teddy departs without Ruth, they have reclaimed their own. Joey and Lenny have won back their hearts' desire from the favored sibling. Joey, the irresistible one who had had "more dolly than" Teddy's "had cream cakes" (p. 66), is happy with Ruth even though he "didn't get all the way" (p. 66). He tells the others: "Sometimes. . .you can be happy. . .and not go the whole hog. Now and again. . .you can be happy. . .without going any hog" (p. 68). Apparently, Joey has associated Ruth with mother, and desire has given way to love. In keeping with this feeling, he complains of Lenny's plan to take her to Greek Street: "I don't want to share her with a lot of yobs" (p. 73). Lenny's satisfaction is different from Joey's. He has taken more pleasure from ousting Teddy than Joey has. After all Teddy is the man who pinched his "specially made cheese roll" (p. 64). As he once enjoyed the bite of the cold, Lenny has enjoyed the contest with Teddy, but he also looks forward to the pleasure of seeing Joey enjoy Ruth. Lenny seems to have handed over to Joey the pleasure of fulfilling sexual desire. Lenny than receives his satisfaction vicariously. Anna Freud cites such behavior as a form of identification called *altruistic surrender*. It occurs in persons who are disappointed with themselves. Consequently, they displace their wishes onto objects who seem better qualified to fulfill them. Anna Freud describes a female patient whose "early renunciation of instinct had resulted in the formation of an exceptionally severe superego, which made it impossible for her to gratify her own wishes. . ." But her impulses were not repressed; "she found some proxy in the outside world to serve as a repository for each of them. . .The patient did not dissociate herself from her proxies but identified herself with them." What she forbade herself, she encouraged in her proxy. She received gratification from their gratification.[69] Such is the way Lenny handles his own sexual impotence. His impulses are not repressed, but he surrenders to Joey the satisfactions of action. Lenny shows this altruistic identification when he yields Ruth to Joey. Lenny has danced with her, even kissed her; but when Joey takes Ruth by the arm, Lenny steps aside.

Joey smiles at Lenny, then sits with Ruth on the sofa, embracing and kissing her (p. 59). Lenny sits on the arm of the sofa and caresses Ruth's hair, while Joey embraces her. Both are happy.

Max is happy, too. He thinks Ruth will be no trouble at all. He tells Ruth she is the first woman they have had in the house since Jessie died. Any other woman would have tarnished mother's image: "But you. . .Ruth. . .you're not only lovely and beautiful, but you're kin. You're kith. You belong here" (p. 75). It is not until the last moment that Max becomes fearful that he will not get his share: "I'm too old, I suppose. She thinks I'm an old man" (p. 81). But he is hopeful to the last. The final line of the play is Max's, "Kiss me" (p. 82).

Sam's wish for mother/Jessie/Ruth is revealed by his great fear. As a withdrawer, he has seen life as one great primal scene. He watched and listened while Mac had Jessie in the back seat of his cab. The same castration fears that he felt as a child during his first primal-scene experience came back to him then. And Mac was a large and fearful man. As he watches and listens to the verbal rape of Ruth, his repressed erotic feelings are stirred too. Subconsciously, he reexperiences the oedipal dream of having his mother, and it is immediately quelled by the fear of castration from father figures — all butchers. Sam collapses in fright as he confesses the only part of his dread secret he dares to acknowledge, even to himself. In his state of collapse, he is blind, deaf, and dumb. He can no longer see and hear primal scenes; therefore, he can no longer have fearful fantasies. He can no longer be burdened with dread secrets. His wish for withdrawal is carried to its ultimate end.

Ruth also gets her wish. She is thirsty for return to fulfillment of animal needs. No more helping Teddy with his lectures! No more pregnancies! No more child care! No more barren sand! And what is more, she will be boss! She will have her own three-room flat, new clothes, and earthy people to interact with. In the final tableau she sits enthroned in father's chair.

She is mistress of the roost—mother of them all. Joey sits at her feet with his head in her lap—happy. Max crawls around her, returned to infancy. Lenny watches; a new satisfaction has been added to his share—the powerful father has been bested as well as the favored sibling. The tableau is the concretization of wish fulfillment—the wish to have mother. In this perception of the play, even Teddy is not devoid of wish fulfillment. He, who early in life withdrew into intellectualism to defend himself against instinctual danger, is safe. He has not been engulfed. He has maintained his "intellectual equilibrium." This was his stated wish: "You won't get me being. . .I won't be lost in it" (p. 62).

Max, Lenny, and Joey, in their acquiescence to mother, have returned to infancy. Thus, the play as wish fulfillment links with the play as a dramatization of regression. The whole play depicts a backward movement. Lenny's clock also records the forward movement of time, and he stifles it when it initiates the move to capture Ruth. Thence forward, time moves backward. At the start of the play all the characters are adult and older; and they all live in an old house bereft of mother. At the end of the play, they make a tableau of madonna and children. Sam has returned to nothingness. Max is a crawling infant. Lenny and Joey are children snuggled close to mother. This tableau of regression concretized is one of the homecomings the play celebrates—the return to mother's lap and love. This return to oral security is the resolution of the sons' earlier expressions of hunger. The tableau also represents the regression from patriarchy back to matriarchy. Mother/Ruth sits in father's chair—dominant over the family.

Regression can also be seen in the backward movement through the developmental phases of life. The movement of the play actually begins with the return of repressed wishes—oedipal wishes. All these returning wishes are also homecomings. Ruth's repressed erotism returns along with the old wish to take mother's place. The family's repressed desires for mother return and take the form of a need to possess and debase her. For Ted there is a return of old fears and angers at seeing father and brothers take mother away. His feeling of helplessness, his passive acceptance, is also a return of that feeling with which a child normally resolves his oedipal strivings. He gives up his mother and seeks sublimation in the outside world. These returning feelings push the family back into the struggle for dominance characteristic of the anal phase. When the play opens, father and sons are set in old anal patterns. Here again the symbolism of the removed wall is applicable; it represents the living room as an anus. The house is scrupulously clean, but the family lives with verbal dirt and bestiality. Their sexual activities, real and fantasied, show their fixation on the anal wish to revel and play in dirt. Lenny's tales are of women dirty with disease. Joey takes his girls "in the rubble" (p. 67). Their anal sadism has been indulged in verbal violence and physical pugnacity. Joey is a boxer. Max clobbers people with his stick. Lenny's tales are full of jabs and kicks. They have, moreover, dehumanized each other. No one is thought of as having feelings. All of these are set patterns, a way of life won long ago. With the advent of Ruth and the surge of old feelings, the struggle for dominance begins all over again. Teddy struggles against Max and his brothers for possession of Ruth. These interpersonal struggles are bestial, savage. This is what Irving Wardle means when he says the play has to be understood in "territorial terms."[70] They also fight merely for position—the dominant position. This struggle is crucial to Peter Hall's interpretation of the play. The struggle for dominance is multifaceted. There is a struggle between Ruth and Teddy, one between Teddy and Lenny, one between Teddy and Max, one between Lenny and Max, one between Max and Sam, and, finally, one between Ruth and her new family. The outcome of all of this struggle is, of course, the return to orality prophesied

at the outset by Lenny's complaints that Max is "a dog cook"—
he thinks he is "cooking for a lot of dogs" (p. 11). In the final
scene when the men take their childish proximities to mother/
Ruth, they illustrate that what they have longed for most was
not sexual satisfaction—the fulfillment of desire, but mothering—the fulfillment of the need to be loved. Joey speaks for them
all: "I've been the whole hog plenty of times. Sometimes. . .you
can be happy. . .and not go the whole hog" (p. 68). The
ultimate homecoming for this family is their regression to the
womb.

Regression calls attention to movement patterns and thereby provides the link to what may be the most resonant determination of this play. *The Homecoming* dramatizes repetition
compulsion. Norman Holland paraphrases Freud's definition
of it as "the tendency human beings have to get themselves into
the same situations over and over. . . ." And he says that it
"manifests itself in a sense of 'I've been here before.' "[71] The title
of this play states that sense. *The Homecoming* is a return to
the nostalgic past. It picks up on Goldberg's speech to McCann:
"Who came before your father's father but your father's father's
mother! Your great-gran-granny" (*The Birthday Party*, p. 81).
The Homecoming shows man's wish to go backward in time, to
return from whence he came. Thus, it coincides again with
Holland's explanation of Freudian theory: "Such a sense [I have
been here before] symbolizes a wish to return to one's warm,
hungerless paradise before birth. . . ."[72] So this determination
interrelates with regression and stresses this play's relationship to
the other plays of its group—the ultimate fulfillment of the wish
to have mother. Repetition compulsion is more than just backward movement, however; it is cyclical movement. Man wishes
to stay in this circular path, to return from whence he came,
to repeat the mistakes of the past, to have a "second wind," to
complete the cycle.

The first scene of this play is overrun with nostalgia, which, incidentally, makes a bizarre combination with the animal imagery and bestial behavior set up in contrast to it. Thus, the atmosphere is immediately dreamlike. The play begins with Max's search for the scissors. The old butcher/castrator, who spent his life working with the chopper and slab, can not even find a pair of scissors now; he is unable to cut the mustard any more. Thus, the play heralds Max's ultimate return to infancy. At the moment, however, Max indulges in rosy memories. He used to be a real "tearaway." He recalls Mac with pride and wonder; he was a "big man." He even remembers Jessie as not "such a bad woman" even though it made him "sick to look at her rotten stinking face" (p. 9). When Lenny chooses a winner for the race at Sandown Park, it is a horse named Second Wind. Max then remembers his expertise with horses. When Sam enters, he looks back fondly on Jessie: "Nothing like your bride. . .going about these days. Like Jessie" (p. 16). Even in his angry reply to Joey, Max unwittingly orders a nostalgic return: "Go and find yourself a mother" (p. 16). Lenny interjects a note of mockery into all this; he says to Max: "You used to tuck me up in bed every night. He tucked you up, too, didn't he, Joey" (p. 17). Still Max returns to sentimental memories of his father dandling him. Across the ocean, Teddy has, apparently, been infected with similar sentimentalism. He has had the urge to come home again. He brings his wife of six years. When he enters the house, he looks around nostalgically: "I mean, it's a fine room, don't you think?" (p. 21). He has positive recollections of Max: "I think you'll like him very much" (p. 22), he says to Ruth.

As the play progresses, an awareness grows that feelings and events are repeating themselves. The nostalgia is more than a wish, it is the symptom of a behavior pattern. Individually, each character in the play repeats past feelings and events. Teddy left home six years ago, the day after he married Ruth. He withdrew from animal instincts and behavior by becoming an intellectual and by removing himself physically from the scene. He moved a long distance away—to America where in his perception all was clean. Yet, he returns home sentimentally, only to rediscover bestial rivalry that he again rejects and again departs from. Ruth comes home and feels the old repressed feelings rising within her. She was different six years ago—a career girl. She was a model; she posed for nude photographs. Since then she has tried to be a faculty wife and mother, but she has found this life arid and insect ridden. At home again in the neighborhood of her childhood, her aggressive instincts and her old erotism come to the fore; she acquiesces to them. She kisses Lenny; she goes to bed with Joey. She demands, makes contracts, conducts business as she did when she was a model. She has returned to the free life of sex and dominance. Lenny and Joey hate women. They revile and defile them to show their resentment at past rejections. They were born to a whore who neglected them. Yet they choose another. They are willing to be her economic slaves for the chance to be her lovers and children again. Max has cared for a sick mother, toiled for a prostitute wife. He gave up his dream of life at the racetrack to slave in the butcher shop and at home. Yet he wants to take Ruth in in Jessie's place. When Teddy objects that Ruth is not well, Max tells him not to worry, that he's used to looking after people who are not well. Max also shows resentment over Jessie's rejections, but he is willing to settle for the hope of a share of Ruth. He finally returns all the way to infancy—crawling on the floor at Ruth's feet. Sam collapses at the prospect of being watcher again. He has always restricted his ego; he has taken the scraps and leavings rather than compete. He drove the car while Mac "banged" Jessie on the back seat. Now he watches while Max and the boys claim Ruth.

Family events repeat themselves, too. It is not difficult to imagine that turning a bride into a wife/mother/whore is an old family custom. Max and Sam remember this was their mother's and father's house. Mother was ill, father was a butcher, and there were three invalid sons. Max followed father into the butcher shop. He married Jessie, who became a whore with three bastard sons. Brother-in-law Sam was her pimp and chauffeur. Mac was her lover. Max was left to be housewife and mother as well as butcher. Then Teddy brings Ruth home and discovers that he has married mother's counterpart. Max and the brothers recognize it, too. Brother-in-law Lenny will now be Ruth's pimp and landlord. Joey will be her lover, while Lenny will watch as Sam did. Teddy will be left out until Ruth is sick and old before her time. Then the family will kick her out as they threaten to dispose of Sam when they think he is a corpse. She will return home for Teddy to nurse as Max had cared for his mother and Jessie. Meanwhile, Ted will have been mother to three sons who will be starved for maternal love, and the whole cycle will repeat itself again. Max verbalizes it all in the first scene with Sam. Sam says: "This was our mother's house." Max replied: "One lot after the other. One mess after the other." Then Sam says: "Our father's house," and Max replies: "Look what I'm lumbered with. One cast-iron bunch of crap after another. One flow of stinking pus after another" (p. 19). Bernard Dukore speaks to this point:

> The title itself indicates a return which one may interpret as a return to an ineluctable condition. As soon as Ruth and Teddy enter, he remarks that the old key still works, for the lock has not been changed. After he finds his old room intact, he states explicitly, "Nothing's been changed. Still the same."[73]

Teddy's words are another reminder of the dream-work's tendency to blend opposites. While this play stresses change — shifting relationships, reversals of feeling, returning instincts, altering needs — it also emphasizes the static quality of the circular path — repeating itself again and again and again.

The concept of the blending of opposites continues the

chain of linking interpretations, for from another point of view this play is built on the splitting apart of opposing facets of character. Other critics have noted the possibility of splitting in these characters; but true to this play's rich ambiguity, they have all perceived the splits in different ways. Esslin sees Lenny and Joey as one person combining "cunning and sexual potency," Max and Teddy as one person combining "senility and wisdom."[74] Hollis sees Sam and Max as "the composite father," and Lennie and Joey as "similar aberrations."[75] It is also possible to see this play as a sequel to *The Dwarfs* in which Len/Teddy returns home from his new sterile life to confront the many facets of himself that he has tried to purge. These old selves are part of Len/Teddy's past, his family heritage that can not be repressed permanently. They rise up again like Riley and the Matchseller to renew old guilts and fears. These return-ing feelings have urged Teddy home. There he encounters all his old discarded selves and their wellsprings. Lenny is the aggressive, domineering, violent self that still shows itself in Teddy's rise in the world. He had the drive to study and the will to succeed and the capability to destroy his past that led him from these lowly origins to his position as a professor of philos-ophy at an American university. Joey is his physical, naive side. It was this need for physical love that caused Teddy to take a wife. It was the naive acceptance of this wife as a longed-for mother that brought on the psychical impotence which makes Teddy unable to satisfy his wife sexually. Lenny and Joey to-gether compose Teddy's original self. Max and Sam are his parental images made part of himself through introjection in childhood. Sam is the gentle side who watches rather than competes; he withdraws to another arena. When Sam could not compete for mother's love at home or for father's respect in the butcher shop, he became the best chauffeur in London. Teddy is a watcher, too. He watches rather than competes, while his brothers and father capture his wife. As a child, he had withdrawn into intellectualism and pursued success in another arena far from home. Teddy can also be perceived as gentle in his early concerns for Ruth's comfort. Max is the harsh but responsible side of Teddy's father image. He carries a big stick, but he also stuck by his bastard sons, bathed them, fed them, and mothered them. Teddy can be harsh. He shows his harshness when he leaves Ruth without entering a single plea. He shows his responsibility when he returns home to be father and mother to his sons. These old selves once filled Teddy's person. The hollow man made sterile by the climb to success had left them all behind. As Disson's success and sterility had made him an arid, impotent father and husband, so have Teddy's. His wife has lost interest in him. Then, feeling his emptiness, Teddy has been urged home by returning yearnings. In this dream Teddy arrives home and watches the many facets of his old self warring with his new self. He sees their interactions with his wife and her returning feelings. He sees that his wife responds to the old selves that won her—the old selves that need her to satisfy desire, to provide maternal love. But Teddy has gone too far, he can not turn back. He chooses his life of sterility and success. He rejects his old selves again, along with his wife this time. On his homecoming he purges them all again. Disson had called them all together for a tea party. Their presence, distorted by his own inner conflicts, destroyed him. Teddy refuses to "get lost in it"; he departs from his homecoming newly alone and cleansed. An alternate ending is equally plausible. Teddy's homecoming results in his becoming a whole man again—one with his past. It is the hollow, empty self who leaves the family home—dispossessed. The old self remains behind in a new and more satisfying relation to his wife.

This reading of the play overlaps with and incorporates a concretization of the house as psyche, which has been seen in many of the earlier plays. In *The Homecoming* the old family house is psychic memory revisited. In *The Room*, the house/

psyche was divided into a conscious mind upstairs and a subconscious in the basement. In *The Caretaker* the house is old, and whole areas of it are locked up, unused. Someday it is to be renovated, redecorated; but at present it is piled with junk; it is leaking upstairs. In *The Dwarfs*, Mark, the successful self, has moved to a fancy new apartment. And, in *The Homecoming* the old family house is to be revisited. It is illumined. It is no longer divided. The conscious and, at least, the preconscious are one large room where past and present can come together. This room is no longer shut off from the entrance hall. Figures can no longer move unseen from one level to the other. All is open, visible, known. All phases of the self live here and can be observed here: the aggressive, violent self/Lenny and the physical, naive self/Joey live here with the selves introjected from the father image—the harsh, responsible self/Max and the withdrawn, watching self/Sam. The dead mother and whore/Jessie is absent only physically. Her spirit lives in this psychic memory, and it blends with Ruth. The two women become one. All aspects of the former self in this house/psyche choose Ruth, and she chooses them because they allow her old self to come out of hiding into the open room. She joins with the old selves in war against the sterile, intellectual, new self that Len became at the end of *The Dwarfs,* that Aston's Buddha represented in *The Caretaker*, that Teddy has become in this play. From here two endings are again possible. Teddy rejects the old selves and their war. He withdraws from the combat. He stands aside and sees it all clearly; he understands it as animalism. He chooses once again to abandon the old psychic memories. He abandons them to live again in his clean, sterile intellect. The alternative interpretation is also viable here. The newly integrated self purges the hollow, sterile, intellectual from the psyche. When Teddy leaves, he leaves the psyche in control of the original self, which has come to terms with its warring facets and which has been reintegrated around a maternal figure whose absence had brought on its earlier disintegration.

This perception of *The Homecoming* as the renewal of acquaintance between the present and the past suggests that this play is indeed the capstone of Pinter's construct of dramas. It is the play in which all the pieces of the puzzle finally come together. From the dream approach, it is the ultimate dream that finishes a series of dreams each of which has examined a different facet of a wish. *The Room* began this series with its study of repression and denial; *The Homecoming* caps the series with its reversal of appearance and reality, its acting out of the usually hidden feelings, its full awareness of the ever-repeating patterns of life. Pinter himself seems to confirm this concept of the play. John Russell Taylor reports:

> Pinter has said that the play came to him all of a piece, with the shattering force of a dark dream and with no more confidence for him that it would mean anything to anyone else than the average dream gives a dreamer foolhardy enough to try and relate his dream experience to someone else.[76]

Thematically, the play is certainly a capstone, for it encompasses the themes and ideas of all the other plays. *The Room* showed that the dangers to the self live within. They spring from the violent self who stifles the repressed wishes that try to come to the surface and call man home. In *The Homecoming* those repressed wishes are allowed to surface, and they carry Teddy and Ruth home where each can examine his desires in a well-lighted room. For Ruth physical desire is acknowledged and no longer denied. For Teddy the open-end still applies. Either his fear of man's animal instincts is sustained, resulting in the loss of Ruth; or his ability to face the past banishes his repressions and enables him to win a new relationship with Ruth. *The Birthday Party* presented a sense of evolving births and deaths within the psyche that in *The Homecoming* is enlarged to a cyclical pattern of repetition compulsion within the family.

Stanley gives a picture of man pressed into being what he does not want to be by guilts that accompany hostility toward parents. This is what appears in Lenny and Joey and Max, also; Teddy runs away from it physically, just as Stanley did. However, when he returns home, he discovers the family is still within him. Repetition compulsion either sends him running away again or forces him back into the pattern. *The Dumb Waiter* displays the terror of the terrorists. Gus and Ben, the hired killers, turn out to be small boys waiting fearfully for a punishing father to take them to the bathroom in the night. Max is a terrorist, too. He is a butcher who carries a big stick, but underneath he wishes to be a baby crawling near mother's chair, begging to be fondled and kissed. Thus, the violent ones emerge as frightened children acting out defiance in order to stem the tremors of their misunderstood guilts. The likeness of *The Homecoming* to *A Slight Ache* has already been partially examined. As Edward lost Flora to the Matchseller whom he himself invited in, so Teddy lost Ruth by bringing her home. As the Matchseller took on Edward's longed-for virility, so Lenny and Joey take on Teddy's. Thus, in each case a wife who ached for sexual fulfillment is won from an arid life. At the end of *A Slight Ache* Flora carries the Matchseller off to bed to nurse him to death. At the end of *The Homecoming*, Max and Joey and Lenny have sacrificed their virility for infancy. They have ceased to be conquering males and have been transformed into suppliant babes. Max would appear to be wrong when he says Ruth will turn them all into animals. They themselves relinquish their own bestiality. This idea of sons castrating themselves by submitting to their own wish to be infants is repeated also from *A Night Out*, as is the focus on male ambivalence toward mothers. As Albert returned to the mother whom he had almost killed with an alarm clock, so Max and Lenny and Joey return to a duplicate of the mother they had reviled. Moreover, in both plays mother is perceived alternately as a whore. *The Caretaker*'s ambivalence of sons toward father is seen in the boys' response to Max. Mick and Aston toss Davies out; Lenny and Joey see Max reduced to a sniveling infant, while Teddy removes himself. In both plays no one really wants to be the caretaker; everyone wants to be the care *receiver*. *The Dwarfs* shows the violence man must direct against himself if he would rid himself of his past. It shows the sterility he must live with if he succeeds. Teddy shows the aftermath of this violent purge. The hollowed man comes back seeking a sentimental image of his insides that he can reclaim. From one point of view the original operation was too successful. Teddy is still unable to exist amid the gobbling, spewing, carping dwarfs. From the alternate view, the feminine spirit takes its effect on the hollow man. It brings back to consciousness the repressed feelings and the forgotten selves, and it brings them together again into a new configuration. *Night School, The Collection, The Lover, The Basement,* and *Tea Party* show how people change to suit shifting relationships and altering needs. So does *The Homecoming*. These four short plays explore the ironic fate of the loved wife and her husband whom psychical impotence robs of the desire she craves. This happened to Max and to Teddy. It happens to Joey. Thus, all of the plays make the point that *The Homecoming* stresses: man is incapable of a total escape from his family and the unconscious forces that childhood interaction leaves behind. Everyman is left with the wish to recapture that love and security he first knew at mother's breast. Everyman scratches and rages with every other man for that favored spot. Everyman adjusts and adapts as he jockeys for that special position. Everyman goes willingly to impotence for the pleasure of being mother's Teddy or Joey or ' 'nny. Some, like Teddy, escape physically; but to do so they renounce all physical pleasure. They escape into intellectualism, but perhaps they all cherish a nostalgic wish to return home. Some never give in to this wish; some eventually reconcile the urges of mind and body. For them the wish to have mother is fulfilled.

The alternative endings to some of the determinations of this play show a lack of the thematic synchronization that characterized earlier plays. Perhaps this is the result of a greater use of conscious control in the writing. Pinter's remarks to Richard Bensky indicate a great deal of revision was done on this "dark dream" that came to him "all of a piece":

> That's my main concern, to get the structure right. I always write three drafts, but you have to leave it eventually. There comes a point when you say that's it, I can't do anything more. The only play which gets remotely near to a structural entity which satisfies me is *The Homecoming*. *The Birthday Party* and *The Caretaker* have too much writing. . .I want to iron it down, eliminate things.[77]

The degree of ironing down and eliminating is clearly greater in *The Homecoming* than in the earlier major works. Moreover, *The Homecoming* was written after Pinter's new emphasis on realism and deliberate ambiguity had begun in the series of short plays that precede it. *The Collection* and *The Lover* begin a new emphasis on ambiguity designed to show truth as unknowable. *The Basement* continues this emphasis by making the difference between dream and reality unrecognizable. *Tea Party* continues it by showing the variations in individual perception, and by leaving no clear indication of the degree of distortion in Disson's vision. The audience can not be sure whether Willy and Diana, and eventually Wendy, are conspiring against Disson or not. The lack of thematic consonance in the various determinations of *The Homecoming* carries through on this trend toward heightened ambiguity. Actually this heightening represents a different source of the ambiguity. In earlier plays, ambiguity sprang intuitively from the condensation of the primary process. This heightened ambiguity results from the secondary process, the consciously applied mechanisms.

Nevertheless, this play does represent the most complete fulfillment of the wish to have mother of any play in this third group. By some determinations, all parties in *The Homecoming* achieve this wish fulfillment. By others, only the family succeeds in fulfilling the wish to have mother. Teddy either gains his wish to avoid engulfment, or he loses mother. In the latter case he may be receiving his punishment for having once been the favorite and for having possessed mother in six years of marriage. If so, *The Homecoming* performs double duty as a dream: it completes the wish inherent in the series of dreams begun by *The Collection*, and it provides a transition to the punishment dreams that follow — *Landscape, Silence, Old Times*, and *No Man's Land*.

5

Punishment Dreams: For the Wish To Have Mother

Pinter's four most recent plays — *Landscape, Silence, Old Times,* and *No Man's Land* — form a final group that can be viewed as punishment dreams because in every case the husband figure is bereft of the wife/mother's love; he is always the loser — punished. In *Landscape* Beth sits in the same room with Duff, but her spirit is totally withdrawn from him. She lives in a private world that he can not penetrate. In *Silence* Ellen and Rumsey and Bates all live in separate worlds; Bates has made his bid for Ellen, but he has lost. It is Rumsey whom she chooses in her memories. In *Old Times* Deeley ends where he begins, slumped in a chair to which he has returned from Kate's apparent indifference. In *No Man's Land* the punishment is complete. Hirst is the totally abandoned male. No woman is present. He lives in an alcoholic stupor where hazy memories can dull sharp regrets. Thus, the four plays parallel that grouping relationship of dreams in which each dream explores a different view of the same material. Each play takes a different approach to the causes and effects of a man's loss of a woman's love.

In this sense of exploring the loss of the loved woman, *Landscape, Silence, Old Times,* and *No Man's land* are anticipated by *Tea Party* and *The Homecoming.* Disson's loss is due to his own guilt over his fixation on the incest wish. Teddy's loss is due to his own retreat into intellectualism, his own wish not to be engulfed. In these two plays, however, events are occurring in the here-and-now. Disson and Teddy have Diana and Ruth when the plays begin. During the course of the plays' events, they suffer their losses. In *Landscape, Silence, Old Times,* and *No Man's Land* the losses have already taken place. The events of the plays are a looking back; these are memory plays. In that sense, *The Homecoming* is again a transition piece. It begins the concern with going back in time, returning. However, *The Homecoming* depicts a physical return, on some levels of meaning, at least. *Landscape* and *Silence* are strictly mental returns. *Old Times* provides the intragroup difference. It is both. There is a seeming physical return, a homecoming of sorts, by Anna; but, at the same time, the characters recall and reenact what has already happened. In *No Man's Land* the return is mental again, but remembering has become difficult. Hirst's past is too painful to be revisited and his future is too empty to be met.

Another intergroup difference is in thematic concern. The third group of plays, *The Collection* through *The Homecoming,* emphasizes change. Personalities and relationships are seen to alter and shift in accordance with personal needs and interpersonal stimuli. The plays of this fourth group present the aftermaths of these changes, but again to differing degrees. *Landscape* and *Silence* show people set in static isolation from one another. *Old Times* shows shifting attitudes within the play, changing memories and revelations, but the basic relationship between husband and wife is the same at the end of the play as it was at the start. Deeley and Kate are set in a static alienation just as surely as Beth and Duff, and Ellen, Bates, and Rumsey are. *No Man's Land* shows the ultimate stasis—forgetfulness. Hirst is forgotten by the loved ones who peopled his past, and their faces are beginning to go blank in his memory. The only shifts occur in his confused recognitions of the relative strangers who occupy his present life.

Pinter has also changed his style again. *Landscape* and *Silence* represent a new and totally different style. They are contrapuntal monologues. *Landscape* differs from *Silence* in that in the latter play the characters speak in complete isolation. In *Landscape*, however, only Beth speaks with complete unawareness of Duff. Duff attempts to communicate to Beth. *Old Times* and *No Man's Land* revert to a style more like that of *The Homecoming*, where manifest realism conceals a latent surrealism.

The adhesive, then, that holds these last four plays together is the loss of a woman's love; this is in each case the punishment the husbandly figure suffers. Duff, Bates, Deeley, and Hirst all aspired to the love of a female character, but all have been bereft of this love. Thus, the other two unifying factors are indicated: *have been* points to the focus on memories; *bereft* points to the focus on incompatibility, alienation, and isolation.

LANDSCAPE

The first of this final group is *Landscape*. It was written for the stage, but first produced on radio in 1968. A year later it was performed at the Aldwych Theatre in London on a double bill with *Silence*. Since *Landscape* is in essence a pair of monologues delivered by two characters fixed in chairs, it seems perhaps more suited to radio than the stage. Although, as Simon Trussler points out, "it is helpful. . .to know that the play's only two characters, Beth and Duff, actually *are* sitting together in the same room,"[1] it is even more helpful to *see* them sitting together but forever apart in their landscape of stillness. After the grunting, growling, pawing movement of *The Homecoming*, here is absence of movement. There are no shifts of relationships. All has happened. All is past. Duff and Beth seem rooted in what Samuel Beckett wrote of in *Proust*—"the calamity of yesterday."[2] Exactly what the calamity was is uncertain; nevertheless there was a calamity, for Beth and Duff are completely lost to one another. Duff makes timid efforts to change this, but he seems unable to reach Beth. Each lives in his own private landscape. Arthur Ganz compares their world to T. S. Eliot's *Wasteland* when he describes it as "an icy, protective sterility."[3]

This cold, static atmosphere pervades the old familiar Pinter room—the kitchen. Beth and Duff are the two people in it. She sits in an armchair to the left of a long kitchen table. He sits in a chair to the right of it. As usual the set is realistic. It contains a sink, a stove, a window. No visitors come into this room, however. The third party to this pair of Pinter people enters only in the minds and memories of Beth and Duff. The third party is Mr. Sykes, a figure too shadowy to be likened to any previous Pinter character. His nature is obscured by the unreliability of Beth's memory. Duff supplies the basic facts: Sykes was a man of some wealth and position who once owned this house. Sykes is dead now, and he has willed the house to his former servants—Beth and Duff, a middle-aged couple like Rose and Bert. Duff, though, is older than Beth. He is in his fifties; she is in her late forties. Duff reverses Bert's pattern in another way as well. Bert was the silent one who resisted Rose's attempts to establish communication. Duff tries occasionally to speak to Beth, but Pinter states that she "never looks at Duff, and does not appear to hear his voice." She speaks as though to herself— but aloud. Pinter says Duff "does not appear to hear her voice" either.[4] Duff has the lonely, lost quality that Mr. Kidd had, but he also displays Bert's violence smoldering underneath. He seems, as well, to harbor within him the vulgarity and the animalism of Max and his sons. Beth displays the purity that all her counterparts only pretended to, but Beth's memories reveal that she, too, may have been adulterous, if only in fantasy.

Beth's monologue shows her fixation on a gentle lover in the past. She remembers him in a scene on the beach. He was asleep there. She wandered between the water's edge and the spot where he lay in the dunes. Beth also remembers him watching her arrange flowers; he touched her gently on the back of her neck. On one occasion they stopped in a hotel bar; on another he picked her up in his car and they drove to the sea. She remembers a blue dress she wore. But mostly Beth remembers lying near her lover in the sand on the beach. He was gentle and her true love.

Duff's monologue deals with more recent times. He tells Beth about his walk in yesterday's rain. He took the dog, and they stepped under a tree for shelter. He tells her about stopping at a pub and meeting a rude man who complained about the beer. Duff also sketches the story of their service for Mr. Sykes. Beth was the housekeeper and cook. Duff was the handyman and chauffeur. He recalls driving Mr. Sykes to the city once and being unfaithful to Beth while he was there. He confessed it to her on his return. Beth had been an excellent housekeeper. Mr. Sykes had bought her the blue dress she wore. He had willed them this house. Duff also remembers a time after Mr. Sykes's death when he had raped Beth crudely, either in reality or fantasy. This final memory of rape contrasts with Beth's final memory of gentle love and captures the antithesis of these two characters.

Martin Esslin singles out the major questions that the play leaves unanswered. Who is the man Beth remembers on the beach?[5] Is the man on the beach the same man who watched her arrange the flowers?[6] "How have Beth and Duff come to their present condition of noncommunication?"[7] Of course, manifestly the answers are lost in the confusion of memory where reality and fantasy are as indistinguishable as they were in Law's basement apartment—where truth is as unknowable as it was in Stella's Chelsea flat.

If the memories of these characters are analyzed as dreams, however, some insights into these questions can be gained. Analysis must begin, in this case, with an objective view of Beth and Duff and then move inside their private landscapes—their dream worlds. An objective overview reveals that *Landscape*, like so many of Pinter's other plays, bears a strong resemblance to *A Slight Ache*. Both plays show the longings of two people—the unfulfilled aches. The big difference is that *A Slight Ache* deals with the anxieties attached to present yearnings. *Landscape* deals with the aftermath, the depression that sets in when the time for gaining fulfillment seems passed. Arieti explains: "Contrary to what happens in anxiety, in depression there is no feeling that a dangerous situation is going to occur. The dangerous event has already taken place; the loss has been sustained."[8] Beth and Duff bear this air of depression which signals that expectation and anxiety are over.

Beth's depression resembles the kind that accompanies mourning. She displays many of the mental symptoms that Freud describes in "Mourning and Melancholia": "Loss of interest in the outside world" and "a turning away from any activity that is not connected with thoughts of him."[9] Beth's mental retreat exemplifies this turning away and loss of interest. Duff's occasional entreaties demonstrate that her retreat is complete and of some duration. He seems to advise her: "You should have a walk with me one day down to the pond, bring some bread. There's nothing to stop you" (p. 12). Later, he suggests she go out to sit in the garden some day. Obviously, Beth has not ventured even that far in a long while because he explains that he has "put in some flowers" (p. 16). Duff also reveals her loss of interest in people when he adds: "No one would see you. There's no one there" (p. 16). Duff has thought of "inviting one or two people" he knows to come to the house "for a bit of a drink once or twice," but he has always "decided against it" (p. 17). Clearly Beth sits every day in the house and loses herself in thoughts of her gentle love. Her total absence of response to Duff shows another symptom Freud names: "Loss of capacity to adopt any new object of love (which would mean replacing him)."[10] Beth even shows the "numbness," the lack of "muscular tone," and the "paresthesias of the skin" that Arieti mentions as physical signs of depression.[11] Beth was once a busy housekeeper. When she went to the beach with her lover, she carried a bag of food all of which she had cooked herself. Even the bread, she had baked. When Mr. Sykes gave a Friday-night dinner party, Beth worked until she was out on her feet; Duff had not helped with the late coffee because he was already too tired. Now, Beth only sits. Her alertness, her readiness are gone. Pinter says that these characters *are relaxed, in no sense rigid*" (p. 7). Beth occasionally remembers that her skin "was stinging" (p. 14); this could well be a displacement of present paresthesias to past memories, especially if the numbness now robs her of all other physical sensation.

Beth's correspondence to Freud's and Arieti's descriptions of mourning goes beyond these external symptoms. Freud says that the mourner's "turning away from reality" is accompanied by "a clinging to the object through the medium of a hallucinatory wishful psychosis."[12] Beth's pictorial memories have this quality of wish-fulfilling visions. Arieti's explanations make this behavior clearer and still more appropriate to Beth. He says that the survivor tries to remove his unacceptable sadness by regrouping his thoughts into different constellations. These rearrangements can take different forms, according to a person's mental predisposition. One form is to "associate the image of the dead person mainly with the qualities of that person which elicited pleasure, so that the image no longer brings mental pain."[13] Beth remembers gentleness. Whoever the man she mourns may be, she remembers him as gentle: he put his arm around her and "cuddled" her (pp. 20-21); his touch was tender on her neck, and his kiss was soft on her cheek (p. 29). Arieti later explains that in "periods of greatly diminished attention" (depression fits this category), conscious thinking is "arrested at a paleologic level."[14] The paleologic that Arieti refers to is that mode of thinking which, developmentally, precedes logic—primary process thinking. It occurs in mental illness and creativity, as well as in dreams. Beth's memories, then, are the product of the same mechanisms that operate in dreams. It will be remembered that one of these mechanisms is condensation, which groups basically dissimilar images according to some one similar characteristic. Beth has chosen gentleness as the organizing image. Therefore, in her mind a variety of different memories are condensed under the image of gentleness. Syke's gentleness, Duff's gentleness, her own gentleness, anybody's gentleness—all become one montage. Thus, dream dynamics provide one explanation for the ambiguity of the identity of Beth's gentle lover; he can very well be *both* Duff and Sykes.

Freud also provides evidence that Beth's mourning probably is for Sykes, whom she had taken for her lover in fantasy:

> The practicing psychoanalytic physician knows how frequently, or how invariably, a girl who enters a household as servant, companion, or governess, will consciously or unconsciously weave a daydream, which derives from the oedipus complex, of the mistress of the house disappearing and the master taking the newcomer as his wife in her place.[15]

If, as in Beth's case, the master of the house were unmarried, he could even more readily become the object of her oedipal fantasies. Beth's memories of Sykes as a gentle lover could, then, be only fancies. As such they need not be any less real to Beth. Freud says:

> Let us be clear that the hallucinatory wishful psychosis—in dreams or elsewhere—achieves two by no means identical results. It not only brings hidden or repressed wishes into consciousness, [but] it also represents them, with the subject's entire belief, as fulfilled.[16]

If Beth is experiencing "hallucinatory wishful psychosis," then these are repressed wishes coming to the surface and being represented as fulfilled. This condition would indicate that no real sexual relationship need have existed between Mr. Sykes and Beth. Nevertheless, Beth entertained fantasies so real to her that she felt she had lost her lover when Sykes died.

Freud also explains that repressed libido frequently gives rise to narcissism:

> When libido is repressed, the erotic cathexis is felt as a severe depletion of the ego, the satisfaction of love is impossible, and the reenrichment of the ego can be effected only by a withdrawal of libido from its objects. The return of the object libido to the ego and its transformation into narcissism represents as it were, a happy love once more. . . .[17]

Beth's fantasies are laced with narcissism. She frequently speaks of her own beauty, and she displays autoerotism in the images of her naked body, which she feels beneath her robe. Moving now into the latent content of Beth's memory/dreams, the flower-arranging scene is also a displacement of her own autoerotism. Freud tells of a dream in which a young lady arranged the center of a table with flowers for a birthday: "The table with its floral centerpiece symbolized herself and her genitals."[18] Later, Freud comments on the girl's use of the phrase "I arrange" in reference to the flowers: "In a deeper layer of the dream, the phrase 'I arrange' . . . must no doubt have an autoerotic, that is to say, an infantile, significance."[19] When Beth speaks of watering and arranging flowers in a bowl, the same autoerotism is apparent. On another occasion, Beth explains herself in these words: "My hands touching my flowers, that is my meaning" (p. 24). Still another sign of narcissism is the presence of a watcher at each of Beth's beach fantasies. Freud says that a "subject's narcissism makes its appearance displaced onto . . . [a] new ideal ego, which, like the infantile ego, finds itself possessed of every perfection that is of value."[20] He explains that there is a special psychical agency that constantly watches the ego to ensure narcissistic satisfaction from the ego ideal. "Recognition of this agency enables us to understand the so-called delusions of being noticed or more correctly, of being watched. . . ."[21] Beth's memories frequently include people staring at her—women passing by, a man in the distance sitting on the breakwater. A breakwater is a structure to break the force of the waves. A man sitting atop it, then, becomes a concretization of this superego structure that guards against Beth's becoming overwhelmed by the tide of her sexual impulses. In other words, it preserves her repression as it ensures her narcissistic satisfaction.

Freud sees the role of such narcissists to be receivers of love rather than givers of it.[22] All of Beth's fantasies focus upon the gentleness she receives. She even recalls receiving gentleness from the surrounding scene; in the sea the water billowed gently around her. Physical contact with her lover has more the character of infantile snuggling for comfort's sake. He cuddles her in his arms. She buries her head in his side. There is never any real adult, heterosexual contact in which she gives love. She watches him sleep; she sees only his eyelids, his belly button. He watches her arrange flowers; he touches only the back of her neck.

Finally, there is Beth's one seemingly nonegocentric desire—the desire for a baby. This is also narcissistic; Freud says:

> Parental love, which is so moving and at bottom so childish, is nothing but the parents' narcissism born again, which, transformed into object-love, unmistakably reveals its former nature.[23]

Beth then is lost to love because her repressions have led to narcissism. She is incapable of loving or being loved. She has shut out the husband who half-heartedly calls to her, and she has fixed herself upon fantasies of narcissistic satisfaction.

Duff, too, shows signs of depression, though not as severe as Beth's. His activity is less. He is no longer the busy man of all work. He brings no one to the house. He goes to the park alone, except for his dog. Lidz seems to be describing Duff:

> Depressive states may be due to loss of love of the self or of self-esteem, or to resentment toward a loved person. Such states relate to the feelings of the small child when deprived of the mother.[24]

Duff shows this sense of deprivation by frequently returning to the pond—symbol of uterine waters. Moreover, he identifies with the traditionally deprived sparrows: he would have fed them in preference to the ducks. His only companion is the faithful dog, and soon even the dog disappears. In the scene by the pond, Duff steps under the trees to avoid the rain, symbol of fertility: he wants no babies, he wants to be one. On the other side of the pond, he sees a man and woman: a mother and father image watch over him.

In Duff's loneliness he goes to the pub where his need

to boast of his prowess as a cellarman testifies to his low self-esteem: "He didn't know I'd been trained as a cellarman. That's why I could speak with authority" (p. 25). As he elaborates on the duties of the cellarman, he discloses his tendency to compensatory sexual fantasies by the double entendre of his imagery: "Spile the bung. Hammer the spile through the center of the bung" (p. 25). This same defense against inadequacy is also obvious in his fantasy of raping Beth. He would have had her "like a man" (p. 29), he says, as though ordinarily he is unable to have her like a man. Duff, like Richard and the others, is apparently a victim of psychical impotence. Because of an "incestuous fixation on mother and sister," Freud says, these men can only love debased women.[25] Duff had found just such a sexual partner on his trip to the city with Sykes. His words to Beth reveal the girl's inferiority in his eyes: "The girl herself I considered unimportant" (p. 22). Such men as Duff reserve their tenderness for the women they associate with mothers or sisters — in Freud's words: "The overvaluation that normally attaches to the sexual object being reserved for the incestuous object and its representations."[26] These insights would indicate that the tenderness Beth recalls is more likely to have come from Duff. Pinter's letter to the director of the first German production of *Landscape* confirms this interpretation. He wrote:

> The man on the beach is Duff. I think there are elements of Mr. Sykes in her memory of this Duff, which she might be attributing to Duff, but the man remains Duff. I think that Duff detests and is jealous of Mr. Sykes, although I do not believe that Mr. Sykes and Beth were ever lovers.[27]

Duff has been the gentle, untouching lover. The coarse exterior he shows to the world is his defense by reversal. Like Max and his sons, Duff hides his sensitivity behind animalism. Beth's withdrawal blocks out this coarse, everyday veneer of

Duff's; and, ironically, in dreams she transfers Duff's tenderness to Sykes.

Duff is also a victim of oedipal and oral fantasies. His concern with "shit" and "bung-holes" and "banging" represents his anality and his perverse sexual aims overlapping and finding fulfillment in his language. The fulfillment he longs for—to have mother—is forever lost to him by the caprice of his own psyche and Beth's.

The play presents a picture of present loneliness and past longings. Two unfulfilled souls live out their emptiness— together but isolated. Their only solace is to long for the love and security they once had at birth. Pinter indicates this regression at the start of the play. The first memories each partner has are of scenes by water. Beth is by the sea. Duff is by the pond. In fact, the very structure of this play shows regression. Lidz says:

> If we listen to children conversing when they are sitting together idly, or when they are engaged in some sedentary activity, we find that although the talk has the form of conversation, it is very likely to be a dual or collective monologue. One child says something to the other and waits for a reply, then the other child speaks but what he says has no connection with what the first child said, and so they continue, each voicing his own preoccupations or fantasies in turn.[28]

The whole play becomes a concretization of alienation and incompatibility highlighted by each character's final memory images—his of debasement and hers of gentleness. This contrast is also implicit in the title of the play; *Landscape* condenses the principal images the play creates. First, of course, it indicates the landscape provided by the play on stage: two alienated people, together in the intimacy of the kitchen, but isolated from one another by the long kitchen table between them. Each one keeps close to one end of this table—

symbol of the nourishing woman, mother. He clings to mother in his psychical impotence; she clings to mother in her infantile narcissism. Thus, it is this mother symbol, the table, that separates them emotionally as well as physically. Next, the title indicates the contrasting memory landscapes described by Beth and Duff. She describes bright, sunlit, sandy beaches by the sea. He describes a pond, trees, rain, shit. Psychologically, their landscapes are equally different. She clings to purity, cleanliness, gentleness — all reaction formations against the dirt and sexuality she fears. He defends against incest and impotence by sexual perversity and masculine vulgarity. Of course, in dream symbolism landscapes also represent the human body. Freud says: "We have earlier referred to landscapes as representing the female genitals. Hills and rocks are symbols of the male organ. Gardens are common symbols of the female genitals."[29] In the earlier reference Freud speaks of he states:

> The pubic hair of both sexes is depicted in dreams as woods and bushes. The complicated topography of the female genital parts make one understand how it is that they are often represented as *landscapes*, with rocks, woods, and water. . . .[30]

Thus, the landscape each character describes is also representative of the body of the opposite sex. She speaks of dunes that are sand hills — symbolic of the male body. She runs from these; they are hot. She loved it better by the shore — symbol of birth. There it was "so fresh" (p. 9). His scene has trees and a pond. He walks in a park; he speaks of the garden. These all suggest female-body symbols, but this landscape has "shit all over the place, all along the paths, by the pond. Dogshit, duckshit,. . . all kinds of shit . . . all over the paths" (p. 12). Each one in these landscapes reveals his sexual attitudes and hang-ups. She fears sex — runs away.

He needs to debase his female object. This montage of images condensed in the title parallels the overdetermination of the play.

Thematically, *Landscape's* realistic reading reasserts the unknowability of truth. It says that memory is just as confused as conscious reality. Through dream analysis, the play says man's ignorance of himself and others is just as great in hindsight as it was in foresight. Beth and Duff have lived together for an adult lifetime, but neither understands his own needs or his partner's needs. He boasts vulgarly to prove his manhood to her who wants only his gentleness. She takes his gentleness for granted and displaces it onto a master. By these ironies man alienates himself from the love and security he thinks he seeks. He thinks he seeks sexual fulfillment, but at bottom he longs to be fondled at mother's breast. It is this longing that lies behind the wish to have mother for which man is continually punishing himself. The longing and the punishment begin with repression. Repression leads to psychical impotence for the male and narcissism for the female. Consequently, neither can give to the other the love that is needed. The result is a misbegotten alliance of misplaced love that ends in alienation and depression.

SILENCE

Silence, the partner of *Landscape*, is also a retrospective view of misplaced love. Perhaps it is a more complex view; it flashes back and forth among more stops along the path to present loneliness. *Landscape* presents Beth and Duff as middle-aged people whose memories take them back to one certain time span when their adult lives were intermixed with Mr. Sykes. *Silence* presents three people at various stages of life. Ellen is in her twenties, Bates is in his thirties, and Rumsey is in his forties. Then time seems to move both forward and backward—forward to old age and backward to youth again. Arthur Ganz suggests that "the ages designated by the stage directions and embodied in the actors are only those at which the decisive choices in their relationships are made."[31] Ganz is probably right. Perhaps Pinter means to suggest that in their memories they remain this age forever. Ellen says: "Am I old now? No one will tell me."[32] The greater complexity of this play results from more than just time, however. Pinter seems to be attempting a more multi-faceted account than *Landscape* gives of how people arrive at such isolation, such silence. Simon Trussler provides a descrip-tion of John Bury's set for the original production that defines this greater complexity better than any other words could. Trussler says that Bury's set, "an elaborate confusion of mirrors at once multiplying angles of vision and entrapping the reflected images in a maze of memory, could scarcely have been more exact or appropriate."[33] What emerges from this elaborate confusion of mirrors is that Bates wants Ellen, Ellen wants Rumsey, and Rumsey wants his freedom—mis-placed loves.

This similarity, however, is only the beginning of the partnership between *Landscape* and *Silence*. *Silence* was first produced in July 1969, by the Royal Shakespeare Company at the Aldwych Theatre in London. It was on a double bill with *Landscape*. In 1970 the two plays were published in one book by Grove Press. Moving to more important factors, they share the same style; both are contrapuntal monologues. *Silence*, however, presents the thoughts of three characters instead of the two in *Landscape*. There is also the difference that in *Silence* the characters do on occasion engage in dialogue. There are two such scenes. Once Bates moves to Ellen and they converse. Second, Ellen moves to Rumsey and they converse. Later a bit of this last dialogue is echoed. Beyond these brief exchanges, the characters are locked in separate mental worlds. To borrow the words of James Hollis, "Each seems caught in the prison of himself, in the strictures of an unrelieved past."[34]

Like *Landscape*, the characters of *Silence* receive visitors only in memory. However, each character lives in a separate room. The room must be his own mind. Pinter's description of the setting says simply: "Three areas. A chair in each area" (31). The monologues make clear that no two of these characters finally live together. They have visited one another in the past, but eventually each is alone. The characters are very like those in *Landscape*, looked at from a different angle of time and vision. Ellen is a girl of clean, pure images. Bates is a man of earthy, vulgar images. Rumsey is a man of property. These three figures are also reminiscent of the girl and two men in *The Basement*. Rumsey, like Law at the outset, has a comfortable house and solitude. Bates, like Stott, stands with his girl outdoors in the cold and rain. Law sitting by his fire might easily be Rumsey in his chosen solitude dreaming of a second chance to win Ellen/Jane from the younger man he sent her to.

This play, again like *Landscape* and *The Basement*, flashes back and forth among mental images. Whereas in *The Basement* these images are pictured on film, in *Silence* they are pictured in words, as they are also in *Landscape*. The chronology seems more disjointed in *Silence* than in either of the other two plays. Simon Trussler says: "Each character is living his or her whole life instantaneously, so that whether any particular experience belongs to childhood, youth or middle-age is often difficult to determine."[35] However, if the fragments are pieced together and rearranged, a story does emerge. Ellen was a young girl caught between the affections of two men. She used to visit the older man, Rumsey, in his house. They also walked together. She visited the younger man, Bates, in the fields. Ellen had a vague preference for Rumsey, one that she could not define. When Bates asked her what she wanted to do, she could only answer: "I don't know" (p. 38). When he invited her to go to town to his cousin's place, she refused. It was Rumsey who really made the choice. He insisted that Ellen find a younger man. Apparently, after this rejection Ellen did go to town with Bates. Perhaps they got married. She claims to remember the wedding. But perhaps this memory is confused like the rest. If Bates's memory is reliable, they did go to his cousin's place, and there they made love. Married or not, they separated sooner or later because in old age they both live in town, but apart. Bates is in a noisy rooming house. Ellen has a city job, walks home through crowded streets, drinks at night with old women. Rumsey stayed in the country where he cares for his animals. Now all remember the past. Bates remembers taking the bus to town with Ellen. Rumsey remembers walking with Ellen, she in her grey blouse. Ellen remembers her two lovers. She remembers colliding with the wind. She remembers her lovers waiting; she remembers kissing them and seeing the last of the lights. Her last words are: "Certainly, I can remember the wedding" (p. 52). Each is alone in the silence with his memories. Martin Esslin suggests that *Silence* resembles "Beckett's *Play*, where the device of repeated fragments of speech running down" indicates those "last moments of awareness" before death. But, he offers an alternative interpretation also: "As we age, our awareness of the past dims and runs down—and the rest is silence."[36] The play also resembles Beckett's *Krapp's Last Tape*. Ellen, Rumsey, and Bates all cling to the memory of a moment that represents lost love just as Krapp plays and replays "spool five" from "box three" to relive that one moment when he drifted among the flags with his lover.[37] That is the only certainty in *Silence*. The details of memory are vague, fragmentary, and inconclusive. But each one clings to the memory of that moment of splendor before love was lost.

The present silence of this play, then, is one in which the three characters are separated from one another by space and time. They are isolated and alienated, living in a world of memory. In the past time of their memories, they lived in a different silence—one in which they spoke but did not hear. They remember not hearing; Rumsey and Bates speak of it in succession. Rumsey says: "She was looking down. I couldn't hear what she said." Then Bates says: "I can't hear you. Yes you can, I said." Then Rumsey speaks again. At first he acknowledges his own deafness. The second time he recalls hers: "What are you saying? Look at me, she said" (p. 43). Bates's next speech follows the same pattern. As he first commented on his not hearing, his second speech points up hers: "I didn't. I didn't hear you; she said. I didn't hear what you said" (p. 44). In their present silence, Ellen, Bates, and Rumsey are caught between that past silence and the future silence that Esslin speaks of—death or the running down of awareness. If this play is to be approached as a dream, it must be through that present silence before awareness is cut off but after events have turned into the uncertainties of memory. Ellen describes her own arrest in this state of time:

> After my work each day I walk back through people but I don't notice them. I'm not in a dream or anything of that sort. On the contrary. I'm quite wide awake to the world around me. But not to the people. . . .It is only later, in my room, that I remember. Yes, I remember. But I'm never sure that what I remember is of today or of yesterday or of a long time ago. And then often it is only half things I remember, half things, beginnings of things. (p. 46)

These memories—they are the dreams, and the images in

each character's private dreams are the key to a fuller interpretation of the play.

Ellen is the fulcrum around whom the dreams turn. Her
present is dark and quiet: "Around me sits the night. Such
a silence" (p. 43). She reiterates her splendid past in one
simple sentence: "There are two" (p. 33). In contrast to her
present loneliness, two men loved her in her remembered past.
There was contact. She spoke to them, looked at them, kissed
them, smiled, and touched them as she turned. She knew them
from girlhood. She was the innocent country lass, a milkmaid
who carried the milk to the top of the hill. The milkmaid's sex
life was fantasized. She ran to the top of the hill—symbol of
the male body. She collided with the wind—the high, un-
predictable feelings that threatened to envelop her. Her sex
life was also autoerotic. Thus, another interpretation can be
added to Ellen's oft-repeated memory of colliding with the
wind. Freud explains that "sexual excitation" or "pleasurable
sensation" provide the reason that children enjoy being thrown
into the air. In a footnote he adds that "some people can
remember that in swinging they felt the impact of moving air
upon their genitals as an immediate sexual pleasure."[38] Ellen
also ran over the grass, and she turned, wheeled, and glided.
"Symbolic representation *par excellence* of masturbation,"
Freud says, "are *gliding* or *sliding*. . . ."[39] The milkmaid's
autoerotism indicates her wish to remain a child, and her
behavior confirms this wish. One man, Bates, clasped her; the
other man, Rumsey, sat her on his knee. She refused to go
away with Bates, and she resisted Rumsey's attempt to send
her off to a younger man. She did not want a younger man.
She preferred the fatherly Rumsey. "I don't like them," she
said, when he ordered her: "Find a young man." "I hate
them," she insisted (p. 44). Even in her dark present, she
clings to dependency and infantilism. She seems lost and calling for help:

Am I silent or speaking? How can I know? Can I know such
things? No one has ever told me. I need to be told things. I seem
to be old. Am I old now? No one will tell me. I must find a
person to tell me these things. (p. 43)

When Rumsey sent her away, she went to the city with Bates.
She may have married him. But like Beth, she feared the
reality of sex. With her young lover, she had passed the dogs
of passion by; she had gone by herself to the top where the
clouds raced. Once in the city, it was no different. Her repression did not lift; her narcissism deepened. Finally, the lights
of passion and the symbolic male body, the hills, are distant
and dim: "A long way a long way a long way over the hills I
can see lights far far away" (p. 45). Her outer self conceals
her dreams: "Nobody could tell, from looking at me, what was
happening" (p. 36). More and more she has withdrawn into
herself. She has become only truly interested in herself and her
dreams. When she walks home from her job, she does not
see the people around her: "I'm quite wide awake to the world
around me. But not to the people" (p. 6). It is only later
in her room that she remembers and comes alive in her
fantasies. She goes out drinking occasionally with an old
woman companion, but Ellen has nothing to tell her. "She
does the talking anyway," Ellen explains. "I like to get back
to my room. It has a pleasant view" (p. 37). Ellen withdraws
into herself and her pleasant view of the past where "there
are two." When they were part of her reality, she did not know
what she wanted. "I want to go somewhere else," she told
Bates. When he asked her where, she said, "I don't know"
(p. 38). Now she hurries home to enjoy them as her repression
always demanded, in narcissistic fantasy. But even there her
passions dim: "As my eyes close I see last of lights" (p. 52).

The memory Rumsey clings to in his present silence is a
walk with his girl. Rumsey's dream shows repression, too. His
girl dresses in grey to please him. He prefers colorlessness,

absence of passion. Rumsey is the lover who walks past the dogs. They walk when the clouds "are racing just before dark or as dark is falling . . ." (p. 33). Dark is the absence of that light which is identified with erotic feelings. It is the light that crushes Ellen. But Ellen and Rumsey "walk through the hills" just before dark when age is dimming passion. Even in fantasy, Rumsey defends against sexuality. He says when he is ready to walk: "Her arm in me her hand in me" (p. 33). Thus, he disguises sexuality by displacement and reversal— displacement to other extremities, arm and hand; reversal of functions—she is inside him instead of his being inside her. Freud maintains that such reversals are quite common in dreams: "We find in dreams reversals of situation, of the relation between two people—a 'topsy-turvy' world. Quite often in dreams it is the hare that shoots the sportsman."[40] Clearly, Rumsey's defense against sexuality, his passionlessness, springs from more than just increasing age. It goes back to his unconscious childhood memories. Rumsey identifies females and passion with fearful primal-scene memories. Ellen's grey clothes are reminders of mother's nightclothes. Darkness, vague movements, shifting shapes are all present in his dream images. Clouds race, dark falls, her hand slips. Later Rumsey identifies the topography of Ellen's female body as "the same": "That the house which grew nearer is the same one she stands in, that the path and the bushes are the same, that the gate is the same" (p. 34). The same "house" can only mean mother. Ellen's body is the same as mother's. When Ellen comes to him, he asks her to cook for him. Rumsey sees and wants mother when he sees and wants Ellen. Moreover, Ellen was once a little girl he knew. Therefore, she has other incestuous identifications, also—daughter, sister. Rumsey's dread of these incestuous feelings has caused him to repress his erotism. He only talks to Ellen: "I tell her my thoughts" (p. 33). Finally, he sends her away to find a younger man. When he does, he tells himself he has lost nothing. His animals are quiet; his passions are stilled. Nothing is now required of him; he who wants mother need not himself become a caretaker. He is not even sure that his horses really need him. And he still has his fantasies. But now that her presence is removed, his fantasies are less threatening. Now he can dream: "She floats . . . under me. Floating . . . under me" (p. 40). But his dreams still occasion primal-scene memories, for immediately he recalls seeing shapes, people, in vague, shifting movements:

> Sometimes I see people. They walk towards me, no, not so, walk in my direction, but never reaching me, turning left, or disappearing, and then reappearing, to disappear into the woods. (p. 40).

Sexual fantasies are still accompanied by oedipal guilt. This is why Rumsey had to send Ellen away. Ironically, however, his repression and his overvaluation of Ellen had been responsible for her preference. He did not threaten her with fears of engulfment in passion. This is why she did not want a younger man. With Rumsey she was safe from adulthood; she could continue her defensive retreat into narcissistic infantilism. But in the aftermath, he, like her, remembers; he remembers that one splendid moment before love was lost, before the "folding" of the light, when: "I walk with my girl who wears a grey blouse" (p. 52).

Bates's first and last words in the play are: "Caught a bus to the town. Crowds. Lights around the market" (pp. 34, 52). This, then, is the moment he clings to, the moment when he took Ellen to town on the bus. When they arrived, he "Brought her into this place, my cousin runs it. Undressed her, placed my hand" (p. 34). But Bates's memory images are like Duff's—dirty and coarse. At the lighted market, there was rain and stink. Lights were bumping. He took Ellen to the dumps. "This way the way I bring you" (p. 34), he says. Clearly, he needs to debase her to satisfy his desire. On another occasion, he waits for her "in the pissing dark" p. 34). There is "mud"; there are "cows" and a "river." Ellen comes across the "field out of darkness" (p. 35). The cows represent the nurturing mother; the river is the birth waters. The elements of debasement are the "pissing dark" and the mud. Bates somehow knows this dark side of his nature would not flourish long with this mother figure, Ellen. He speaks of the shadow she sees as a big bird coming to rest in a tree. The shadow, or shape as he calls it, has primal-scene connotations. As such it represents his oedipal guilts that would repress his birdlike passion that flys "up and down in the wind" (p. 40). Once it came to rest on a tree, a female symbol, his passion would die. The tree, Ellen, would meld with memories of mother, and incestuous feelings would deprive Bates of desire. Ironically, then, Bates, whom Ellen rejected, would have allowed her to be the little girl she yearned to return to. Ellen saw only the debasing passion, however. In the town, with the barking cars and the lights, she "clutched" Bates. Clutching suggests her fear and discomfort. When Bates kissed her, he pressed the smile off her face. Ellen probably ran from this harsh passion, leaving Bates alone. Now in his present silence, Bates is an old crank. The young people call him "Grandad." He complains about their racket. He can not sleep at night. The landlady calls him grumpy and asks: "Surely you have smiled, at a thing in your life? At something? Has there been no pleasantness in your life? No kind of loveliness in your life?" (p. 43). He answers: "I've had all that. I've got all that. I said" (p. 43). And he repeats it later to convince himself. But his projections deny his insistence. When he hears the noisy young men in the next room, he envisions them with "their tittering bitches, and their music, and their love" (p. 36). When the young people are silent, he imagines:

"Sleep? Tender love?" (p. 45). Then he protests again: "It's of no importance" (p. 45). But his protest is false and hollow. Bates is the real loser in this trio of silent estranged dreamers. The other two are somewhat content. Rumsey chose his solitude and freedom from responsibility. Ellen goes nightly to her dreams as a welcome escape from people. Bates however, feels frustrated, hemmed in. He "can't get out of the walls, into a wind" (p. 39). When he presses his forehead, draining out the dust and bringing a calm moment, it is funny: "Funny moment. That calm moment" (p. 41). Calm is such a rarity for Bates that when it comes it is funny, strange. He feels lost and uncertain. "What can be meant by living in the dark?" (p. 36), he asks. Thus, he speaks his discontent with his dark, passionless life in the silence. And like the others he calls to mind his one splendid moment: "Caught a bus to the town. Crowds. Lights around the market." Then the stage directions read: *"Long silence. Fade lights"* (p. 52).

When the lights have dimmed, the silence persists and calls up the afterimage of three separate souls, lost to loves that were ironically misplaced. The silence that surrounds them has the depth of three dimensions in time—past, present, future. But each character has his own personal silence as well. Ellen's is a kind of emotional paralysis. She does not know or think: "I sometimes wonder if I think" (p. 36). She does not grow or live with reality: "Am I old now? No one will tell me" (p. 43). She passes through people "noticing nothing" (p. 46). She lives in a time capsule inside her memory where she can hear her own heart beat: "Such a silence. Is it me? Am I silent or speaking?" (p. 43). Rumsey's silence comes from an inner satisfaction with his unthreatening, undemanding world. "Pleasant alone and watch the folding light. My animals are quiet. My heart never bangs" (p. 35), he says. He no longer needs to fear his passions; they are stilled. He spends his evenings quietly reading. Nothing is required of him. Bates's silence is an unwelcome one—outside himself, a silence from absence of love and companionship. His landlady asks: "Why do you live alone? . . . What do you do with yourself? . . . Are you nothing but a childish old man, suffocating himself?" (p. 43). His silence contrasts with the noise of his young neighbors: "I'm at my last gasp with this unendurable racket" (p. 35). All three of these characters, separately and together, are entombed in that silence which Holland says is a defense against primal-scene fantasies. All three cling to silent memories because old, childhood guilts made them afraid of the loving relationships they remember as so splendid. The play seems to say that the anxieties and fixations of childhood motivate the adult choices that dictate the patterns of men's lives. As a result of these choices, people must endure in loneliness, and they understand this final isolation no more than they understand the original choices. They latch onto the memory of pleasant moments with which they block out the dark realities. Soon fantasy and memory become one in the stillness and the silence.

OLD TIMES

Old Times combines with Landscape and Silence to make one of the closest-knit threesomes in Pinter's repertory. Despite the two-year lapse between their stage debuts (Old Times was first produced at the Aldwych in 1971, while Landscape and Silence had appeared in 1969), these plays cling to the same themes and very similar characters. Old Times is true to its group relationship in that it continues to examine lost or misplaced loves, misbegotten alliances. In Landscape Duff loves Beth while Beth loves a phantom of memory and dream—Sykes, Duff, and an ideal lover all rolled into one. In Silence Bates loves Ellen, and Ellen loves Rumsey whom she fantasizes as a father image. Rumsey loves Ellen but, like Beth and Ellen, he prefers the dream of love to the reality of it. In *Old Times* Deeley loves Kate, Anna seems to love both Deeley and Kate, but Kate loves only herself. Such a brief statement of these misplaced loves, however, runs the risk of oversimplification. The feelings and the relationships of these plays are both nebulous and complex because they spring out of unconscious desires and guilts and are overlaid with blends of memory and fantasy. In *Landscape* Beth is in sight of Duff but out of his reach as she blends all the gentle moments of two men and her fantasies about them into one dream. In *Silence* Ellen, Bates, and Rumsey are forever apart as they dream. Moreover, Ellen keeps her memories of the two men somewhat distinct, but events and occasions mix and shift with need and desire. The men, too, cling to memories and attitudes that satisfy the moment. In *Old Times* three characters are together again. Nevertheless, each stirs up his own blend of memory and seemingly deliberate fantasy, and each of these mixtures is thrown into a "casserole" with each of the others. The result is a concoction that can never be precisely defined.

The characters of *Old Times* are quite clear, however. Kate seems cut from the same cloth as Beth and Ellen. All are self-contained, narcissistic dreamers. Deeley has the coarseness of Bates and Duff, but it is covered over with a refined veneer like Edward's. He also resembles Lenny in his relish of verbal combat. Anna opposes Kate's passivity with the same restlessness that Bates provided in contrast to Ellen. Anna also opposes Deeley with the same strength and will to power that Ruth employed against Lenny.

The basic Pinter situation is more explicitly recognizable in *Old Times* than in *Landscape* and *Silence*. The play begins with two people in one room; they receive a visitor who is physically present—whatever she may represent. Indeed, as Arthur Ganz points out, the "basic dramatic situation recalls that of *The Room*."[41]Deeley and Kate live in silence like Bert and Rose. Deeley, however, is the talker like Rose, and Kate is silent like Bert. Both men leave home for business trips. Deeley claims to jaunt around the globe, and Bert runs across town in his van. Both women are visited by a specter from the past who seems to call them back to "old times." Within that basic pattern the plays run their differing courses — again a tribute to Pinter's ingenuity and development.

Old Times begins with a dim, silent tableau. Anna's figure is in the background; she looks out a window. Deeley is slumped in an armchair. Kate is curled on one of the two sofas that grace the living room of their converted farmhouse. The lights come up on Kate and Deeley while he questions her, somewhat anxiously, about Anna, whom they expect for a visit. She and Kate were roommates twenty years ago. Deeley's questions reveal he is threatened by Anna's return. When Anna moves into the scene, she paints a picture of a happy, busy city life the two girls led together, which contrasts with the quiet country life Kate and Deeley lead. Deeley seems to be fighting back when he describes meeting Kate at a movie, *Odd Man Out*, where two lesbian usherettes caught his notice. Anna retaliates with a story about a man who visited Kate in their apartment one night. He had been sobbing in the armchair. He approached both girls' beds; Anna would have nothing to do with him; Kate let him lie across her lap until he withdrew to the armchair, sobbing again. Deeley tells the next tale. He paints himself as a world traveler, knowledgeable about the idle, corrupt life in Sicily where Anna lives. In one breath he indicates he is a pimp, dealing always in prostitutes. In the next breath, he calls himself Orson Welles. He seems to imply disbelief in Anna's story of her life in a Sicilian villa. Next Anna and Kate are oblivious to Deeley as they seem to relive the days when they were together and Anna made all of Kate's decisions and catered to all of her wishes. The first act ends as Kate retires for her nightly bath.

Act two takes place in the bedroom where "the divans and armchair are disposed in precisely the same relation to each other as the furniture in the first act, but in reversed positions."[42] A faint glow comes from the bathroom door to indicate Kate's presence inside. Deeley still seems to spar with Anna. He remembers seeing her at the Wayfarers Tavern. He sat and stared up her dress. She allowed it. Then they discuss Kate's sensuous baths, and Anna suggests Deeley dry Kate himself. Deeley counters by suggesting that he powder Kate while Anna watches. When Kate emerges from the bath, she and Anna seem once more to return to their former life when Anna invited men, of Kate's choosing, to visit them. Kate chose them for their gentleness and their humor. When Deeley reenters the conversation, it returns to a sparring match which ends in Kate's revelation that Anna had once been in love with Deeley. Then Kate takes over the conversation as she recalls Anna's symbolic death, initiated by Kate's plastering her face with dirt. Anna's corpse was conveniently gone when Kate brought Deeley into the room. His male presence was a relief to Kate until he expected her "to be sexually forthcoming" (p. 73). Then she tried to plaster his face with dirt, but he resisted. He suggested marriage instead. At about that time, Deeley asked Kate who had slept in the other bed before he had. Kate replied: "No one at all." Those are the last words spoken. Silence falls. Deeley begins to sob. Then he goes to Anna's divan, turns away, moves to the door, turns and approaches Kate's divan, lies across her lap. Then after a long silence, he goes to his armchair and slumps there as at the beginning of the play. The lights come up to very bright revealing Deeley in his chair, Anna lying on a divan, and Kate sitting on the other divan.

In this realistic account of events, the play emerges as an enigma reminiscent of *The Collection*. There seems to be the same mixture of homosexual and heterosexual relationships, the same mixture of fantasies and lies about past events, the same jealous combat over a sexual partner, and the same unknowability of the truth. The play raises many questions in the spectator's mind. Simon Trussler puts into words the principal ones:

> Did Deeley really desire Anna as well as Kate? Did Anna desire Kate in her own deceptively prim fashion, while not exactly repelling Deeley's voyeuristic advances? Did Kate, tenuous as her very existence sometimes seems to become, ever manage to focus her emotions sufficiently to desire anybody?[43]

Trussler decides that all these questions are unanswerable and that this play is guilty of "emotional trickery."[44] Trussler is certainly right in that definitive, dogmatic answers can probably never be given to these questions. He is also right that this play shows Pinter's continuing exercise of strong structural control. However, the play also shows that Pinter's intuition is still on target. This play, like all of Pinter's plays, allows several layers of meaning all of which coincide with Freudian theory. This much truth can hardly be tossed aside as "emotional trickery."

The layers of meaning in *Old Times* are condensed under the symbol contained in the title. Just as dreams most often feature some real experience of the preceding day, this play begins in the present. But the present reality of the characters result from past events, old times, which the characters remember. The past events that they remember result from old times that they do not remember—childhood experiences lost in the unconscious. Freud says that there is a "peculiar amnesia which, in the case of most people, . . . hides the earliest beginnings of their childhood up to their sixth or eighth year."[45] Yet, he explains, people react with great passion to those early events, and "the very same impressions that we have forgotten have none the less left the deepest traces on our minds and have had a determining effect upon the whole of our later development."[46] *Old Times* begins with a present in which the characters look back to old times that are underlaid with old times that go back to these deepest traces covered over by amnesia but still exercising their controls.

In the present reality Kate, Deeley, and Anna are all reaping the arid harvest of their neurotic pasts. Kate and Deeley live in a landscape of silence almost as separate from one another as Beth and Duff. They live far away from town in a converted farmhouse. It is so quiet, Deeley says: "You can hear the sea sometimes if you listen very carefully" (p. 19). Moreover, they very "rarely get to London" (p. 18), Deeley volunteers. Within this mutual landscape, they live in separate silences. Kate's is very like Beth's and Ellen's. She lives within herself: "She was always a dreamer" (p. 23), Anna says. "She hasn't made many friends, although there's been every opportunity for her to do so" (p. 23), Deeley explains. In fact, she is quite alone most of the time. Deeley's work takes him away quite often, but Kate stays at home. She takes long walks by the sea where, "There aren't many people" (p. 20). Even when Deeley is at home, there is little communication between them, judging from the reluctant, terse answers she gives to his questions about Anna. She is even sharp with him in some of her responses: "Oh, what does that mean?" (p. 8), she says when he asks if Anna was her best friend. Later when he almost accuses Anna and Kate of lesbianism—"why should I waste valuable space listening to two—" Kate says: "If you don't like it go" (p. 67). Deeley's silence is unwanted like Bates's. Deeley gets away, but his is a restless travel—around the globe, he says. But when Kate tells him to go if he does not like it, he answers, "Go? Where can I go?" (p. 67). He shows his feeling of rejection by his anxiety over Anna's coming and his combative attitude toward her after she arrives. His distrust of Anna's relationship with Kate shows his own exclusion from Kate's intimacy. Finally, as he ends his anxious interrogation about Anna, he reveals his hopelessness: "Anyway, none of this matters" (p. 17). But his sobbing at the end of the play makes clear that it does matter.

The present nature of Anna's silence is clouded by the lies and fantasies she exchanges with Deeley. They make it appear that she lives a voluptuous life in a fine villa in Sicily. But Anna's loneliness is clearly demonstrated by her visit to Kate. It has been twenty years since their friendship, but Anna returns to it with fond memories. Moreover, Deeley points up that Anna's husband must not miss her since she feels so free to come and visit Kate. The busy life in London with Kate, which Anna describes as so appealing, contrasts sharply with life in a Sicilian villa high on the cliffs. And Anna has admitted, "But I would miss London. . ." (p. 20).

These silent, separate lives are a natural outgrowth of the old times when their paths last crossed. Kate, Deeley, and Anna all evidence some kind of neurotic adjustment to their sex instincts. Freud calls such deviations by the name *inversion*, and he notes the variety of behavior found in inverts. Some require at all times a sexual object of the same sex; others show no such exclusiveness, and respond to either sex; still others are only occasionally inverted, and can find gratification with the same sex when a suitable love object from the opposite sex is unattainable. Other varieties among inverts stem from their attitudes toward inversion. Some inverts accept their preferences as normal while others fight against and even try to conceal their inversion. One final variety Freud describes is a "periodic oscillation between a normal and an inverted sexual object. . . ."[47] Kate, Deeley, and Anna appear to be inverts of differing varieties. Perhaps this is the double entendre implied in the repeated reference to Kate's *casserole*. A casserole is a mixture of various kinds of food all cooked together in one pot. When they think Anna might be bringing her husband, Deeley says: "At least the casserole is big enough for four" (p. 14). Deeley implies their group can take one more variety into the pot. Later when Deeley says to Anna: "I wish I had known you both then" (p. 20), Anna replies: "You have a wonderful casserole . . . I mean wife . . ." (p. 20). She indicates he did not need to know them both because he already has variety in Kate. This interpretation of *casserole* is also suggested by Deeley's invitation to Anna:

> Well, any time your husband finds himself in this direction my little wife will be only too glad to put the old pot on the old gas stove and dish him up something luscious if not voluptuous (p. 41).

Inversion may also be the symbolic referent of the reversed furniture arrangement in the bedroom for act two. These characters live with one apparent relationship, but sleep in a variety of other relationships. Deeley's comment about the versatility of the beds buttresses this interpretation:

> The great thing about these beds is that they are susceptible to any amount of permutation. They can be separated as they are now. Or placed at right angles, or one can bisect the other, or you can sleep feet to feet, or head to head, or side by side. It's the castors that make all this possible. (p. 48)

Deeley makes repeated references to his own varied inversion. He identifies himself with the movie title *Odd Man Out*, and he also speaks of himself as "off center." "Odd man out" seems to indicate that his attraction to Kate left him outside her homosexual attachment to Anna. His reference to "off center" and later comments about traveling east or in certain directions are appropriate to a conclusion about dream symbolism that

Freud gives approval to: "Thus 'left' may represent homosexuality, incest, or perversion, and 'right' may represent marriage, intercourse, with a prostitute, and so on, always looked at from the subject's individual moral standpoint."[48] If Deeley is "off center," he can deviate in either direction. During the movie he was attracted to Robert Newton and vented his arousal on Kate. Deeley also indicates that he has been associated with "prostitutes of all kinds" (p. 42). Thus, the impression reigns that he may, like Lenny, be a pimp. There are strong indications, as well, that Deeley's sexual relations never go beyond the intermediate stage. Freud describes the intermediate relations to the sexual object as "touching and looking at it."[49] He calls it a perversion to "linger over the intermediate relations to the sexual object which should normally be traversed rapidly on the path toward the final sexual aim."[50] Deeley admits this perversion when he says: "Sometimes I take her face in my hands and look at it" (p. 24). In this context, of course, *face* represents a displacement upwards. Touching may always have been Deeley's sexual aim with Kate. Even in his first attraction to her he speaks of their naked bodies meeting, and he wonders what Robert Newton would think about it: "As I touched her profoundly all over" (p. 31). Anna recognizes this perversion in Deeley when she suggests that he dry Kate after her bath. His reply is, "In her bath towel?" (p. 55). He would prefer to "do it with powder" (p. 56). Deeley was indulging his voyeurism when he stared up Anna's skirt at a party at "someone's flat, somewhere in Westbourne Grove" (p. 51).

Deeley indicates that Anna did not object to his gaze. In fact, she found it "perfectly acceptable" (p. 51). Moreover, Anna, too, is a voyeur. She likes to watch. She says: "Sometimes I'd look at her [Kate's] face. but she was quite unaware of my gaze" (p. 26). Deeley repeats the word: "Gaze?" In this context, he repeats the word less to indicate his interest in words, as many critics have suggested, than to emphasize his recognition of another voyeur. He makes this point again when he offers to let Anna supervise while he dries and powders Kate. Anna's love of watching, however, is more than just a wish to see genitalia. She indulges herself in all kinds of watching entertainments. She and Kate had visited "that gallery, or this theatre, or that chamber concert. . .there was so much, so much to see and to hear, in lovely London then. . ." (p. 38). Anna's principal neurosis, however, was her altruistic surrender in favor of Kate. Anna's relationship to Kate fits Anna Freud's description of the patient who "had projected her own desire for love and her craving for admiration onto her rival and, having identified herself with the object of her envy, she enjoyed the fulfillment of her desire."[51] There is much evidence to indicate Anna was attracted to Deeley. Kate speaks about it openly to Deeley: "She was prepared to extend herself to you. . .She fell in love with you" (p. 70). Deeley's notice of Anna at the party in Westbourne shows he may have returned this feeling to the extent that he was capable. The present sparring between Anna and Deeley reveals some attraction still exists between them, for Freud says: "An inclination to physical struggles with some one particular person, just as in later years an inclination to *verbal* disputes, is a convincing sign that object-choice has fallen on him."[52] However, Anna withdrew in favor of Kate. That night when Deeley approached her bed, Anna did not move to accept him. She submitted to symbolic death to allow Kate to experience love with Deeley. Later, when she heard Kate was married to Deeley, her "heart leapt with joy" (p. 36). She had also devoted herself to filling Kate's every need, inviting in the men Kate wanted to see, advising her on the most attractive blouse to wear, fixing the hem of her black dress, drawing her bath. And, of course, admiring Kate's beauty. Anna verbalizes her feelings to Deeley: "All I wanted for her was her happiness. That is all I want for her still" (p. 69). Anna had tried to identify herself with Kate by wearing Kate's underwear. Then when Anna permitted Deeley's gaze, it was as if he were also staring at Kate. When she was with Deeley, Anna imitated Kate. Deeley says to Kate: "She thought she was you, said little, so litte. Maybe she was you" (p. 69).

This attempt to become one with Kate was, of course, Anna's mistake. Kate's hostility was aroused by Anna's wish to be like her. In Kate's eyes, Anna was stealing from her: "She was a thief. She used to steal things" (p. 10). Underwear is a Freudian symbol for female genitalia. By borrowing the underwear, Anna appeared to be stealing Kate's femininity, and Kate was a narcissist who could not give, only receive. Like Beth before her, Kate was one of those beautiful women who develop a certain self-contentment. They love only themselves and have no need for loving but for being loved.[53] Thus, Kate was content to be cared for by Anna, to accept her services and her altruistic surrender. Kate's self-containment, her withdrawal from people was a symptom of her narcissism. Her sensuous baths in which she "soaps herself all over" and gives herself "a comprehensive going over" are obvious signs of her autoerotism. Anna's and Deeley's love of looking complemented Kate's love of admiration. Kate's absorption is so intense that her only animated response is to Anna's and Deeley's comments on her beauty. Then she explains her preference for a blurred world. She wishes awareness only of herself. Anna comments on Kate's tendency to dreaming. Kate, like Beth, lived more in fantasies than in reality. This narcissism is, of course, a return to an infantile state, and Freud explains that narcissists sometimes develop "a crippling dependence" upon their helpers in need.[54] Kate's remembered past showed signs of such a total dependence on Anna. Therefore, when Kate felt betrayed by Anna's thievery, she resorted to animism to be rid of her. Norman Holland says that "animistic fantasies seem to deal with the child's sense of helplessness. . . ."[55] Therefore, in her helplessness, Kate fancied her wish to be rid of Anna as an accomplished fact. Moreover,

Freud testifies that animism is a frequent companion to extreme narcissism.[56] Kate dirtied Anna's face, thereby turning her into a loathsome thing. Freud says that loathing opposes scoptophilia, the desire for looking, and can eventually abolish it.[57] The dirt on Anna's face, then, brought about her disintegration. Anna, in her altruism, accepted her demise and removed herself. Kate explains: "When I brought him into the room your body of course had gone" (p. 72). Kate then transferred her need to Deeley. Deeley, with his love of looking and touching, could supply Kate's narcissistic needs without expecting her to give. When Deeley did act as though he thought Kate was going to be "sexually forthcoming," she tried to turn him, too, into a loathsome symbolic corpse. But "he resisted. . . with force" (p. 73). He suggested a change instead—marriage. Kate accepted because "neither mattered." Thenceforth, Deeley accepted the only love she had to give, a pat on the head when he lay across her lap. With his fixation at a pregenital stage of development, this infantile substitute for adult love was not unacceptable to Deeley, but his sobbing indicated his wish for an unknown more. Each character in his striving committed himself to emptiness and the loss of truly satisfying love.

Old Times also shows old times repeating themselves. In the present of the play, Anna returns. Consequently, Deeley feels threatened with a more total loss of his illusive sex object, so he spars with Anna. Their litany of song acknowledges their mutual recognition of Kate's narcissism and withdrawal. Deeley begins with, "Lovely to look at, delightful to know?" (p. 26). He continues with, "Blue moon, I saw you standing alone. . ." Thus, he indicates Kate's narcissism, his voyeurism, and the loneliness that results from the combination. Anna's responses convey the same message: "Oh but you're lovely, with your smile so warm. . ." and then, "You are the promised kiss of springtime. . ." She pays homage to Kate but indicates a return of love is only a promise. Deeley echoes that sentiment with,

"And someday I'll know that moment divine/When all the things you are, are mine!" (p. 27). Later she indicates all is lost now—even the promise, "When a lovely flame dies. . . ." He, too, mourns a loss, "The sigh of midnight trains in empty stations" (p. 28). So while it is true that Anna and Deeley do "vie with each other in singing snatches of old popular songs" (as Arthur Ganz points out),[58] they are also engaging in an exchange of information that establishes their joint relationship as losers at Kate's shrine. They correspond quite neatly to Freud's explanation of the narcissist's suitors:

> For it seems very evident that another person's narcissism has a great attraction for those who have renounced part of their own narcissism and are in search of object-love. The charm of a child lies to a great extent in his narcissism, his self-contentment and inaccessibility, just as does the charm of certain animals which seem not to concern themselves about us, such as cats and the large beasts of prey.[59]

Kate, however, keeps Deeley's anxiety alive by her show of preference for Anna. She lapses into the relationship they had in old times. She suggests they stay home; she responds to Anna's suggestion of inviting someone over—just as if Deeley were no longer there. In the next act, however, the situation is reversed like the setting. The reversal occurs when Kate becomes the one threatened. Anna has unwittingly supplied Deeley with a trump card; her story about wearing Kate's underwear provides Deeley with a device for having Kate reject Anna. Deeley tells Kate that he knew Anna before, that Anna had pretended to be Kate. Kate recognizes that Anna had loved Deeley. Now she is threatened, and she resorts again to animism. In telling the story of Anna's former symbolic death, Kate kills her again. She makes it clear when she answers Deeley's question about who had slept in the other bed: "I told him no one. No one at all" (p. 73). Again Anna accepts and walks

toward the door as a sign of her withdrawal. Then to high-
light the repetition compulsion, the whole scene is reenacted.
Deeley sobs. Anna lies down on her divan. Deeley approaches
Anna, but she makes no move to accept him. Deeley goes to the
door, returns to Kate, and lies across her lap. Then after a long
silence the initial tableau appears again. Deeley is slumped in
his armchair. Kate is sitting on her divan. Anna is no longer
alive and standing. She is lying dead on her divan. They are
all losers again. They have had their second chance to live it all
over again, and they have duplicated the pattern of old times.

This compulsion to repeat is an involuntary process
resulting from old times that lie forgotten in the unconscious.
The silence to which they have all retreated is in itself a defense
against fearful fantasies developed in childhood. Anna, in
particular, demonstrates this inhibition. Anna Freud says that
altruistic surrender is a "defensive process" that "has its origin in
the infantile conflict with parental authority about some form
of instinctual gratification."[60] Norman Holland says that
"primal-scene fantasies" are the basis for "later interest in watching drama and other performances,"[61] which is certainly
appropriate to Anna. Deeley's psychical impotence, which he
demonstrates by his fixation at the intermediate stage of
sexual relations and by his need to debase these women as
prostitutes or lesbians, undoubtedly sprang also from some kind
of oedipal fears. Kate's withdrawal into narcissism is indicative
of a similar disturbance.

The verbal combats between Anna and Deeley certainly
show leftovers from anal conflicts in both these characters. Each
is still fighting the battle for dominance that is the product of
the defiance-submission antithesis of anality. Each wishes to
possess and control Kate, and yet each submits ultimately to
Kate's control, which emanates from her ability to withhold
love—a weapon always available to parents. Arthur Ganz
compares this facet of Kate to Ruth in *The Homecoming*: "As

the desired sexual object she [Kate], like Ruth, has power over those who desire her, though Ruth's power lies in the promise of sexuality, Kate's in the denial."[62] Kate controls them, then, by responses they learned as children. Moreover, all three characters tend to resort to the old anal device of dehumanization. Anna and Deeley speak of Kate as though she were dead. Kate dirties their faces (or would have dirtied Deeley's) as though they were feces which she can then discard as inanimate objects. Their greatest carryover from orality is, of course, their dispossession anxiety. Anna confesses it: "I would not want to go far, I would be afraid of going far, lest when I returned the house would be gone" (p. 19). House, of course, is a womb symbol. Deeley replies, "Lest?" Again his interest in words is only a cover for his concern with the idea that follows *lest*. He is threatened by Anna's thought of returning, for he fears it would mean his own dispossession. Deeley's orality reveals itself also in his constant innuendoes about food. Kate's inversion makes her a casserole. People are vegetarians or the opposite, meat eaters, depending on their sexual dispositions. Kate, of course, shows the greatest arrest in orality. Her narcissism is a return to infantile gratification. Her dependence on Anna is like a child's dependence on her mother. She was even satisfied to have no other friend but Anna—a repeat of the original mother-child relationship. All three of these characters show the effects of the oldest of all times—infancy.

Old Times presents still another possible interpretation. The title could refer to the Kate that was. Anna then becomes the other half of Kate. Ronald Hayman briefly suggests this possibility: "One interpretation is that Kate and Anna are two different sides of the same woman, Anna representing whatever survives of that part of the girlish self which seems to be put aside on marrying."[63] Arthur Ganz also views "Anna as an aspect of Kate—her passionate self, from which she has retreated in heterosexual, domestic relationship with Deeley." Ganz argues that "no actual roommate—however possessed of *sang froid*—is likely to retire quietly to bed under the circumstances Anna describes."[64] Ganz's objection stresses the validity of approaching this play as a dream where behavior is bizarre and characters are frequently split in accordance with the antithetical forces warring within them. Such a condition certainly applies to Kate and Anna, and Freud describes it:

> An especially prominent part is played as factors in the formation of symptoms in psychoneuroses by the component instincts, which emerge for the most part as pairs of opposites and which we have met with as introducing new sexual aims—the scoptophilic instinct and exhibitionism and the active and passive forms of the instinct for cruelty.[65]

Kate and Anna are opposites in almost every regard. Kate is an exhibitionist. Deeley and Anna get pleasure from watching her. While Anna did allow Deeley to gaze up her skirt, this occurred when she had identified with Kate by wearing her underwear. Anna is principally a watcher. Kate is the cruel sadistic one; she can snuff out people by a magical thought or a ritual of dirtying and never express regret. Anna is the passive side of the instinct for cruelty—the masochist. She allows Kate to snuff her out, not once but twice. They are opposites in other ways as well. Anna is the busy, active one. She recalls the hustle and bustle of their lives: "But what stamina, and to work in the morning, and to a concert, or the opera, or the ballet, that night, you haven't forgotten?" (p. 17). Kate "continues" in the silence of her country home, or occasionally she walks to the sea where "there aren't many people" (p. 20). Anna is the doer: she gives out invitations, fixes hems, draws baths. Kate is the receiver: she sits and wishes or asks or orders. Anna gives; she wants to celebrate Kate's happiness; she steps aside in Kate's favor. Kate resents sharing; she views Anna's borrowings as thievery, her identification as cause for annihilation. Anna's attraction to Deeley was sexual; she would have extended herself. Kate's relationship with Deeley is infantile; she accepts him only as a submissive child to be patted on the head.

Occasionally in the play Anna and Kate are indicated as one person. When Deeley first met Kate at the movie, *Odd Man Out*, there was only one person in the theater, seated dead center. But Anna claims they went to this movie together. When Deeley took Anna out for coffee, he explains: "Maybe she was you. Maybe it was you, having coffee with me, saying little, so little" (p. 69). When Kate disintegrated Anna, Anna bore signs of being Kate:

> You tried to do my little trick, one of my tricks you had borrowed, my little slow smile, my little slow shy smile, my bend of the head, my half closing of the eyes, that we knew so well. . . .(p. 72)

Indeed, Anna can easily be considered the earthy, sensual self that Kate felt the need to repress. Her spirit, of course, lies there in the dark unconscious to which Kate has relegated it. But like all repressed instincts, it returns. As the play opens, Anna's figure stands dimly in the shadows; she is a specter still coming between Deeley and Kate. Deeley wanted her and feared her. His sexual instinct called out to her, but his need to repress erotism made him repel her. Deeley chose Kate because his own neurosis forbade him to take the sex object he had made attractive by mental debasement. He returned instead to the vision of purity who would pat him maternally and punish him with rejection. To Kate, Anna is also the mother figure — introjected. She can protect and nurture and cherish. This is the relationship Kate always establishes with Anna in the play. When Anna becomes her rival, however, Kate wants to be rid of her, as the girl child wishes to be rid of the mother who steals father's attentions. When Kate kills Anna, then, she accomplishes two needs: she kills the passionate side of herself to avoid incurring oedipal guilt and, at the same time, she kills the hated rival. She was going to kill Deeley, too, because he threatened to arouse her repressed libido and thus bring Anna back. But he offered Kate marriage instead. Once Kate had married this father figure, she was forced to retreat to orality to avoid her guilt over having taken father away from mother. Deeley, of course, has helped Kate drive away her sensual side as his own self-punishment. Consequently, at the close of the play, Deeley and Kate sit in their separate, silent landscapes — alienated and isolated. And Anna? Anna lies dormant in the dark — waiting until some memory, some event, some instinct will cause her to rise into consciousness again, to disturb the silence once more.

Old Times provides a more thorough look at incompatibility and misplaced loves than *Landscape* and *Silence* do. This longer play shows once more how helpless man really is to direct his own love choices. *Old Times* by its very title emphasizes the importance of the past in propelling man into misbegotten alliances. However, it also shows that given a second chance, man will repeat his mistakes just as unwittingly as he made them in the first place. The ironic element is in man's striving, his energetic effort, to gain the goals that will commit him to emptiness and loss of love. Deeley struggles against Anna only to win Kate's selfish withdrawal. Moreover, Deeley had already known dissatisfaction with Kate's nature, but still he fought to keep her from Anna, to keep her for himself. Once he has vanquished Anna, he suffers again his own loss. He expresses it loudly with his sobs. *Old Times* also reveals that altruism is no less neurotic than narcissism or striving for unwanted goals. Kate's seeming generosity is really a form of masochism. Indeed, *Old Times* presents neuroses, inversions, and even perversions as standard household equipment. As such they provide a built-in defeat for man's wish to have mother. This wish itself long ago, in very old times, made man a sure loser.

NO MAN'S LAND

No Man's Land intensifies the image of loss. It seems to distance itself from Landscape, Silence, and Old Times by moving deeper into man's loneliness. This distance is paralleled by the time lapse between Old Times and No Man's Land. Old Times first appeared at London's Aldwych Theater in 1971, and No Man's Land had its first production by London's National Theater at the Old Vic in April 1975. Four years intervened — Pinter's longest pause, broken only by the B.B.C. broadcast of the short piece, Monologue, in April 1973. Monologue presents one solitary male addressing an empty chair. No Man's Land illumines the space around an equally deserted figure. In this last play, love has been totally misplaced; it is absent. Even its memory is tainted. Spooner questions whether Hirst ever truly loved his wife. Moreover, No Man's Land is, by displacement, no woman's land: not a single female character is present in this play. The punishment for the wish to have mother is complete.

Like the other plays of its group, No Man's Land explores the nebulous world of fantasy and memory, but the memories are dimming out. Today's people fuse with those of yesterday, fading in and out of a barely perceived present where reality is not in clear focus. Consequently, the characters seem vague at first, but a steady gaze soon distinguishes them. Hirst is the collapsed man so frequently encountered at the end of Pinter's plays. At the end of The Birthday Party Stanley is led away dressed in his morning suit for the funeral of his real self. At the end of A Slight Ache Edward is abandoned, prostrate on the floor, as Flora begins anew with the Matchseller. At the end of Tea Party, Disson is frozen in his chair — silent, unseeing, and unhearing. In No Man's Land Hirst is collapsed from the outset. In a self-willed punishment, he has allowed Eros, love and life, to be annihilated by Thanatos, destruction and death. The punishment is administered by Hirst's own hand in the continuous motion of taking alcohol to his mouth.

Spooner is the mysterious stranger from the outside like Riley in *The Room*, like the Matchseller in *A Slight Ache*. Like Davies in *The Caretaker*, he has been brought home by the occupant of this room. Spooner even seems to be down on his luck as Davies was. Sometimes, however, he shifts into a returning friend like Stott in *The Basement* or like Anna in *Old Times*. Moreover, he has Stott's former expertise in games as well as his competitiveness over girls. Spooner also shares Anna's readiness for altruistic surrender. The other two characters in the play, Foster and Briggs, are reminiscent of the all-male family in *The Homecoming*. Foster is capricious and distrustful like Lennie; Briggs is harsh and rough-spoken like Max. Yet together they care for the abandoned Hirst as Max cared for his motherless sons.

The play opens in typical Pinter fashion: two people are in a room. One is quiet—Hirst; one is talkative—Spooner. Foster and Briggs enter the room, but from another part of the house. Actually it is they who live with Hirst; they are his care-takers, his nursemaids. Spooner is the visitor from outside. The only other visitors are the specters of memory.

However, the room in this play is neither the familiar kitchen nor the upper-middle-class living room. This is an elegant room in a fashionable house in North West London. This is such a room as Mick dreamed of in *The Caretaker*. One wall is bookshelves; the occupant of this room is an educated man. In a central spot stands an antique cabinet with a top of marble and brass; the occupant is a wealthy man. The shelves of the cabinet contain a large collection of liquors and beers; the occupant is an alcoholic. This word, however, is never spoken. Since it is concretized by Hirst's continuous drinking, the word would be redundant. Thus, Pinter proceeds by his usual method of indirection.

On the realistic level, *No Man's Land* unfolds within this elegant room as the blur between drinking and passing out. When the play begins, Hirst, precisely dressed, is pouring drinks for himself and Spooner, a shabbily dressed man whom Hirst has apparently met in a pub. Spooner, however, identifies himself as an intellectual, a poet and friend of the arts, a man of strength by the absence of being loved. The conversation progresses to mutual memories of earlier times. Then Spooner becomes accusatory: he suggests Hirst never loved his wife; he salutes Hirst's impotence. When Hirst is briefly riled, Spooner responds with an offer of friendship—an offer he claims is foreign to his usual aloofness. Hirst rejects the offer on the excuse that he lives in no man's land where all is still, icy, and silent. So saying, he falls to the floor and crawls from the room. The incident stirs within Spooner a sense of déjà vu.

Foster and Briggs enter. Foster introduces himself as Hirst's son. They accept the presence of a stranger in the house as a normal occurrence, but their hostility to Spooner communicates their resentment of intruders, their fear of dispossession.

When Hirst returns, he shows no recognition of Spooner. He is greatly disturbed by a dream he has just awakened from—a dream of someone drowning, but not himself. When Spooner claims to be the drowning man in the dream, Hirst collapses again, and Briggs takes him off to bed. Foster snaps off the light, leaving Spooner in the darkened room.

Act Two opens with Spooner's awakening—again with a sense of déjà vu. Briggs interrupts, bringing breakfast and a long tale that establishes a new identity for Foster as Briggs's old friend. When Hirst enters, he calls Spooner, Charles; he calls Briggs, Denson. He treats Spooner like an old friend from his days at Oxford, and Spooner accepts that role. A new confusion about identities occurs. However, when Spooner recounts Hirst's past exploits with other men's wives, Spooner seems truly to be an old acquaintance. Meanwhile, Hirst becomes outraged, calls for Briggs, and begins to babble about faces in his album. When Briggs refuses to give Hirst any more drinks, Spooner brings Hirst the whiskey bottle. In fact, Spooner offers Hirst his all;

he even proposes to challenge death for Hirst. His final offer is to put Hirst back in touch with his public through a poetry reading.

Hirst rejects everything, demanding the subject be changed for the last time. He declares his intention to remain forever in this static environment with his caretakers, Foster and Briggs. Then he recalls his drowning dream. Spooner reassures him that he, Hirst, is not dead but in the icy stillness of no man's land. Hirst drinks to that. A slow fade ends the drama.

Once the spell is broken, the usual questioning begins. Did Spooner and Hirst really know each other in the past? If not, are their recollections lies or fantasies? Is Foster Hirst's son or a hired helper and old acquaintance of Briggs? What is the meaning of Hirst's dream? Truly, this is one of Pinter's most enigmatic plays. Indeed it must be if form is to echo content, for this play tiptoes around the edges of the most intimate parts of the heart and mind—where, Hirst says: "no living soul. . .has . . .or can ever. . .trespass."[66] It peeps into the void, that empty space between being and nonbeing. Pinter announces this loudly in his title. The Oxford English Dictionary says *no man's land* was originally "the name of a plot of ground, lying outside the north wall of London, and used as a place of execution." In World War I *no man's land* became that area of a battlefield which lay between the combatants' trenches. The phrase is also universally defined as a piece of wasteland to which no one has a recognized title. This arid, unclaimed, and deadly place is a meaningful metaphor for the world in which these characters dwell. Pinter has Hirst and Spooner describe it as icy and silent, unchanging and unmoving. Indeed, it is a still point—between numerous and various dualities.

The identifications of these dualities and the explorations of their meanings must begin at the realistic level. Only after the seeming gaps in the play's logical overlay are filled, can the dream structure of the play be seen most clearly. And in truth, the gaps can be filled by implication. They begin to fade when the play's primary image is brought into focus—the alcoholic. Hirst is an alcoholic who lives in the no man's land between awareness and oblivion. He begins drinking and blurring his consciousness the minute he awakens, and he drinks until he blanks out. It is safe to assume that in between he has difficulty recognizing people. Apparently he has met Spooner at a pub in Hampstead Heath. In his alcoholic haze he considers Spooner a stranger. Spooner has been drinking too, but he may well recognize Hirst as his friend from long ago. Perhaps he plays the role of stranger because he realizes Hirst is too drunk to remember and because he knows the long years since their last meeting have rendered them virtual strangers. Spooner's use of a new name seems justified when he reveals his hostility over Hirst's having once stolen his wife. In Act Two, after a long sleep, Hirst recognizes Spooner and calls him by his real name, Charles Wetherby. Their mutual memories are no mystery under these circumstances. The confusion in the identities of Foster and Briggs allows the same kind of explanation. Presumably they are hired helpers, but in various stages of awareness Hirst identifies them with other people he has known. Foster, a young man, might easily be mistaken by a drunken old man as the absent son whom he longs for. Foster may even enjoy playing this role on occasions for the sense of importance it gives him— especially if his true identity is a beachcombing playboy summoned by his old friend Briggs, especially if he is a would-be poet in need of a patron. He may occasionally play this role in order to evict, with greater authority, the bums and unidentified drinking companions whom Hirst frequently brings home. Brigg's job as chief cook, butler, and nursemaid to an alcoholic must be so difficult and unpleasant that Hirst may well have had many others; Denson and Albert may have been two of Briggs's forerunners. Accurate identification of his nursemaid is probably so unimportant to Hirst that he constantly confuses the names. He cares only for the drinks that Briggs keeps him supplied with. Briggs, however, knowing he can not be easily replaced, can, when his disgust mounts, bully Hirst and refuse to serve him. Usually, though, both Briggs and Foster humor Hirst, play his games, and answer to whatever names he assigns them.

Looking at these characters through a telescope of familiar psychological principles brings them into even sharper focus. They are all captured, during the time of the play, in the ambivalence of the Hirst household: they all live between love and hate. Hirst loves the presence of the others when he awakens from his nightmare; they prevent his complete aloneness. Yet he treats them as things by failing to know their identities, and when Spooner offers him total friendship, Hirst rejects it. Spooner, on the other hand, has oscillated between this generous offer and the angry memories of Hirst's affairs with other men's wives. Foster and Briggs care for Hirst's physical needs and protect him from intruders, and Foster explains to Spooner that they do it out of love (p. 49). Yet each knows disgust with Hirst. Foster complains about wasting his time "looking after a pisshound" (p. 52). When Hirst wonders sentimentally what he would do without Briggs and Foster, Briggs replies cynically that Hirst would crawl after a bottle and "stuff it between his teeth" (p. 45). Nevertheless, the hired helpers resent Spooner's claim of friendship with Hirst. Briggs denigrates Spooner by insisting he is a "pintpot attendant" at the Bull's Head in Chalk Farm (p. 48). Briggs expresses the violence he feels for Spooner when he says: "I've seen Irishmen chop his balls off" (p. 49). Foster offers to kick Spooner's head off if he tries to make nonsense out of the family life in Hirst's household (p. 50). Yet, later, they all drink together in amiability. Even Briggs's show of affection for Foster is punctuated with anger. At one moment he recalls trying to save Foster from the wasted life of Bolsover Street, and at another he calls him "a cunt" (p. 85).

In brief, the spaces between these characters are also no man's lands. They approach each other, but no one is allowed to make a genuine contact; this would be trespassing. They peep at each other, but they do not truly see one another. Foster says as much, in Pinter's oblique fashion, through the story of the tramp "out East" and the disappearing coin (p. 42). Foster explains that the tramp asked him for a few bob (approached him) but he saw the tramp was not to be trusted (refused to make contact). Foster noted that the tramp and his dog had only about one eye between them (could not see clearly). As if to compensate for the rejection, Foster threw the tramp a coin. The tramp retaliated, in distaste, by tossing the coin back. When Foster automatically clutched at it, the coin disappeared; even an inanimate object was destroyed by venturing into the no man's land between people. Foster's story is also a warning to Spooner that they are mutually repellent. Thus, the characters in this play maintain distance from one another. Like the people in *Landscape*, *Silence* and *Old Times*, they are alienated and isolated, each in his own silent space.

Inside, these characters carry another no man's land, created by the warring opposites within themselves. Hirst is the prime example. Karl Menninger, in *Man Against Himself*, describes the alcoholic as a person in a "hopeless impasse."[67] Menninger classifies alcoholism as a form of slow suicide that frequently begins only after the achievement of significant success.[68] Hirst conforms to this pattern; he is a rich, powerful, accomplished poet. In Foster's words, "nothing ersatz" (p. 50). Requests for critical essays still come to Hirst; yet in private he knows personal defeat. He is, therefore, trapped in the stillness between success and failure. According to Menninger, the alcoholic is initially a jolly, popular person who strives to be loved;[69] but eventually these unfortunate people frustrate and alienate their parents, estrange their wives, and lose all their friends.[70] Hirst is amiable; Spooner says he is kindness itself

(p. 17), and Hirst's past popularity is demonstrated by all the ladies he once won and by all the charming and tender faces in his album. But they are all gone now, nothing but memories. Hirst has only Briggs and Foster, hired helpers, to prevent him from waiting forever for a stranger to fill up his glass (p. 45). Hirst dwells near the negative end of the continuum that extends from friendship to desertion. Menninger says the alcoholic suffers from a deep but irrational inferiority caused by the unconscious guilts that accompany an unforgivable and unforgettable disappointment endured in childhood. Drinking helps to further repress these threatening memories.[71] Hirst's disjointed babbling is pervaded with disappointment and distress—never fully remembered. In Act One he mentions dreaming of a beautiful woman who was all poison (p. 46). In Act Two he speaks of blackened tennis balls, under dead leaves—centuries old, lost, and dead (p. 81). Hirst suffers between remembering and forgetting. Hirst's need not to remember is linked with his fears. Menninger states that the "alcoholic suffers secretly from unspeakable terror." Unable to face it, he tries drowning his terror in drink, but the cure "becomes worse than the disease."[72] Hirst's dream expresses both this unknown terror and the new one that results from the cure—the fear of dying. In his dream someone is following him; then he sees a body floating in the water; but when he looks again, no one is there (p. 95). He assures himself the drowning man was not he (p. 44). This, then, is Hirst's major no man's land: that icy, silent, still place he speaks of lies between the fear of living and the fear of dying. He can only tolerate the anesthetized present; the past is frozen in pain and fear while the future holds only the uncharted void. Hirst states the alternatives matter-of-factly as he thanks Briggs for another drink. He asks what he can do between drinks: "Look through my album? Make plans for the future?" (p. 45).

Spooner's still point lies between rejection and identification. Dressed as a shabby old tramp, he appears to be rejected. He admits to Hirst that he is down on his luck and pleads to be an all-around servant, performing such menial tasks as cooking and dusting (pp. 88-89). On the other hand, he is by his own admission a rejecter, one who retreats into intellectualism. He describes himself as a "man of intelligence and perception" who feels acute alarm in the face of interest or "positive liking" (p. 17). As a "betwixt twig peeper," he keeps a proper distance between himself and others (pp. 18-19). Moreover, in this effort he can be harsh and vulgar, as his questions about Hirst's wife illustrate: did she respond to "finger spin," how fast did she come off the wicket, "did she google?" (p. 30). On the other hand, he identifies with Hirst as a prominent man of letters—not only in the past but also in the present. He keeps open house for young poets (p. 27); he is acquainted with the impeccably aristocratic Lord Lancer (p. 66). He is able to organize a poetry reading for Hirst that will include: a guaranteed full house, a host committee, a dinner party at a fine Indian restaurant, and a press conference tailored to Hirst's pleasure. He empathizes with Hirst as well. When Briggs unceremoniously pulls Hirst up from a fall, Spooner interferes; and, leading Hirst gently to a chair, he says: "We are of an age. I know his wants. Let me take his arm. Respect our age" (p. 47). This empathy and identification amount, finally, to an altruistic surrender equal to Anna's in *Old Times*. He declares himself willing to challenge death for Hirst, ready to be entombed for the sake of Hirst's dignity.

Briggs's no man's land is suggested by his name. In the American military the "brig" is a prison. Briggs is not quite the jailed masochist and not quite the sadistic jailer. He is hemmed in by his job of caring for Hirst. The whole of his speech about Bolsover Street is an indirect statement about his confinement in Hirst's household. He warns Foster against wasting his youth there with its gray-faced, despair-ridden occupants (p. 62). On the other hand, he is a jailer too. Clearly he is Hirst's keeper; he also carries the keys that unlock Spooner at the opening of Act Two. He is something of a masochist for staying in this situation, which he sometimes finds unpleasant and disgusting, for serving so faithfully a master who can not even remember his name. His sadism erupts in verbal abuse: he calls Spooner a "pisspot attendant" (p. 48) and Foster a "vagabond cock" (p. 52). Occasionally he behaves disrespectfully and defiantly to Hirst. He jerks Hirst up off the floor once, and another time he refuses to give the master a drink.

Foster's name also indicates the opposites between which he lives. He is almost a foster son and almost a foster father. His youth allows him to masquerade as a son, but his yearning for the pleasures of the immature life are more important to this extreme. He misses the girls in Siam who always took an immediate shine to him (p. 38) and were always prepared to give him a "giggle and a cuddle" (p. 51). Briggs testifies to Foster's love of idleness and concretizes it as being served hot toddies in a fourposter bed in the Malay Straits (p. 52). Nevertheless, Foster's service to Hirst is mature and almost parental in character. He protects Hirst from corruption and evil (p. 49); he feels proud of his position of trust (p. 86). At Briggs's summons Foster left Bali voluntarily (p. 86), and presently he feels satisfaction in being where he is needed (p. 83). Even his pleasure in indolence is balanced by ambition. He is a would-be poet who finds it nourishing to be in touch with the special intelligence of Hirst (p. 87).

On the whole, then, *No Man's Land* is a womanless household of alienated males whose focal point is Hirst. Hirst is the great sufferer; his guilts are revealed, his punishment displayed. As an alcoholic he has withdrawn into living death or dying life. Perhaps this is the significance of his name, which sounds very much like *hearse*. In this near-dead state, he is visited by a man from his past, Spooner, who feeds his memory and soothes his fears. Thus Spooner, too, resembles his name, for *spooner* means one who feeds with a spoon—indulges and coddles. Hirst needs all the care and pampering that Briggs, Foster, and Spooner can give him, because he has lost love.

Viewed as a dream, this play is clearly a punishment dream for the forbidden wish to have mother. The terrors that Hirst seeks to drown in drink are his oedipal fears. Menninger says that the inferiority the alcoholic feels stems from aggressive urges springing out of repressed hostility, usually toward the father.[73] Frequently, the alcoholic has had a father who oscillated between maudlin sentimentality and savage highhandedness.[74] Consequently, the child turned to his mother who, out of her own frustrations, overwhelmed him with love and intensified his fear of the castrating father. The child, therefore, could only accept his mother's love as a suckling infant.[75] Clearly, such parents offered the child only ambivalence, love plus thinly disguised hate.[76] The ambivalence that dominates Hirst's household presents a meaningful parallel.

Within this ambivalence-ridden punishment dream, oedipal, anal, urethral, and oral imagery are abundantly condensed. To begin with the obvious, mother has been replaced by males. Thus, the dreamer denies wanting mother. Foster and Briggs are a split parent figure; father and mother have been combined. They show this by the physical care they provide. Briggs is chiefly occupied with bringing the bottle to Hirst. He also brings food. As jailer and jailed, he rarely leaves the house. He, like mother, is possessive and ever present; he has been trapped here in Bolsover Street. Foster, in male fashion, comes into the play from outside, both in the present of Act One and in the remembered past when he was summoned from Bali. Foster appears also as the protective male who threatens intruders and guards the child, Hirst, from evil, corruption, and craft (p. 49). These roles are, however, interchangeable.

Foster sometimes pours drinks and sometimes supplies food. Apparently it is he who has to cope with the financial adviser's changing tastes for breakfast (p. 51). Foster also claims cleaning the house as his responsibility (p. 51). Moreover, Briggs can as easily be the protective one who has been out in the world. It is he who threatens Spooner by claiming to have seen him collecting beer mugs at the Bull's Head in Chalk Farm (p. 37). In summary, Briggs himself comments to Spooner that he and Jack "share all burdens" (p. 61). As the split parent figure, the ambivalence Briggs and Foster display to Hirst is appropriate to the parents of an alcoholic.

Not only does the dreamer/protagonist deny mother, but he also splits himself. The play is replete with clues to the oneness of Spooner and Hirst — their mutual experiences, for example. Both were at Oxford; both are poets; both had cottages where tea was served on the lawn. Primarily, both recall looking into a woman's face. Spooner remembers pure malevolence in his mother's eye (p. 26); Hirst dreamed of beauty that was all poison (p. 46). Moreover, Hirst knows, without being told, what Spooner did to provoke his mother's hatred. He volunteers: "You'd pissed yourself" (p. 26). He even knows that Spooner was twenty-eight at the time (p. 27). Thereby, he shows the same condensation of wife and mother, infancy and adulthood that Spooner is experiencing. A new significance for Spooner's name now emerges. A *spoonerism* is an unintentional interchange of sounds in two or more words — Sheets and Kelly for Keats and Shelley. When these slips of the tongue reveal a secret association, they are known as Freudian slips. Thus, the name *Spooner* can be considered to reveal this interchange of identities between Hirst and himself.

The function of the splitting is, of course, defensive. However, it is not the good/bad split of Ben/Gus in *The Dumb Waiter*. Nor is it the love/hate split of Aston/Mick in *The Caretaker*. This more complex split divides, basically, between the activity and passivity of the oral period. Hirst is the passive side. He sits in his chair and submits to the care of the parent figures. Spooner is the active side. He moves about the room easily and challenges the parent figures. Thus, Hirst is imprisoned and dependent, while Spooner is free and strong. Hirst is flabby and empty, while Spooner is intelligent, perceptive, and still creative. Hirst is fearful of life as well as death. Spooner is resourceful and brave, able to promote a literary event for Hirst or to challenge death for him. Alternately, they project their pain and guilt upon one another. This split is compatible with the inner conflicts of the alcoholic. Menninger explains that the alcoholic's drinking is a substitute for parental love and also a form of infantile revenge. It is symptomatic of his fear of giving up the love objects he wishes to destroy. It allows him to escape the destruction he fears by destroying himself.[77]

Oedipal fears, such as Menninger describes, intermingled with elements from other developmental stages, underlie all the major images of the play. Spooner's peeping, for example, is clearly connected with primal-scene fantasies so frightening that they must be denied. Spooner insists he does not peep on sexual relations. In such cases, he sees only the whites of eyes at very close range. He prefers to keep space in his vision, lots of it (p. 19). In Spooner's "Amsterdam waiter" speech (p. 39), the oedipal wish is concretized more emphatically. Spooner is sitting outside of a cafe by a canal. The cafe is a feeding place; the canal, as water, is suggestive of the birth waters. Thus, he is near mother. Appropriately, a rigid man sits in shadow at the next table—the threatening father whose rigidity represents the death he can deliver. Together they observe a happy scene full of life and love and sunshine. A fisherman catches a fish, which he lifts high. Fish, like snakes, are phallic symbols,[78] and the rising action can readily be interpreted as erection. The waiter cheers and claps. He, as in *The Dumb Waiter*, can be a displacement of the child waiting to be taken to the bathroom. As he waits, he fantasizes himself as the fisherman seeking love. A little girl passes by and laughs, and two lovers kiss and move on. These are the separate images that show the female object and the erotic contact. The fisherman is flushed with pleasure, but all the while the shadowed man whistles and waits. Spooner has tried to remove himself from this dangerous scene by becoming the artist who paints it rather than the man who experiences it. As a painting, it is a still life depicting the proximity of life and love to death and destruction. No man's land is in between.

Hirst's drowning dream (p. 46) is similarly fraught. Holland identifies drowning and wetting with the urethral phase of development during which the child thinks of consequences rather than whims and impulses.[79] Furthermore, Mack and Semrad link erotic sensation with urination in this pregenital stage.[80] Apparently, then, this dream recalls primal-scene fantasies associated with urination needs at night. Hirst reports seeing shadows and young lovers gamboling in the bushes. These are typical primal-scene images. Then he reports water falling, a lake, someone drowning. These images were blinding. In other words, they were castrating. When the sounds stopped, he felt freezing. To turn cold is to die. He dreamed he was being blotted out, suffocated—by a perfumed muff. Someone was doing him to death. Clearly, in this part of his dream, he was being smothered by sexual love. It was at this point in his dream that "she" looked up and staggered him with her beauty—that was poison. Again love equals death. Hirst can only block it out, remember nothing. He asks: "Am I asleep? There's no water. No one is drowning" (p. 46). At the end of the play, Hirst recalls this dream again. This time he is walking toward a lake. Someone, whom he loses, is following him. Then he sees a body floating in the water (p. 95). The drowning in all these versions of the dream is overdetermined. It represents Hirst's current fear of killing himself by drink, his childhood fear of drowning in mother love (her milk), his oedipal fear of destruction by the father (the man following him), and his fear of his own wish to kill the father (who in this determination is the drowned man). Whether the drowned man is himself or his father, the dream is so fearful that he must insist he was mistaken. He saw no body. Spooner, the less fearful self, knows it is he who drowns—he, the creative, active man now dying inside the empty shell that is Hirst. Even Hirst's photograph album overlies primal-scene imagery—vague shapes, shifting and changing. Hirst speaks of faces, shadows, eyes beneath hats. All of these wisps of people remind him of others long dead. Who else but parental ghosts? These ghosts still beckon to him with sidelong glances, but his fears require these faces to be fixed and dead.

Hirst also concretizes his own castration. Under the dead leaves and twigs in the country gullies, Hirst sees blackened balls (p. 81). In the displacement of dreams, however, the balls are tennis balls, and the dread deed was performed by girls and children, not fearsome fathers. These balls were lost and dead centuries ago, just as Hirst has long since been impotent, made so by his own fear of loving mother. Spooner testifies openly to Hirst's impotence and salutes it (p. 33). And he also obliquely acknowledges the impotence of himself, the better half. He confesses having an unconsummated affair with Arabella Hinscott. He blames the failure on Arabella's wish, but then he admits she was contented by her own particular predilection—"consuming the male member" (p. 76). Seemingly, Spooner, too, was castrated by woman. He contents himself now with voyeurism, but even in his peeping he is fearful of sex.

Hirst/Spooner has other perversions as well. Having spent himself on one woman after another, Hirst eventually corrupted Geoffrey Ramsden (p. 76). In addition, at Spooner's open houses, both women and men were admitted, whether they were poets or not—most of the men were not. These parties featured young bodies that lay in dim light. Here the images of homosexuality blend with the primal-scene imagery of the wife moving among the dark shadows in a long dress (p. 28). These various forms of sexual behavior are the result of fierce oedipal concerns, and they are also typical of alcoholics. Menninger asserts that alcoholics exhibit great heterosexual activity although secretly they fear women and lack normal sexual powers. They seek solicitude, not sexual gratification.[81] He also states that "many alcoholics indulge in homosexual (or in heterosexual) relations only when they are drunk."[82] Only if their terror has been anesthetized can they seek Eros, the creative half of life. The rest of the time the alcoholic, like Hirst, must deny sex and fantasize that he is one of those old men who will be garlanded by the village church for dying virginal and unloved (pp. 29-30). This self-deception relates to Menninger's description of the alcoholic as "flagrantly hypocritical."[83]

This deception is also present in the dream. In this first determination, the play appears to be pure punishment—abandonment of the wish to have mother, acceptance of male substitutes. Yet, in this dream the child is alone with his mother substitute. Even a substitute for mother's milk is there. The dream's appearance is deceiving; mother is absent only by reaction formation. The wish to have her is still there, and it is fulfilled in disguise.

As the play progresses, Hirst's dream deepens; he regresses to an even earlier oral fantasy—the wish for oneness with mother. Immediately after birth, the infant is unaware of the outer world of objects. He knows only sensitivity to pain and pleasure. Even these sensations can barely be distinguished. He seeks relief from hunger and other discomforts in sleep. Gradually his waking hours increase and certain sensations become familiar. By constantly testing the borders between his senses and the external world of reality, he differentiates himself from his mother.[84] Erik Erikson says the infant's "first social achievement . . .is his willingness to let mother out of his sight."[85] This earliest level of life, before differentiation, is the focus of the latter part of this play as a dream.

The setting can, from the outset, be perceived as a womb-room. This one is darkened by heavy curtains across the windows. Occasionally, Hirst tests the reality of the outside world by drawing the curtains aside. He looks out only briefly, however, and then lets them fall shut again. The most prominent feature of this room is the cabinet that holds Hirst's liquor; thus, it is symbolic of mother's breast. Only one other presence is required —the infant. To satisfy this need, all four characters must be viewed as part of one self. Such a blending is not beyond the process of condensation. Spooner is already clearly a part of Hirst. Foster, too, can be seen as summoned into Hirst's self. When Foster wonders how he came to be called here from Bali, Spooner's explanation is that Hirst called to him as a result of an imaginative leap (p. 86). Furthermore, Foster's youth in Bali resembles Hirst's youth by its great show of sexual activity with the ladies. Foster is also a would-be poet. Thus, he represents Hirst's youth and early ambition, and Hirst maintains, when speaking of his album, that his youth can never leave him (p. 45). Briggs represents the middle-aged Hirst trapped by responsibility and imprisoned by love—that "intricate one-way system" leading to Bolsover Street (p. 62). Together the harshness and vulgarity of Foster and Briggs are the violent part of Hirst's nature. Hirst alludes to it when he speaks of the easy change from a sensitive, cultivated man to the bully, cutpurse, and brigand (p. 78). Moreover, Briggs and Foster live within the same house —with Hirst. In dream symbolism, then, they are with him in this womb. The final evidence comes from Erik Erikson, who states that the early differentiation process is the origin of projection and introjection. By the former, the infant achieves the feeling that outer goodness is part of his inner self. By the latter, he experiences inner pain as an external force.[86] Thus, the infant, Hirst, can project Briggs and Foster outside himself or incorporate them into himself. This very sense of oneness is created by the final dialogue of the play. Hirst announces that they will change the subject for the last time (p. 91). From that moment, Briggs, Foster, and Hirst seem to lose their separate identities and individual qualities. They begin to speak with the sameness of one person, almost echoing Hirst. One finishes the other's sentences. Hirst says: "It's night." Foster echoes: "And will always be night." Briggs continues: "Because the subject—," and Foster completes the line: "can never be changed" (p. 94). There is silence; then Hirst repeats his dream, ending in the usual self-assuring words: "There is nothing there." After another silence, Spooner integrates into this whole by echoing Hirst's earlier description of no man's land (p. 95). The entire episode gives the effect of a chorus illustrating Erikson's comment that many sick individuals try to "recover social mutuality" by testing the boundaries "between words and social meanings."[87]

Beyond this oneness with mother, there is only the death wish, the tendency to return to the totally inanimate state. This wish and the fear of it lie in the nethermost layer of this dream. The déjà vu that Spooner experiences repeatedly is evidence of the death wish. Mack and Semrad point out that Freud saw repetition compulsion as a phenomenon of the death instinct because it reveals man's tendency to repeat ill-advised behavior and to seek satisfaction for his need to suffer.[88] Hirst reveals this need; and his more conscious self, Spooner, highlights the repetition of painful experiences by his déjà vu. When Hirst collapses and crawls from the room (p. 34), when Spooner awakens to a silent house and a locked door (p. 59), when Briggs takes orders from an upstairs room (p. 68)—in each case Spooner feels he has known this experience before.

The presence of death is implicit in the darkness of the room, the frequent references to the dying of light, the blankness of the faces in the album. Even conscious literary allusions to death blend with the dream images. Father figures are always synonymous with death in oedipal fantasies, and Briggs refers to Spooner as the "shithouse operator," thereby likening him to the memory of father during toilet-training years. Hirst defends Spooner as a good man and then comments that he hears a fly buzzing (p. 88). Thus, he raises Emily Dickinson's image of an uneventful death. Earlier, the role of the kindly, courteous death so often present in Emily Dickinson's poems is projected onto Spooner. He offers himself to Hirst as a friendly boatman to help him cross a river. The river is likened to a tomb; it is a "deep and dark architecture" (p. 33). Death is also implicit in many waiting images, such as Hirst's reference to waiting for a stranger to fill his glass. In the same speech he hints at the absence of a future (p. 45).

Hirst's fear of death, of course, recurs in his telling and retelling of his drowning dream. Death follows him, a body floats in the water, some one is drowning—but the dead one is never Hirst. Spooner identifies with death on each of these occasions. Persistently, he says the man drowning or drowned is he. Yet, the parts of the dreamer's self reverse positions when Spooner offers to challenge death. He would fight against it by regenerating the man of letters through his poetry reading and press conference. Hirst, however, rejects life by changing the subject— for one final time (p. 91). But death never comes. Only the wish for death is present in the dream. The equally strong force, the fear of it, keeps the composite Hirst in no man's land—that silent, still place where he is one with mother. It lies between differentiation from her and the total return to mother earth. The dream life of this play is a testing of those boundaries between barely living and completely dying. Hirst, in his fear, would prefer never to move to one limit or the other. He refuses to renew life, but he also refuses to die. He prefers that still point in between, "which never changes. . .but which remains forever, icy and silent" (p. 95).

Thus, the last of the memory plays shifts its focus to forgetting. Man's need not to remember his pain and guilt becomes the root of an even greater isolation—isolation from life itself. Accompanying this isolation is a deeper alienation—alienation from the contructive part of the self. For, appropriately, this play about an alcoholic has as its major theme—self-destruction. On the realistic level, Hirst has had a kingly portion of the world's bounty. He has enjoyed enough charm and good looks to win the affectionate attention of many women. Even as an alcoholic he is able to command the friendship and loyalty of the other three men in the play. He has had the intelligence and talent to achieve fame and fortune in the literary world. But despite all these gifts, he has sunk into despair and depression. In the time of the play he can still grasp Spooner's offer of friendship, but he spurns it. He can still attempt to renew his literary prominence, but he rejects the opportunity. He chooses to seek oblivion—in drink. Thus, this play takes the step beyond lost loves, beyond isolation, beyond depression; it peeps fearfully into the face of death. On the psychoanalytic level, the play discloses that the wish to have mother can deepen into a wish to return to the womb, which becomes the death wish—man's ultimate self-punishment. Clearly, man is not set on this path to self-destruction by his present losses, but, ironically, by early ones beyond his understanding. That first disappointment in parental love set the pattern for his self-defeat, and man keeps reliving that experience. Mother once looked on the infant Hirst/Spooner with pure malevolence; subsequently, Hirst/Spooner saw this same poison in the face of his wife. His constant search for love with other men's wives hastened his ultimate loss of his own. His wish for revenge against those who disappointed him boomeranged and destroyed his capacity to love or be loved. Indeed, eventually his anger moved him beyond alienation and began to destroy life itself. But *No Man's Land* discloses that the man who can not face life is no better equipped to meet death. His self-destruction can not be deterred until it propels him into the final fear—fear of death. Then it is that he becomes trapped in no man's land, the world of the living dead. The irony is that the fearful side of man can drown the free, creative self and leave the empty shell to live out life. The power of Pinter's presentation of this theme is in its understatement and its objectivity. The play does not plead for sympathy nor wallow in self-pity. Neither does it preach, accuse, or excuse. It tells its tale obliquely and poetically and leaves the audience to search out its meaning and judge it for themselves. The psychoanalytic approach reveals the universality of the wishes, guilts, and fears that unconsciously motivate man to destroy himself. In the presence of this universality men can not condemn. They can only hope to avoid no man's land themselves by trying to accept both life and death.

CONCLUSION

Now that the last play has unfolded and drawn to a close, the Pinter enthusiast has the urge to take a backward look, much as the playwright has done in these last four plays. This retrospective view of Pinter's dramatic world reveals it spinning in the same pattern of repetition compulsion that regulates the lives of the characters that people it. The examination of each individual play has revealed a family of basically similar characters operating in a basically similar situation. The first play began with isolated, incompatible people living in fear of intruders from the outside world, especially a dark figure from the basement. The last play presents equally isolated people, but the intruder is present and friendly. The protagonist has extended his fear to that dark figure from another world—death. The pattern has completed its cycle. Outward changes seem small, yet a great deal has happened. The inner self has been explored, not Pinter's inner self but man's inner self. Northrop Frye comments on the possibility of avoiding private symbolism as "already present in Freud's treatment of *Oedipus Tyrannus* . . . The dramatic and psychological elements can be linked without any reference to the personal life of Sophocles, of which we know nothing whatever."[89] Moreover, the parallel between these plays and Freudian theory makes their universality clear. In the early plays the connection between man's violence and his own anxiety and guilt has been explored. Then man's concern with his identity has been examined. His impotence and inadequacy are viewed in relation to his ambivalence toward his family. These feelings are seen to develop into a wish to be someone else—role playing, fantasizing. Then, human character and personality become fluid as people adapt and adjust to shifting perceptions of themselves and others. At this point wives come under the scrutiny that was heretofore reserved for the self and the family. Gradually, understanding seems to grow, and finally, there is a looking back through memory. The looking back is necessary because man finds that after all this experience he has returned to the same lonely, isolated state from which he began. Thus, he realizes that looking back yields no more surety than looking forward did, that memory is just as faulty as prophecy, that understanding has been an illusion, and, finally, that death is as fearsome as life. The changes in man's condition are few. Originally, he withdrew from the world because of the anxiety wrought by his repression. Then he rejects the world because of the depression that is the aftermath of his anxiety. Looking forward, man lives in anxiety; looking backward, he lives in depression. The flight from depression leads through regression back to the womb and to the brink of the tomb. That is the final message of Pinter's plays from *The Room* to *No Man's Land*. In no man's land man must stop until he gains the courage to choose a new beginning or the final ending. Meanwhile his memories dim until all that remains is the sense of having been there before. At this point, man's déja vu and Freud's theory of repetition compulsion coalesce with Northrop Frye's cyclical approach to literature. The montage also takes in Pinter's words, "I'm dealing with these characters at the extreme edge of their living. . .";[90] these words blend into Frye's description of the point of demonic epiphany—"the prison of endless pain."[91] Frye likens man's perspective from this point to Dante's vision of Satan from the bottom of hell, which Dante locates "at the center of the spherical earth." Frye calls it a "dead center" beyond which we "finally see the gentlemanly Prince of Darkness bottom side up."[92] This is what happens on a trip through Pinter's dramatic world. One travels through the dark center of man's being where the unconscious speaks in a strange language—the language of dreams. This center is hell, and to pass through it seems to turn man inside out. When one emerges on the other side, however, he realizes that man is only upside down. All is the same; only the view is changed. Instead of a forward look, there is a backward look, and this regression leads not to the womb but to the tomb. Instead of a topside view of Satan, there is an underview; and instead of awesome space above, there is the dreadful void below. The reader, like man himself, has traveled through learning and understanding back to ignorance and confusion. Has the journey, then, been worthwhile?

Some critics would say no. Ronald Hayman says of *Old Times*: "*Old Times* is not a puzzle to be solved; it is an elaborate construction of words, echoing silences and images which ought to be enjoyed as such." Then he adds: "The critic can best help us to relish the writing by weaning us away from trying to solve the mysteries."[93] If he is right, and the rest of the Pinter scholars are wrong, then intellectual curiosity has suffered a lethal blow, and one more attempt has been made to conceal from men the pleasures of their minds. Most important, however, the advice of all the sages since Socrates—know thyself—has come to naught, for Pinter's plays present the same puzzles to man that his own dreams present. These puzzles are the mysteries of the unconscious mind that mankind has always tended to ignore. Carl Jung says: "People measure their self-knowledge by what the average person in his social environment knows of himself, but not by the real psychic facts which are for the most part hidden from them."[94] These psychic facts are hidden in man's dreams and in that parallel to his dreams—his artistic creations. Therefore, Pinter's plays can be partially unraveled by the same techniques that Freud applied to dreams. That the unraveling is only partial is no reason never to unravel at all. After all, in *No Man's Land* the dark figure of *The Room* is no longer relegated to the basement; it no longer compells violent murder. The dark figure can now be identified as death —still frightening perhaps, still mysterious, but also patient and polite.

Clearly, the dream approach has answered many of the questions posed by Pinter's plays. It has shed light on many of the obscure symbols. It has shown that man is not unmotivated but unconsciously motivated. The dream approach has, however, left the plays' poetic ambiguity intact. It has not ruled out other interpretations, it has merely added to them. It has delineated new themes while reaffirming the familiar ones of dispossession, struggle for dominance, and betrayal. It has also shown man's self-ignorance and his self-punishment. It has illustrated his cyclical patterns and his universal inadequacies and neuroses. Most of all, it has demonstrated how Pinter's plays group around the oedipal wish—the classic theme of all great literature and the universal problem of all mankind.

As these plays are universal, however, they are forever open-ended, forever overdetermined. In *Modern Man in Search of a Soul*, Carl Jung separates visionary literature from the conventional kind drawn from the "realm of human consciousness." He describes visionary literature in these words:

It is a primordial experience which surpasses man's understanding. . .It arises from timeless depths; it is foreign and cold, many-sided, demonic and grotesque. A grimly ridiculous sample of the eternal chaos—. . .it bursts asunder our human standards of value and of aesthetic form.[95]

Unquestionably, Jung's description fits Pinter's plays. Unquestionably, such primordial experience can never be fully plumbed. Freud's words echo in the mind: "The possibility always remains that the dream may have yet another meaning."[96] The possibility also remains that other meanings are still forthcoming from other approaches. This poetic ambiguity is the wellspring of the power Pinter's plays have to grip their audiences. As Edward and Flora project different images onto the Matchseller, so individual spectators can project differing interpretations onto Pinter's plays. Walter Kerr has seen the plays as existential; Kathleen Burkman has seen them as ritual; Martin Esslin has seen them as psychological and archetypal. This psychoanalytical interpretation of Pinter's plays as dreams is, therefore, merely another approach to the meaning in Pinter. The plays hold eternal promise—of new readings, new insights, new pleasures!

Notes

CHAPTER 1

1. Martin Esslin, *The Peopled Wound: The Work of Harold Pinter* (New York: Doubleday and Co., 1970), p. 30.

2. Judith Crist, "A Mystery: Pinter on Pinter," *Look*, 24 December 1968, p. 78.

3. Northrop Frye, *Anatomy of Criticism: Four Essays* (New York: Atheneum Press, 1969), p. 105.

4. Sigmund Freud, *The Interpretation of Dreams*, in *The Standard Edition of the Complete Psychological Works of Sigmund Freud*, 24 vols., trans. and ed. James Strachey (London: The Hogarth Press, 1953) 5:597. (All subsequent references to Sigmund Freud will be to this collected edition and will be cited by volume and page.)

5. Sigmund Freud, *On Dreams*, 5:649.

6. Harold Pinter, *The Birthday Party and The Room: Two Plays* (New York: Grove Press, Inc. 1961), p. 95. (Subsequent references to *The Room* will appear in the body of the text.)

7. Sigmund Freud, *The Interpretation of Dreams*, 5:354.

8. Frye, p. 137.

9. Sigmund Freud, *On Dreams*, 5:653.

10. Sigmund Freud, *The Interpretation of Dreams*, 4:91.

11. Ibid., 5:375.

12. John Russell Brown, "Dialogue in Pinter and Others," in *Modern British Dramatists: A Collection of Critical Essays*, ed. John Russell Brown (Englewood Cliffs, N.J.: Prentice-Hall, Inc., 1968), p. 126.

13. Sigmund Freud, *The Interpretation of Dreams*, 4:219.

14. Ibid., 4:284.

15. Sigmund Freud, "Revision of the Theory of Dreams," 22:11.

16. Norman Holland, *The Dynamics of Literary Response* (New York: Oxford University Press, 1968), p. 35.

17. Frieda Fromm-Reichmann, "Psychiatric Aspects of Anxiety," in *Identity and*

Anxiety: Survival of the Person in Mass Society, ed. Maurice R. Stein, Arthur J. Vidich, and David Manning White (Glencoe, Ill.: The Free Press, 1960), p. 131.

18. Holland, p. 37.

19. Theodore Lidz, *The Person* (New York: Basic Books, Inc., 1968), p. 193.

20. Holland, p. 39.

21. John Mack and Elvin Semrad, "Classical Freudian Psychoanalysis," in *Interpreting Personality: A Survey of Twentieth-Century Views*, ed. Alfred M. Freedman, M.D., and Harold I. Kaplan, M.D. (New York: Atheneum Press, 1972), pp. 23-24.

22. Lois Gordon, *Stratagems to Uncover Nakedness* (Columbia, Mo.: University of Missouri Press, 1970), p. 18.

23. Sigmund Freud, "Repression," 14:147.

24. Holland, p. 43.

25. Max Schur, "The Ego in Anxiety," in *Drives, Affects, Behavior*, 2 vols., ed. Rudolph M. Lowenstein, M.D. (New York: International Universities Press, 1953) 1:83.

26. Frye, p. 160.

27. Anna Freud, *The Ego and the Mechanisms of Defense* in *The Writings of Anna Freud*, 2 vols., trans. Cecil Baines, 1st rev. ed. (New York: International Universities Press, Inc., 1966), 2:114.

28. Holland, p. 49.

29. Sigmund Freud, *The Interpretation of Dreams*, 5:354.

30. Holland, p. 45.

31. Ibid., p. 46.

32. Sigmund Freud, *The Interpretation of Dreams*, 5:355.

33. Ibid.

34. Holland, p. 49.

35. John Pesta, "Pinter's Usurpers," in *Pinter: A Collection of Critical Essays*, ed. Arthur Ganz (Englewood Cliffs, N.J.: Prentice-Hall, Inc., 1972), p. 125.

36. Holland, p. 49.

37. Anna Freud, 2:173-74.

38. Sigmund Freud, *The Interpretation of Dreams*, 4:316.

39. Sigmund Freud, "Revision of the Theory of Dreams," 22:26.

40. Ibid., 22:27.

41. Ibid.

CHAPTER 2

1. Sigmund Freud, *Introductory Lectures on Psychoanalysis*, 15:213.

2. Ibid., 15:219.

3. Arnold P. Hinchliffe, *Harold Pinter* (New York: Twayne Publishers, Inc., 1967), p. 40.

4. Mack and Semrad, p. 67.

5. Lidz, pp. 73-74.

6. Mack and Semrad, p. 66.

7. Sigmund Freud, *The Interpretation of Dreams,* 4:329.

8. Fromm-Reichmann, p. 131.

9. Pinter, *The Birthday Party and The Room,* p. 81. (Subsequent references to *The Birthday Party* will appear in the body of the text.)

10. Esslin, *The Peopled Wound,* p. 85.

11. Silvano Arieti, *The Intrapsychic Self: Feeling, Cognition, and Creativity in Health and Mental Illness* (New York: Basic Books, Inc., 1967), pp. 270-71.

12. Erik H. Erikson, *Childhood and Society,* 2d ed. (New York: W. W. Norton and Co., 1963), pp. 258-61.

13. Esslin, *The Peopled Wound,* p. 84.

14. Ibid., p. 75.

15. Sigmund Freud, *The Interpretation of Dreams,* 5:401.

16. James T. Boulton, "*The Caretaker* and Other Plays," in *Pinter: A Collection of Critical Essays,* ed. Arthur Ganz (Englewood Cliffs, N.J., Prentice-Hall, Inc., 1972). p. 97.

17. Gordon, p. 27.

18. Holland, p. 40.

19. Ibid., p. 39.

20. Ibid., p. 42.

21. Ibid., p. 44.

22. Lidz, p. 190.

23. Sigmund Freud, *The Interpretation of Dreams,* 5:384.

24. Ibid., 5:372.

25. Sigmund Freud, "The Theme of the Three Caskets," 12:295.

26. Gordon, p. 27.

27. Anna Freud, 2:94.

28. Harold Pinter, *The Caretaker and The Dumb Waiter* (New York: Grove Press, Inc. 1961), p. 90. (Subsequent references to *The Dumb Waiter* will appear in the body of the text.)

29. Gordon, p. 33.

30. Sigmund Freud, *The Interpretation of Dreams,* 5:403-4.

31. Mack and Semrad, p. 23.

32. Ibid.

33. Lidz, p. 177.

34. Sigmund Freud, *The Interpretation of Dreams,* 5:354.

35. Holland, p. 43.

36. Ibid.

37. Alrene Sykes, *Harold Pinter* (New York: Humanities Press, 1970), p. 15.

38. Sigmund Freud, "The Theme of the Three Caskets," 12:295.

39. Esslin, *The Peopled Wound,* p. 73.

40. Simon Trussler, *The Plays of Harold Pinter* (London: Victor Gollancz, Ltd., 1973), p. 58.

41. Esslin, *The Peopled Wound*, p. 87.

42. Harold Pinter, *Three Plays: A Slight Ache, The Collection, The Dwarfs* (New York: Grove Press, Inc. 1961), p. 9. (Subsequent references to *A Slight Ache* will appear in the body of the text.)

43. John Russell Taylor, *The Angry Theatre: New British Drama* (New York: Hill and Wang, 1962), p. 106.

44. James R. Hollis, *Harold Pinter: The Poetics of Silence* (Carbondale, Ill.: Southern Illinois University Press, 1970), p. 55.

45. Esslin, *The Peopled Wound*, p. 91.

46. Sigmund Freud, *Introductory Lectures on Psychoanalysis*, 15:158.

47. Sigmund Freud, *The Interpretation of Dreams*, 5:366.

48. Ibid., 5:401.

49. Ibid., 5:358.

50. Arieti, p. 268.

51. Ibid., p. 270.

52. Ibid., p. 268.

53. Ibid., p. 289.

54. Hinchliffe, p. 69.

55. Kathleen Burkman, *The Drmatic World of Harold Pinter: Its Basis in Ritual* (Columbus, Ohio: Ohio University Press, 1971), p. 60.

56. R. F. Storch, "Harold Pinter's Happy Families," in *Pinter: A Collection of Critical Essays*, ed. Arthur Ganz (Englewood Cliffs, N.J.: Prentice-Hall, Inc., 1972), p. 142.

57. Sigmund Freud, *The Interpretation of Dreams, 5:408.*

58. Mack and Semrad, p. 34.

59. Sigmund Freud, "A Metapsychological Supplement to the Theory of Dreams." *14:230.*

CHAPTER 3

1. Sigmund Freud, "Revision of the Theory of Dreams," 22-27.

2. Martin Esslin, *The Theatre of the Absurd* (Garden City, N.Y.: Doubleday and Co., 1961), p. 212.

3. Sigmund Freud, *Introductory Lectures on Psychoanalysis*, 15:214-15.

4. Ibid., 15:215.

5. Ibid., 15:216.

6. Taylor, *The Angry Theatre*, p. 251.

7. Harold Clurman, *The Naked Image: Observations on the Modern Theatre* (New York: The Macmillan Co., 1966), p. 105.

8. Trussler, pp. 90-91.

9. Lawrence M. Bensky, "Harold Pinter: An Interview," in *Pinter: A Collection of Critical Essays*, ed. Arthur Ganz (Englewood Cliffs, N.J.: Prentice-Hall, Inc., 1972), p. 24.

10. Sigmund Freud, *Introductory Lectures on Psychoanalysis*, 15:216.

11. Ibid., 15:217.

12. George Wellwarth, *The Theater of Protest and Paradox: Development in the Avant-Garde Drama* (New York: New York University Press, 1967), p. 207.

13. Storch, p. 142.

14. Harold Pinter, *A Night Out, Night School, Revue Sketches: Early Plays* (New York: Grove Press, 1961), p. 33. (Subsequent references to *A Night Out* and *Night School* will be included in the body of the text.)

15. Esslin, *The Peopled Wound, p. 95.*

16. Taylor, *The Angry Theatre*, p. 252.

17. Sigmund Freud, *The Interpretation of Dreams*, 5:387.

18. Ibid., 5:403.

19. Holland, p. 39.

20. Lidz, p. 186.

21. Sigmund Freud, *The Interpretation of Dreams*, 5:356.

22. Mack and Semrad, p. 34.

23. Esslin, *The Peopled Wound*, p. 113.

24. Harold Pinter, *The Caretaker and The Dumb Waiter* (New York: Grove Press, Inc., 1961), p. 67. (Subsequent references to *The Caretaker* will appear in the body of the text.)

25. Burkman, pp. 87-88.

26. Hinchliffe, p. 88.

27. John Russell Brown, "Mr. Pinter's Shakespeare," *Critical Quarterly* 5, no. 3 (Autumn 1963):251.

28. Holland, p. 60.

29. Ibid., p. 54.

30. Esslin, *The Peopled Wound*, p. 111.

31. Anna Freud, 2:114.

32. Sigmund Freud, *The Interpretation of Dreams*, 5:358.

33. Lidz, p. 33.

34. Esslin, *The Peopled Wound*, p. 109.

35. Gordon, p. 41.

36. "Harold Pinter Replies," *New Theater Magazine* 11, no. 2 (January 1961):9.

37. Holland, p. 49.

38. Ibid.

39. "Harold Pinter Replies," pp. 9-10.

40. Sykes, pp. 37-38.

41. Taylor, *The Angry Theatre*, p. 254.

42. Ibid.

43. Esslin, *The Peopled Wound*, p. 118.

44. Hinchliffe, p. 113.

45. Mack and Semrad, p. 59.

46. Bensky, p. 24.

47. Ibid.

48. Ibid.

49. Pinter, *Three Plays*, p. 86. (Subsequent references to *The Dwarfs* will be included in the body of the text.

50. Bensky, p. 24.

51. Esslin, *The Peopled Wound*, p. 126.

52. Taylor, *The Angry Theatre*, p. 256.

53. Arieti, p. 270.

54. Ibid.

55. Ibid., p. 286.

56. Ibid., p. 272.

57. Sigmund Freud, *Introductory Lectures on Psychoanalysis*, 15:156.

58. Arieti, p. 271.

59. Ibid., p. 229.

60. Sykes, p. 54.

61. Storch, p. 143.

62. Arieti, p. 281.

63. Storch, p. 143.

64. Sigmund Freud, *The Interpretation of Dreams*, 5:354-55.

65. Ibid., 5:355.

66. Ibid., 5:356.

CHAPTER 4

1. Esslin, *The Peopled Wound*, p. 171.

2. Taylor, *The Angry Theatre*, p. 255.

3. Trussler, p. 105.

4. Ronald Hayman, *Harold Pinter* (New York: Frederick Ungar Publishing Co., 1973), p. 17.

5. Pinter, *Three Plays*, p. 67. (Subsequent references to *The Collection* will appear in the body of the text.)

6. Holland, p. 105.

7. Lidz, pp. 402-3.

8. Holland, p. 38.

9. Lidz, p. 403.

10. Holland, p. 43.

11. Ibid., p. 47.

12. Sigmund Freud, *Introductory Lectures on Psychoanalysis*, 15:157.

13. Sigmund Freud, *The Interpretation of Dreams*, 5:355.

14. Esslin, *The Peopled Wound*, pp. 33-34.

15. Sigmund Freud, "On the Universal Tendency to Debasement in the Sphere of Love (Contributions to the Psychology of Love II)," 11:188-89.

16. Hayman, p. 81.

17. Walter Kerr, *Harold Pinter: Columbia Essays on Modern Writers* (New York: Columbia University Press, 1967), p. 33.

18. Harold Pinter, *The Lover, Tea Party, The Basement* (New York: Grove Press, Inc., 1967), p. 5. (Subsequent references to *The Lover* will appear in the body of the text.)

19. Trussler, p. 114.

20. Sigmund Freud, "On the Universal Tendency to Debasement in the Sphere of Love," 11:189.

21. Ibid., 11:183.

22. Ibid., 11:180.

23. Ibid., 11:182.

24. Ibid., 11:183.

25. Ibid.

26. Ibid., 11:186.

27. Sigmund Freud, *The Interpretation of Deams*, 5:377.

28. Sigmund Freud, "On the Universal Tendency to Debasement in the Sphere of Love," 11:187.

29. Ibid., 11:184.

30. Sykes, p. 113.

31. Esslin, *The Peopled Wound*, p. 171.

32. Hinchliffe, p. 137.

33. Pinter, *The Lover, Tea Party, The Basement*, p. 102. (Subsequent references to *The Basement* will appear in the body of the text.)

34. Hayman, p. 117.

35. Esslin, *The Peopled Wound*, p. 175.

36. Trussler, p. 152.

37. Sykes, p. 113.

38. Holland, p. 49.

39. Mack and Semrad, p. 34.

40. Hinchliffe, p. 125.

41. Pinter, *The Lover, Tea Party, The Basement*, p. 43. (Subsequent references to *Tea Party* will appear in the body of the text.)

42. Sykes, p. 112.

43. Hayman, p. 97.

44. Esslin, *The Peopled Wound*, p. 171.

45. Sigmund Freud, "Some Character-Types Met with in Psychoanalytic Work," 14:316-31.

46. Ibid., 14:317.

47. Ibid., 14:317-18.

48. Ibid., 14:331.

49. Sigmund Freud, *The Interpretation of Dreams*, 5:349.

50. Holland, p. 40

51. Sigmund Freud, *Introductory Lectures on Psychoanalysis*, 15:156

52. Holland, p. 60.

53. Sigmund Freud, *Introductory Lectures on Psychoanalysis*, 15:157.

54. Ibid., 15:158.

55. Sigmund Freud, "On the Universal Tendency to Debasement in the Sphere of Love," 11:186.

56. Trussler, p. 134.

57. John Lahr, Introduction to *A Casebook on Harold Pinter's The Homecoming*, ed. John Lahr (New York: Grove Press, Inc., 1971), p. xiii.

58. Arthur Ganz, Introduction to *Pinter: A Collection of Critical Essays*, ed. Arthur Ganz (Englewood Cliffs, N.J.: Prentice-Hall, Inc., 1972), p. 15.

59. Bert. O. States, "Pinter's *Homecoming:* The Shock of Nonrecognition," in *Pinter: A Collection of Critical Essays*, ed. Arthur Ganz (Englewood Cliffs, N.J.: Prentice-Hall, Inc., 1972), p. 150.

60. Margaret Croyden, "Pinter's Hideous Comedy," in *A Casebook on Harold Pinter's The Homecoming*, ed. John Lahr (New York: Grove Press, Inc., 1971), p. 45.

61. Harold Pinter, *The Homecoming* (New York: Grove Press, Inc., 1965), pp. 79-80. (Subsequent references to *The Homecoming* will appear in the body of the text.)

62. Esslin, *The Peopled Wound*, pp. 157-60.

63. Peter Hall, "Peter Hall on Pinter," *The American Film Theatre/Cinebill* 1, no. 2 (1973).

64. Anna Freud, 2:165-66.

65. Sigmund Freud, *The Interpretation of Dreams*, 5:357.

66. Hugh Nelson, "*The Homecoming:* Kith and Kin," in *Modern British Dramatists*, ed. John Russell Brown (Englewood Cliffs, N.J.: Prentice-Hall, Inc., 1968), p. 148.

67. Sigmund Freud, *The Interpretation of Dreams*, 5:354.

68. Anna Freud, 2:96-97.

69. Ibid., p. 125.

70. Irving Wardle, "The Territorial Struggle," in *A Casebook on Harold Pinter's The Homecoming*, ed. John Lahr (New York: Grove Press, Inc., 1971), p. 40.

71. Holland, p. 44.

72. Ibid., p. 45.

73. Bernard Dukore, "A Woman's Place," in *A Casebook on Harold Pinter's The Homecoming*, ed. John Lahr (New York: Grove Press, Inc., 1971), p. 115.

74. Esslin, *The Peopled Wound*, p. 162.

75. Hollis, p. 105.

76. John Russell Taylor, "Pinter's Game of Happy Families," in *A Casebook on Harold Pinter's The Homecoming*, ed. John Lahr (New York: Grove Press, Inc., 1971), p. 65.

77. Bensky, p. 26.

CHAPTER 5

1. Trussler, p. 154.

2. Samuel Beckett, *Proust* (New York: Grove Press, Inc., 1931), p. 3.

3. Arthur Ganz, "Mixing Memory and Desire: Pinter's Vision in *Landscape*,

Silence, and *Old Times,"* in *Pinter: A Collection of Critical Essays,* ed. Arthur Ganz (Englewood Cliffs, N.J.: Prentice-Hall, Inc., 1972), p. 161.

4. Harold Pinter, *Landscape and Silence* (New York: Grove Press, Inc., 1970), p. 7. (Subsequent references to *Landscape* will appear in the body of the text.)

5. Esslin, *The Peopled Wound,* p. 185.

6. Ibid., p. 180.

7. Ibid., p. 183.

8. Arieti, p. 116.

9. Sigmund Freud, "Mourning and Melancholia," 14:244.

10. Ibid.

11. Arieti, p. 116.

12. Sigmund Freud, "Mourning and Melancholia," 14:244.

13. Arieti, p. 117.

14. Ibid., p. 126.

15. Sigmund Freud, "Some Character-Types Met with in Psychoanalytic Work," 14:330-31.

16. Sigmund Freud, "A Metapsychological Supplement to the Theory of Dreams," 14:230.

17. Sigmund Freud, "On Narcissism," 14:99-100.

18. Sigmund Freud, *The Interpretation of Dreams,* 5:374.

19. Ibid., 5:376.

20. Sigmund Freud, "On Narcissism," 14:94.

21. Ibid., 14:95.

22. Ibid., 14:89.

23. Ibid., 14:91.

24. Lidz, p. 35.

25. Sigmund Freud, "On The Universal Tendency to Debasement in the Sphere of Love," 11:180.

26. Ibid., 11:183.

27. Esslin, *The Peopled Wound,* p. 187.

28. Lidz, p. 194.

29. Sigmund Freud, *Introductory Lectures on Psychoanalysis,* 15:158.

30. Ibid., 15:156.

31. Ganz, "Mixing Memory and Desire," p. 166.

32. Pinter, *Landscape and Silence,* p. 43. (Subsequent references to *Silence* will appear in the body of the text.)

33. Trussler, p. 169.

34. Hollis, p. 113.

35. Trussler, p. 166.

36. Esslin, *The Peopled Wound,* p. 195.

37. Samuel Beckett, *Krapp's Last Tape and Other Dramatic Pieces* (New York: Grove Press, Inc., 1960), p. 23.

38. Sigmund Freud, "Three Essays on the Theory of Sexuality," 7:201.

39. Sigmund Freud, *Introductory Lectures on Psychoanalysis,* 15:156.

40. Ibid., 15:180.

41. Ganz, "Mixing Memory and Desire," p. 170.

42. Harold Pinter, *Old Times* (New York: Grove Press, Inc., 1971), p. 47. (Subsequent references to *Old Times* will appear in the body of the text.)

43. Trussler, p. 174-75.

44. Ibid., p. 174.

45. Sigmund Freud, "Three Essays on the Theory of Sexuality," 7:174.

46. Ibid., 7:175.

47. Ibid., 7:136-37.

48. Sigmund Freud, *The Interpretation of Dreams*, 5:357-58.

49. Sigmund Freud, "Three Essays on the Theory of Sexuality," 7:149.

50. Ibid., 7:150.

51. Anna Freud, 2:127.

52. Sigmund Freud, "Three Essays on the Theory of Sexuality," 7:203.

53. Sigmund Freud, "On Narcissism," 14:89.

54. Ibid., 14:101.

55. Holland, p. 44.

56. Sigmund Freud, "On Narcissism," 14:75.

57. Sigmund Freud, "Three Essays on the Theory of Sexuality," 7:157.

58. Ganz, "Mixing Memory and Desire," p. 171.

59. Sigmund Freud, "On Narcissism," 14:89.

60. Anna Freud, 2:130.

61. Holland, p. 45.

62. Ganz, "Mixing Memory and Desire," p. 171.

63. Hayman, p. 146.

64. Ganz, "Mixing Memory and Desire," p. 173.

65. Sigmund Freud, "Three Essays on the Theory of Sexuality," 7:166.

66. Harold Pinter, *No Man's Land* (London: Eyre Methuen, Ltd., 1975), p. 84. (Subsequent references to *No Man's Land* will appear in the body of the text.)

67. Karl Menninger, *Man Against Himself* (New York: Harcourt, Brace, and World, Inc., 1938), p. 144.

68. Ibid.

69. Ibid., p. 148.

70. Ibid., p. 144.

71. Ibid., p. 148.

72. Ibid., p. 146.

73. Ibid., pp. 156-57.

74. Ibid., p. 153.

75. Ibid., p. 154.

76. Ibid., p. 150.

77. Menninger, p. 149.

78. Sigmund Freud, *Introductory Lectures on Psychoanalysis*, 15:155.

79. Holland, p. 41.

80. Mack and Semrad, p. 19.

81. Menninger, p. 158.
82. Ibid., p. 159.
83. Ibid., p. 145.
84. Mack and Semrad, p. 22.
85. Erikson, p. 245.
86. Ibid., pp. 248-49.
87. Ibid., p. 248.
88. Mack and Semrad, p. 34.
89. Frye, p. 111.
90. Esslin, *The Peopled Wound*, p. 26.
91. Frye, p. 239.
92. Ibid.
93. Hayman, p. 148.
94. Carl G. Jung, *The Undiscovered Self,* trans. R. G. C. Hull (Boston: Little, Brown and Co., 1957), p. 7.
95. Carl G. Jung, *Modern Man in Search of a Soul,* trans. W. S. Dell and Cary F. Byrnes (New York: Harcourt, Brace and Co., 1933), p. 157.
96. Sigmund Freud, *The Interpretation of Dreams*, 4:279.

Selected Bibliography

PRIMARY SOURCES

Plays

Pinter, Harold. *The Birthday Party and The Room: Two Plays.* New York: Grove Press, Inc., 1961.

_____. *The Caretaker and The Dumb Waiter.* New York: Grove Press, Inc., 1961.

_____. *Three Plays: A Slight Ache, The Collection, The Dwarfs.* New York: Grove Press, Inc., 1961.

_____. *A Night Out, Night School, Revue Sketches: Early Plays.* New York: Grove Press, Inc., 1961.

_____. *The Homecoming.* New York: Grove Press, Inc., 1965.

_____. *The Lover, Tea Party, The Basement.* New York: Grove Press, Inc., 1967.

_____. *Landscape and Silence.* New York: Grove Press, Inc., 1970.

_____. *Old Times.* New York: Grove Press, Inc., 1971.

_____. *No Man's Land.* London: Eyre Methuen, Ltd., 1975.

Interviews

Bensky, Lawrence M. "Harold Pinter: An Interview." *Pinter: A Collection of Critical Essays.* Edited by Arthur Ganz. Englewood Cliffs, N.J.: Prentice-Hall, Inc., 1972.

"Harold Pinter Replies." *New Theater Magazine* 11, no. 2 (January 1961): 8-10.

288

SECONDARY SOURCES

Arieti, Silvano. *The Intrapsychic Self: Feeling, Cognition, and Creativity in Health and Mental Illness*. New York: Basic Books, Inc., 1967.

Beckett, Samuel. *Krapp's Last Tape and Other Dramatic Pieces*. New York: Grove Press, Inc., 1960.

————. *Proust*. New York: Grove Press, Inc., 1931.

Boulton, James T. "*The Caretaker* and Other Plays." In *Pinter: A Collection of Critical Essays*. Edited by Arthur Ganz. Englewood Cliffs, N.J.: Prentice-Hall, Inc., 1972.

Brown, John Russell. "Dialogue in Pinter and Others." In *Modern British Dramatists: A Collection of Critical Essays*. Edited by John Russell Brown. Englewood Cliffs, N.J.: Prentice-Hall, Inc., 1968.

————. "Mr. Pinter's Shakespeare." *Critical Quarterly* 5, no. 3 (Autumn 1963): 251-65.

Burkman, Kathleen. *The Dramatic World of Harold Pinter: Its Basis in Ritual*. Columbus, Ohio: Ohio University Press, 1971.

Clurman, Harold. *The Naked Image: Observations on the Modern Theatre*. New York: The Macmillan Co., 1966.

Crist, Judith. "A Mystery: Pinter on Pinter." *Look*, 24 December 1968, pp. 77-80.

Croyden, Margaret. "Pinter's Hideous Comedy." In *A Casebook on Harold Pinter's The Homecoming*. Edited by John Lahr. New York: Grove Press, Inc., 1971.

Dukore, Bernard. "A Woman's Place." In *A Casebook on Harold Pinter's The Homecoming*. Edited by John Lahr. New York: Grove Press, Inc., 1971.

Erikson, Erik H. *Childhood and Society*. 2d ed. New York: W.W. Norton and Co., 1963.

Esslin, Martin. *The Peopled Wound: The Work of Harold Pinter*. New York: Doubleday and Co., 1970.

————. *The Theatre of the Absurd*. Garden City, N.Y.: Doubleday and Co., 1961.

Freud, Anna. *The Ego and the Mechanisms of Defense*. Vol. 2 of *The Writings of Anna Freud*. 2 vols. Translated by Cecil Baines.

1st rev. ed. New York: International Universities Press, Inc., 1966.

Freud, Sigmund. *The Interpretation of Dreams. The Standard Edition of the Complete Psychological Works of Sigmund Freud.* 24 vols. Translated and edited by James Strachey. Vols. 4, 5. London: The Hogarth Press, 1953.

_____. *Introductory Lectures on Psychoanalysis.* In *The Standard Edition of the Complete Psychological Works of Sigmund Freud.* 24 vols. Translated and edited by James Strachey. Vol. 15. London: The Hogarth Press, 1961.

_____. "A Metapsychological Supplement to the Theory of Dreams." In *The Standard Edition of the Complete Psychological Works of Sigmund Freud.* 24 vols. Translated and edited by James Strachey. Vol. 14. London: The Hogarth Press, 1957.

_____. "Mourning and Melancholia." In *The Standard Edition of the Complete Works of Sigmund Freud.* 24 vols. Translated and edited by James Strachey. Vol. 14. London: The Hogarth Press, 1957.

_____. *On Dreams.* In *The Standard Edition of the Complete Psychological Works of Sigmund Freud.* 24 vols. Translated and edited by James Strachey. Vol. 5. London: The Hogarth Press, 1953.

_____. "On Narcissism: An Introduction." In *The Standard Edition of the Complete Psychological Works of Sigmund Freud.* 24 vols. Translated and edited by James Strachey. Vol. 14. London: The Hogarth Press, 1957.

_____. "On the Universal Tendency to Debasement in the Sphere of Love (Contributions to the Psychology of Love II)." In *The Standard Edition of the Complete Psychological Works of Sigmund Freud.* 24 vols. Translated and edited by James Strachey. Vol. 11. London: The Hogarth Press, 1957.

_____. "Repression." In *The Standard Edition of the Complete Psychological Works of Sigmund Freud.* 24 vols. Translated and edited by James Strachey. Vol 14 London: Hogarth Press, 1957.

_____. "Revision of the Theory of Dreams." In *The Standard Edition of the Complete Psychological Works of Sigmund Freud.* 24 vols. Translated and edited by James Strachey. Vol. 22. London: The Hogarth Press, 1964.

_____. "Some Character-Type Met with in Psychoanalytic Work." In *The Standard Edition of the Complete Psychological Works of Sigmund Freud.* 24 vols. Translated and edited by James Strachey. Vol. 14. London: The Hogarth Press, 1957.

_____. "The Theme of the Three Caskets." In *The Standard Edition of the Complete Psychological Works of Sigmund Freud.* 24 vols. Translated and edited by James Strachey. Vol. 12. London: The Hogarth Press, 1953.

_____. "Three Essays on the Theory of Sexuality." In *The Standard Edition of the Complete Psychological Works of Sigmund Freud.* 24 vols. Translated and edited by James Strachey. Vol. 7. London: The Hogarth Press, 1953.

Fromm-Reichmann, Frieda. "Psychiatric Aspects of Anxiety." In *Identity and Anxiety: Survival of the Person in Mass Society.* Edited by Maurice R. Stein, Arthur J. Vidich, and David Manning White. Glencoe, Ill.: The Free Press, 1960.

Frye, Northrop. *Anatomy of Criticism: Four Essays.* New York: Atheneum Press, 1969.

Ganz, Arthur. Introduction. In *Pinter: A Collection of Critical Essays.* Edited by Arthur Ganz. Englewood Cliffs, N.J.: Prentice-Hall, Inc., 1972.

_____. "Mixing Memory and Desire: Pinter's Vision in *Landscape, Silence,* and *Old Times.*" In *Pinter: A Collection of Critical Essays.* Edited by Arthur Ganz. Englewood Cliffs, N.J.: Prentice-Hall, Inc., 1972.

_____, ed. *Pinter: A Collection of Critical Essays.* Englewood Cliffs, N.J.: Prentice-Hall, Inc., 1972.

Gordon, Lois. *Stratagems to Uncover Nakedness.* Columbia, Mo.: University of Missouri Press, 1970.

Hall, Peter. "Peter Hall on Pinter." *The American Film Theatre/Cinebill* 1, no. 2 (1973).

Hayman, Ronald. *Harold Pinter.* New York: Frederick Ungar Publishing Co., 1973.

Hinchliffe, Arnold P. *Harold Pinter.* New York: Twayne Publishers, Inc., 1967.

Holland, Norman. *The Dynamics of Literary Response.* New York: Oxford University Press, 1968.

Hollis, James R. *Harold Pinter: The Poetics of Silence*. Carbondale, Ill.: Southern Illinois University Press, 1970.

Jung, Carl G. *Modern Man in Search of a Soul*. Translated by W.S. Dell and Cary F. Byrnes. New York: Harcourt, Brace and Co., 1933.

_____. *The Undiscovered Self*. Translated by R.F.C. Hull. Boston: Little, Brown and Co., 1957.

Kerr, Walter. *Harold Pinter. Columbia Essays on Modern Writers*. New York: Columbia University Press, 1967.

Lahr, John, ed. *A Casebook on Harold Pinter's The Homecoming*. New York: Grove Press, Inc., 1971.

_____. Introduction. In *A Casebook on Harold Pinter's The Homecoming*. Edited by John Lahr. New York: Grove Press, Inc., 1971.

Lidz, Theodore. *The Person*. New York: Basic Books, Inc., 1968.

Mack, John, and Semrad, Elvin. "Classical Freudian Psychoanalysis." In *Interpreting Personality: A Survey of Twentieth-Century Views*. Edited by Albert M. Freedman, M.D., and Harold I. Kaplan, M.D. New York: Atheneum Press, 1972.

Menninger, Karl. *Man Against Himself*. New York: Harcourt, Brace and World, Inc., 1938.

Nelson, Hugh. *"The Homecoming:* Kith and Kin." In *Modern British Dramatists*. Edited by John Russell Brown. Englewood Cliffs, N.J.: Prentice-Hall, Inc., 1968.

Pesta, John. "Pinter's Usurpers." In *Pinter: A Collection of Critical Essays*. Edited by Arthur Ganz. Englewood Cliffs, N.J.: Prentice-Hall, Inc., 1972.

Schur, Max. "The Ego in Anxiety." In *Drives, Affects, Behavior*. 2 vols. Rudolph M. Lowenstein, M.D., ed. Vol. 1. New York: International Universities Press, 1953.

States, Bert O. "Pinter's *Homecoming:* The Shock of Nonrecognition." In *Pinter: A Collection of Critical Essays*. Edited by Arthur Ganz. Englewood Cliffs, N.J.: Prentice-Hall, Inc., 1972.

Storch, R.F. "Harold Pinter's Happy Families." In *Pinter: A Collection of Critical Essays*. Edited by Arthur Ganz. Englewood Cliffs, N.J.: Prentice-Hall, Inc., 1972.

Sykes, Alrene. *Harold Pinter*. New York: Humanities Press, 1970.

Taylor, John Russell. *The Angry Theatre: New British Drama*. New York: Hill and Wang, 1962.

_____. "Pinter's Game of Happy Families." In *A Casebook on Harold Pinter's The Homecoming*. Edited by John Lahr. New York: Grove Press, Inc., 1971.

Trussler, Simon. *The Plays of Harold Pinter*. London: Victor Gollancz, Ltd., 1973.

Wardle, Irving. "The Territorial Struggle." In *A Casebook on Harold Pinter's The Homecoming*. Edited by John Lahr. New York: Grove Press, Inc., 1971.

Wellwarth, George. *The Theatre of Protest and Paradox: Developments in the Avant-Garde Drama*. New York: New York University Press, 1967.

Index